The Art and Craft of Poetry

Keat's *The Eve of St. Agnes*

THE FINAL VERSION AND FIRST DRAFTS OF STANZA 24*

The art ...

A casement high and triple-arch'd there was,
All garlanded with carven imag'ries
Of fruits, and flowers, and bunches of knot-grass,
And diamonded with panes of quaint device,
Innumerable of stains and splendid dyes,
As are the tiger-moth's deep-damask'd wings;
And in the midst, 'mong thousand heraldries,
And twilight saints, and dim emblazonings,
A shielded scutcheon blush'd with blood of queens and kings.

and craft ...

[A Casement [ach'd] tripple arch'd and diamonded
   With many coloured glass fronted the Moon
In midst [of which] wereof a shilded scutcheon shed
   High blushing gules: [upon] [she kneeled saintly down]
And inly prayed for grace and heavenly boon;
The blood red gules fell on her silver cross
And [her] whitest hands devout]

[There was A Casement tipple archd and high
   All garlanded with carven imageries
   Of fruits & [trailing] flowers and sunny corn ears parched]

A Casement high and tripple arch'd there was
   All gardneded with carven imageries
Of fruits and flowers and bunches of knot-grass;
   And diamonded with panes of quaint device
Innumerable of stains and splendid dies
[As is the wing of evening tiger moths;]
As is the tger moths [rich] deep [damasked] sunset wings
[And] in [the] midst whereft 'mong [man] thousand heraldries
And [dim] [twilight] twilight saints and dim emblasonings
A shielded scutcheon blush'd with Blood of Queens & Kings–

of poetry

*Interlinear insertions have been brought into the lines in order of
writing. Brackets indicate deletions. See p. 9.

The Art and Craft of
POETRY
AN INTRODUCTION

by Lawrence John Zillman

The functions of the poetical faculty are
twofold: by one it creates new material for
knowledge, and power, and pleasure; by the
other it engenders in the mind a desire to
reproduce and arrange them according to a
certain rhythm and order which may be
called the beautiful and the good.

—Shelley: *Defence of Poetry*

The Macmillan Company

Fourth Printing 1969

The Macmillan Company

Library of Congress catalog card number 66-14218

Printed in the United States of America

ACKNOWLEDGMENTS

The Atlantic Monthly, for "Waking of a City," by Douglas Malloch. Copyright June, 1932, by The Atlantic Monthly Company. Reprinted by permission.

The Clarendon Press, Oxford, for the manuscript version of Wordsworth's "She dwelt among the untrodden ways . . ." from the de Selincourt edition of *The Poetical Works of William Wordsworth,* Vol. ii, 1944, by permission of The Clarendon Press, Oxford.

The John Day Company, Inc., for "The Griesly Wife," by John Manifold. Copyright © 1946 by The John Day Company. Reprinted from SELECTED VERSE by John Manifold, by permission of The John Day Company, Inc., publisher.

Doubleday & Company, Inc., for "I Knew a Woman, Lovely In Her Bones," copyright 1954 by Theodore Roethke, from WORDS FOR THE WIND. Reprinted by permission of Doubleday & Company, Inc.

Harper & Row, Inc., for "An Afternoon in Artillery Walk," from GUINEA FOWL AND OTHER POULTRY by Leonard Bacon. Copyright 1927 by Harper & Row, Publishers, Inc. Reprinted by permission of the publishers.

Ethelyn Miller Hartwich, for "What Shall Endure," first published in *The World Tomorrow* (World Tomorrow, Inc.), September, 1930. Reprinted by permission.

Harvard College Library, for permission to transcribe the draft manuscript stanza from Keats's *The Eve of St. Agnes*. Printed by permission of the Harvard College Library.

Holt, Rinehart and Winston, Inc., for "A Soldier," from COMPLETE POEMS OF ROBERT FROST. Copyright 1928 by Holt, Rinehart and Winston, Inc. Copyright renewed © 1956 by Robert Frost. Reprinted by permission of Holt, Rinehart and Winston, Inc.

Glenn Hughes, for translations from *Three Women Poets of Modern Japan*, by Glenn Hughes and Yozan T. Iwasaki. University of Washington Chapbooks, #9, University of Washington Bookstore. Copyright 1927 by Glenn Hughes. Reprinted by permission.

Indiana University Press, for "To My Friend, Whose Parachute Did Not Open," by David Wagoner. Reprinted by permission of Indiana University Press from A PLACE TO STAND by David Wagoner. Copyright © 1958 by Indiana University Press.

The Macmillan Company, for "Poetry," by Marianne Moore. Reprinted with permission of The Macmillan Company from COLLECTED POEMS by Marianne Moore. Copyright 1936 by Marianne Moore. For "Mr. Flood's Party," by E. A. Robinson. Reprinted with permission of The Macmillan Company from COLLECTED POEMS by Edwin Arlington Robinson. Copyright 1921 by Edwin Arlington Robinson. Renewed 1949 by Ruth Nivison. And for "Night Song at Amalfi," by Sara Teasdale. Reprinted with permission of The Macmillan Company from COLLECTED POEMS by Sara Teasdale. Copyright 1915 by The Macmillan Company. Renewed 1943 by Mamie Y. Wheless.

New Directions, for "In the Naked Bed, in Plato's Cave," from IN DREAMS BEGIN RESPONSIBILITIES by Delmore Schwartz. Copyright 1938 by New Directions. Reprinted by permission of the publishers, New Directions.

The New York Public Library, for permission to use the draft stanza of "Mr. Flood's Party," by Edwin Arlington Robinson, from the Lewis M. Isaacs Collection of Robinsoniana in the New York Public Library.

October House, Inc., for "Sonnet to My Mother" by George Barker, from COLLECTED POEMS, 1930–1965, copyright © 1965 by George Barker. Reprinted by permission of October House, Inc.

Oxford University Press, Inc., for "The Windhover," from *Poems of Gerard Manley Hopkins*, Third Edition, edited by W. H. Gardner. Copyright 1948 by Oxford University Press, Inc. Reprinted by permission; and for nine lines from the Robert Whitelaw translation of Sophocles' *Antigone*, from *Fifteen Greek Plays*, translated into English by Gilbert Murray, Benjamin Buckley Rogers and others. Copyright 1943 by Oxford University Press, Inc. Reprinted by permission.

Random House, Inc., for "The Express" (POEMS BY STEPHEN SPENDER). Copyright 1934 and renewed 1961 by Stephen Spender. Reprinted from COLLECTED POEMS, by Stephen Spender, by permission of Random House, Inc.; and for "The Fly," copyright 1942 by Karl Shapiro. Reprinted from POEMS 1940-1953, by Karl Shapiro, by permission of Random House, Inc.

Karl Shapiro, for permission to print a manuscript note on "The Fly" as first transcribed by Phyllis Bartlett for *Poems in Process* (Oxford University Press, 1951).

The Tribune Publishing Company, Tacoma, Washington, and the authors for permission to reprint "Early Fishermen" (1956), by Carlin Aden, and "Two Mountains Men Have Climbed" (1954), by Pauline Barr Starkweather, first published in the "Washington Verse" column of *The Tacoma News Tribune*.

The Viking Press, Inc., for "The Way My Ideas Think Me," from HAVE COME, AM HERE by José Garcia Villa. Copyright 1941, 1942 by José Garcia Villa. Reprinted by permission of The Viking Press, Inc.

David Wagoner, for permission to transcribe the draft manuscript of "To My Friend Whose Parachute Did Not Open."

The Laocoon illustration is from Gotthold Lessing's *Laokoon*, edited by Ludwig Schunck. Munster, 1905

Contents

PREFACE

PART ONE: THE POET AND HIS ART

1 THE FAMILY OF THE ARTS   3
    Art and Craft   6
    The Fine Arts   8

2 THE POET AS ARTIST   16

PART TWO: THE POET AND HIS CRAFT

3 THE CREATIVE PROCESS   31

4 POETIC TOOLS: DEVICES FOR RHYTHM AND SOUND   37
    Devices for Rhythm   37
      The Syllable   38
      The Foot   39
      The Verse   45
      Medial Pauses and Verse Endings   49
    Devices for Sound   52
      Rime   52
      Refrain and Parallelism   56
      Alliteration, Assonance, and
      Onomatopoeia   58

5 POETIC TOOLS: STANZA AND POEM FORMS   64
    Stanza Forms   65
      Blank Verse   65
      Heroic and Octosyllabic Couplets   68
      Terza Rima   70
      Quatrains   71
      Stanzas of Six to Eight Verses   73
      Spenserian Stanza   75
      Longer Stanzas   75
    Poem Forms   77
      The Sonnet   77
      The Ode   79
      Free Verse   84

Contents

Sprung Rhythm 88

The French Forms 89

The Limerick 93

The Japanese Forms 94

*An Interlude: The Heroic Couplet, Blank
Verse, and the Sonnet—A Historical View* 96

6   POETIC TOOLS: IMAGERY AND FIGURES OF SPEECH 109

Simile 110

Metaphor 112

Conceit 113

Personification 113

Apostrophe 114

Hyperbole 115

Antithesis 115

Synecdoche 116

Metonymy 116

PART THREE: THE POET AND HIS POEM

7   THE RANGE OF POETRY 123

Narrative Poetry 123

The Ballad 124

The Epic 133

The Metrical Romance 137

The Metrical Tale 143

Dramatic Poetry 144

Poetic Drama 144

Dramatic Poems 147

Dramatic Dialogue 147

The Aside 149

The Soliloquy 151

The Dramatic Monologue 154

Combined Types 156

The Character Sketch 157

The Lyric and Its Modern Voice 160

Cities 164

Love 167

The House Fly 172

Man and God 175

Death 179

Contents

8 THE POET AND HIS POEM: A READING
OF SIX SONNETS FROM FIVE CENTURIES   185
  Shakespeare's *Sonnet XXX*   186
  Milton's *On His Blindness*   196
  Keats's *On First Looking into Chapman's*
   Homer   204
  Hopkins' *The Windhover*   214
  Frost's *A Soldier*   233
  Barker's *Sonnet to My Mother*   243

SELECTED TITLES FOR ADDITIONAL READING   258

INDEX OF TOPICS   262

INDEX OF NAMES, TITLES, AND FIRST LINES   266

As always: For Lorene

Preface

THIS book is concerned with what Marianne Moore has called "the genuine" in poetry—with those qualities that, properly understood, can give a sense of discrimination to the reader and bring him into a fascinating and moving world not to have experienced which must leave him poorer. For poetry finds its fullest enjoyment in the mind of the reader who shares an awareness of the creative process and the creative personality that brought it into being, and the present introduction is designed to offer background material to assist in such understanding. It will deal with the poet as artist and craftsman, and with the basic principles underlying English poetry of all periods. The aim has been to present only such material as the average serious reader should know well, and to employ only such terms as are in generally accepted use.

Particular care has been taken to indicate something of what the reader should "look for" and "listen for" in his reading, in order that he may not only be better able to grasp the overall effect of a poem but also to have some awareness of the manner in which the overall effect has been accomplished. The usual features of such a book have been supplemented by frequent limited explications, and the last chapter has been given over to a much fuller extension of this approach, especially with respect to poetry as an audible art, than is usually found in an introductory work of this kind. While no one can hope that he has all the answers in such explications, he can hope that the method demonstrated, even in an interpretation about which there may be considerable difference of opinion, will be of value and will give the reader a wider grasp of the possibilities inherent in the experience of reading than he might otherwise have had.

LAWRENCE J. ZILLMAN

University of Washington

Part One: The Poet and His Art

⤙ 1 ⤚

The Family of the Arts

D EFINITIONS in the arts seldom achieve "the truth, the whole truth, and nothing but the truth," yet they may serve as starting points for exploration of the many facets with which the beginner is faced as he attempts to think seriously about his subject. And even the beginner may come closer than he realizes to certain essentials if he will but try. Thus when one student spoke of "that stuff that doesn't quite reach the margins of the page" he showed an awareness of an important (and not always superficial) aspect of poetry: its appearance, its shape if you will, by which the reader is guided in his phrasing, and by which the thought of the poem is unfolded for his consideration. When another student wrote that "The poet uses different words to mean exactly the opposite to what they are usually referred to as" he was admittedly ungrammatical beyond the call of duty, and somewhat extreme in his judgment, but he clearly had experienced the suggestive power of poetic expression, the connotative rather than the denotative possibilities of words. And when a third suggested that "Prose is not hidden under ornamental words but can usually be summed up in one sentence; there is no excess of detail or rumpling thoughts," he too was conscious of the suggestive power of words, but also of the emotional impact communicated by a well written poem: the "rumpling thoughts."

The import of the latter phrase, indeed, is not far removed from Emily Dickinson's statement that, when reading, "If I feel physically as if the top of my head were taken off, I know that is poetry"; or A. E. Housman's that "I could no more define poetry than a terrier can define a rat, but [we both recognize]

[3]

the object by the symptoms which it provokes in us"—and he added that "Experience has taught me, when I am shaving of a morning, to keep watch over my thoughts, because, if a line of poetry strays into my memory, my skin bristles so that the razor ceases to act. This particular symptom is accompanied by a shiver down the spine." I suspect that had either Miss Dickinson or Housman thought of the phrase they would have agreed that they were experiencing "rumpling thoughts."

To some readers, of course, such reactions are perfectly silly, and it is difficult for them to realize that when they, too, have "shivers down the spine," for whatever reason, there are those who would consider them a bit naïve also. But blasé, sophisticated, "realistic," or whatever we try to be, we are in fact creatures of sense and sensitivity, we have our emotions, we respond to the imaginative impulse as expressed in the arts, we even try at times to convey something of what we feel by groping toward the expression of our own feelings. So we are not entirely without a basis for understanding some of the more formal definitions of poetry; such, for example, as the famous statement by Wordsworth that "Poetry is the spontaneous overflow of powerful feelings," to which he added, "it takes its origin from emotion recollected in tranquillity"; or by Byron that "poetry is the lava of the imagination, whose eruption prevents an earthquake"; or by Shelley that it is "the expression of the imagination"; or by Keats that

> A drainless shower
> Of light is poesy; 'tis the supreme of power;
> 'Tis might half slumbering on its own right arm;

or by Emerson that "Poetry is the perpetual endeavor to express the spirit of the thing, to pass the brute body and search the life and reason which causes it to exist." But something is lacking in these definitions.

What is lacking is not the element that once formed a significant part of such discussions, namely that poetry should teach as well as delight (Sir Philip Sidney), or, in Samuel Johnson's words, that "Poetry is the art of uniting pleasure with truth, by calling imagination to the help of reason." Coleridge pretty well disposed of this when he argued that "Poetry is that species of composition, which is opposed to works of science, by proposing for its *immediate* object pleasure, not truth," a statement in which he agreed with Wordsworth's insistence that "The poet writes under one restriction only, namely, the necessity of giving immediate pleasure to a human being possessed of that information which may be expected from him, not as a lawyer, a physician, a mariner, an astronomer, or a natural philosopher, but as a man."

The difficulty is that most of these "definitions" do not define. They are as applicable to the other arts as they are to poetry. Most fine arts are involved in "the spontaneous overflow of powerful feelings," or "the lava of the imagination," or "a drainless shower of light," or any other of the general characterizing suggestions. But poetry uses words, and unless the definition incorporates reference to verbal language it falls short. Thus Poe avoided a confusion with music when he noted that "The poetry of words I would describe as the rhythmical creation of beauty"; and Shelley recognized the problem when he wrote: "But poetry in a more restricted sense expresses those arrangements of language, and especially metrical language, which are created by that imperial faculty, whose throne is curtained within the invisible nature of man," a statement not too far removed from one of the most satisfactory modern definitions, that of Lascelles Abercrombie: "Poetry is the expression of imaginative experience, valued simply as such and significant simply as such, in the communicable state given by language which employs every available and appropriate device." Here, although there are echoes of the other "definitions," the phrase "in the communicable state given by language" separates it from the other arts, and the recognition that there are "available and appropriate" devices separates it from other forms of literary expression.

Yet there is an element of truth in each of the definitions we have considered, and perhaps only in a combination of all could a satisfactory description be compounded. For poetry has intangible overtones of sound and rhythm that strike the reader's ear as does music; rhythmical movement that invites a kinesthetic response as does the dance; visual suggestions that appeal to the "inward eye" as do painting and sculpture to the sense of sight; and elements of form whose description as "architectonics" suggests their relationship with architecture. But beyond these elements of the other fine arts there is in poetry the power to develop in words a high thought, feeling or action that can hold the reader and wring from him an imaginative or emotional response *more exact in its nature* than can any other art. Let us examine these relationships to the other arts—and first, art itself.

Art and Craft

In general usage the word "art" is frequently confused with "skill" or "craft." We may speak of a skilled golfer as "an artist with a putter," or of a machine operator as a "fine craftsman" or "an artist when it comes to meshing gears." But in each instance we are referring to manual dexterity only. If we consult *Webster's Dictionary of Synonyms* we find the following pertinent and helpful distinctions:

Both words [art and craft], as here considered, are also affected by their use as designations or pursuits, . . . *craft* tending to be applied to a lower kind of skill or inventive power revealing itself in the mastery of materials or technique, and in effects that can be analyzed and imitated, and *art* to a higher creative power capable of expressing a personal vision and of achieving results which defy analysis and imitation; thus, an artist may demonstrate his *craft* in painting sunlight but he manifests his *art* in painting a scene that conveys his feeling to the spectator. [p. 74] . . . *Craft* is not always clearly distinguished from *trade*, but it tends to be used of those pursuits that involve not only manual or mechanical labor but allow more or less freedom for the exercise of taste, skill, ingenuity, and the like. . . . When qualified, *art* is applied usually only to such pursuits as involve an elaborate technique, great skill, definite ends to be achieved, and the exercise of personal judgment or taste. [pp. 842–43][1]

In the context of our present study, the foregoing can be translated into the two terms *versifier* and *poet*. The poet, as we shall see shortly, is the artist; the versifier is the craftsman. The product of the versifier is verse, the product of the artist is poetry. Verse may be ever so skillfully done in the mechanical

---

[1] Reprinted by permission. From *Webster's Dictionary of Synonyms*, copyright 1951 by G. & C. Merriam Co., publishers of the Merriam-Webster Dictionaries.

exercise of its techniques, but it will lack individuality of expression, personal judgment and taste—it will lack, in Abercrombie's phrase, "the expression of imaginative experience." It may be pleasantly musical but it will usually be indistinguishable from hundreds of efforts in the same area, easily imitated because it, too, in all probability, rests on imitation (consciously or unconsciously); and the easy phrase, the trite image, the commonplace expression will dominate it.[2] For many readers the verse will be easier to read (for there is also an "art" of reading), just as it was easier to write than would have been the distinguished poem, but it must remain verse rather than poetry, the product of the craftsman rather than the artist. It is this second-rate product, produced by "half poets," that a modern writer, Marianne Moore, in *Poetry*, "dislikes," for it lacks the "genuine":

I, too, dislike it: there are things that are important beyond all this
> fiddle.
Reading it, however, with a perfect contempt for it, one discovers in
it, after all, a place for the genuine.
> Hands that can grasp, eyes
> that can dilate, hair that can rise
> > if it must, these things are important not because a

high-sounding interpretation can be put upon them but because they
> are
useful. When they become so derivative as to become
> unintelligible,
the same thing may be said for all of us, that we
> do not admire what
> we cannot understand: the bat
> > holding on upside down or in quest of something to

eat, elephants pushing, a wild horse taking a roll, a tireless wolf
> under
a tree, the immovable critic twitching his skin like a horse that
> feels a flea, the base-
ball fan, the statistician—
> nor is it valid
> to discriminate against 'business documents and

[2] Compare Emerson in his essay, *The Poet*: "The poet is the sayer, the namer, and represents beauty. He is a sovereign, and stands on the centre. . . . Criticism is infested with a cant of materialism, which assumes that manual skill and activity is the first merit of all men, and disparages such as say and do not, overlooking the fact, that some men, namely, poets, are natural sayers, sent into the world to the end of expression, and confounds them with those whose province is action, but who quit it to imitate the sayers."

school-books'; all these phenomena are important. One must make a
    distinction
    however: when dragged into prominence by half poets, the result
        is not poetry,
    nor till the poets among us can be
      'literalists of
      the imagination'—above
        insolence and triviality and can present

for inspection, imaginary gardens with real toads in them, shall we
      have
    it. In the meantime, if you demand on the one hand,
    the raw material of poetry in
      all its rawness and
      that which is on the other hand
        genuine, then you are interested in poetry.

The Fine Arts

But "art" is applicable to all of the fine arts, and rightly so,
for with all of their differences they have in common the quality
of imaginative experience, just as they all rest on the effectiveness of the creative personality and the creative process, to be
considered below. The generally recognized basic fine arts are,
then, architecture (concerned more than are the others with
matters of science also), painting, sculpture, the dance, music,
and poetry (or prose when the elements of art predominate).
For those who would also include drama or opera it should be
pointed out that these are actually related arts and are represented in those named above: drama as a written art under
poetry or prose, as an acted art under the dance (pantomime),
as set design under architecture, painting and sculpture; and
opera in its many aspects under all of these, with music added.

It will be noted that architecture, painting, sculpture and the
dance are visual arts, in that impressions of them come through
the eye, while music and poetry are, correspondingly, audible
arts; and that architecture, painting and sculpture are arts of
space and surface and are relatively permanent, while the dance,
music and poetry are the arts of tempo and rhythm, and are
transitory but readily reproduced. The transitory nature of these

three is indicated by the fact that in a very real sense music is never truly music until it is played, poetry never truly poetry until it is read, or conceived of as read, aloud, and dance never truly such until it is danced. The notes, the words, and the printed choreography are but clues to the final experience of the auditor or viewer.

Each art, thus, has its distinctive qualities, and it is interesting to consider briefly what poetry can do that some of the others cannot, and what poetry cannot do, or cannot do as well as can the others. Let us consider two examples, one fairly simple, the second more complex.

Imagine first, if you will, a stained-glass window, beautiful in its coloring, with a carved frame showing some natural objects, and the window itself depicting a coat of arms. Clearly, if all you had to recommend it was the preceding prose sentence, there would be little temptation to walk more than a few steps to see it. But let John Keats describe the window for you, as he does in *The Eve of St. Agnes*:

> A casement high and triple-arch'd there was,
> All garlanded with carven imag'ries
> Of fruits, and flowers, and bunches of knot-grass,
> And diamonded with panes of quaint device,
> Innumerable of stains and splendid dyes,
> As are the tiger-moth's deep-damask'd wings;
> And in the midst, 'mong thousand heraldries,
> And twilight saints, and dim emblazonings
> A shielded scutcheon blush'd with blood of queens and kings.

Here "every appropriate and available device" has been used by the poet to flesh out the starved sentence at the beginning of this paragraph. The rhythm, the rimes, the stanza form, the devices for sound, all conspire to hold the attention and to integrate the details of the description. And what of the details? The prosaic window above has become "a casement high and triple-arched"; the carved frame is a "garland" with "carven imag'ries / Of fruits, and flowers, and bunches of knot-grass"; the stained glass has become "diamonded with panes of quaint device, / Innumerable of stains and splendid dyes," and so on to the rich fullness of the images which follow, including one that vividly calls up the sense of touch as well as sight: "As are the tiger-moth's deep-damask'd wings."[3]

Clearly, the poetry has gone so far beyond the prose that its advantages here are obvious. But what of its relationship to the stained-glass window itself, an art form related to painting? Rich and compelling as is Keats's stanza, it is no substitute for the thing described: he is writing *about* color, not giving us color; he takes nine lines to convey what the eye would grasp immediately as a unit (even though considerable time might be taken thereafter to search out each detail visually); he creates, in this stanza and others, a remarkable awareness of the room in the castle, but it is not as if we were standing in the cold room looking at the warm colors of the casement.

Is painting, or stained-glass artistry, then superior to poetry? Not at all. Each is *different from,* not *superior to* the other. The poem can give us this window in the context of a story, and make it part of a perfect setting for the lovers; it can perform the important job of selection; it can qualify by choice of words what we might see in the actual window; it can help us find words for what might otherwise be a pleasant but unarticulated response.

No art need be on the defensive with respect to any other art, as will be clear from the following more complex illustration in which several of the arts are involved.

Let us imagine a piece of symphonic music in which a clear feeling of struggle and stress is communicated to the listener, who may share a sense of the tortured, twisting, driving force that lies behind the composition. With no title to guide him, how specific can the listener be in interpreting such music? Will he think of two warriors in combat? of two wrestlers competing for a prize? of a mountain storm or of a storm at sea? of someone seeking answers to imponderable questions? Any one of these or many other situations might be conjured up by what he is hearing. But his response will center around some *general* inter-

---

[3] "Deep-damask'd" is an illustration of the perfect word-choice that sets poetry apart from mere versecraft. (See frontispiece for Keats's draft of this stanza.) Consider also the word "liquefaction" and the kinesthetic response called upon by Robert Herrick's *Upon Julia's Clothes,* p. 170. See also pp. 48*n* and 212*n.*

pretation; he cannot be sure without additional help just what the composer intended beyond this broad emotional impact.

If, then, he is shown the accompanying picture of a man and two boys in the coils of serpents, he may decide that the music is, rather, an attempt to capture in sound something of the powerful effort of the man to prevent destruction of himself and the others. The music described above would fit such a situation; and note that a more specific interpretation of it is now possible. But if we are told that the title of the composition is not "Old Man Protecting Boys" but "The Tempest," this title with its attendant associations will immediately dispose of the warriors, the wrestlers, the philosophically disturbed individual, even the picture which offered such a tempting clue. The listener will, however, still have a problem of identifying the kind

and location of the tempest. If, at last, he is told that the music
he is hearing is Jean Sibelius' "Incidental Music to Shakespeare's
The Tempest" the storm is immediately localized (provided he
knows the play), and the attendant circumstances as described
by Shakespeare, which were in Sibelius' mind as he composed,
will give the listener a surer grasp and a clearer understanding
of the musical intent.[4]

Thus music without title has the possibility, more fully than
has any of the other arts (even abstract painting or sculpture),
of evoking individual responses to a fairly general emotional
expression. The listener will normally not be far removed from
the broad intent of the composer, but only with the help of
words (or of painting, sculpture, or the dance) can the more
specific details be conveyed to him.

In use of the accompanying illustration as a possible clue to
the music, another distinction among the arts has been suggested: the response to the picture is instantaneous (note how
the "architectural" triangular pattern draws the eyes very
quickly to the powerful face of the principal figure), and we
may feel our muscles straining in sympathy with the effort of
the old man to hold off the serpent. It takes time for the music
(assuming that our guess as to its subject had been correct)
to develop this sense of sharing, time that may result in a more
complete and intensified involvement on the part of the listener,
but with a loss in the sense of immediacy that the picture gives.
But the picture, we should remember, is of a statue, a three-
dimensional sculpture that affects the viewer in a manner impossible to the pictured representation, which is flat. True, we
may be able to imagine the three-dimensional quality as we
look at the illustration but, like painting, it is limited to surface,
whereas the sculpture has the added dimension of space and

---

[4] The storm is but one of several scenes from *The Tempest* treated
musically by Sibelius, and the close relationship between music and
poetry is suggested by David Hall's statement that "Shakespeare's great
play receives a magnificent tonal dress from the Finnish bard. This is
perhaps the finest incidental music ever written. Certainly it took the hand
of a master to weave the hypnotic spell of 'The Oak Tree' or the distorted
Caliban character picture." Yet everything said in the present discussion
about the initial difficulty of interpreting the music is equally or more
true of the other musical passages as they relate to Shakespeare's lines.

thus comes closer to the world of experience in which we participate.

The sculpture itself, however, while immediate and visual in its impact, is lacking in other respects. Who are the three persons involved in this struggle? how did they get into this predicament? what was the outcome? The sculpture does not tell us, nor would a musical interpretation of the situation do so, although a ballet might give more information. There are few hints, however, in the work itself. Unless these are three unfortunate hikers from a nudist camp, we would immediately conclude (if we have any knowledge of art) that the lack of clothing is probably indicative of a classical setting; and we may remember that there are many representations of struggle in the sculpture and literature of the period. But beyond that we cannot go if we stay within the limits of this art.

Again we will require the assistance of words, just as we would probably need program notes if the scene of which this is the climax were developed for us in either music or the dance. When we are told, then, that this is the famous Laocoon group of the first century B.C. we may still be in the dark (as we were with respect to "The Tempest" if we did not know the details of Shakespeare's play). And it is at this point that one element of the difference of poetry from the other arts becomes evident: there may be less of the immediate visual appeal of the painting, sculpture, or the dance; less of the broadly generalized and emotionally stirring ambiguity of the music; but there will be opportunity for the incorporation of specific detail and cumulative progression of story, accompanied by "every available and appropriate device" (to quote again from Abercrombie), devices that offer some of the advantages of music (through rhythm, rime, etc.) and (through vividness of imagery) of painting— but without the possibility of the vertical harmony in the chords of the former or the immediacy and physical color of the latter.

Poetry, in other words, contains its own "program notes"; it offers the background we may lack for the full understanding of the other arts, or if it does not offer it, it indicates by allusion the sources to which we can go for information. Clearly, the broader our knowledge the more enjoyment we will find in

allusive poetry, just as we will respond more fully to other arts
if we are aware of the backgrounds, either of subject matter or
style, of which they are the expression.

If we apply these principles to the present case we will discover, either through use of reference books or because we have
read and remember Greek myth or Book II of Vergil's *Aeneid*,
that Laocoon has profaned the temple of Apollo, has attempted
to dissuade the Trojans from admitting the wooden horse into
Troy, and must die. The sculptor, as we have seen, leaps directly
to the high climactic moment. Vergil, of course, tells the whole
story, from which the following pertinent lines (from Dryden's
translation) are taken. These lines should be compared carefully
with the illustration:

> Laocoon, Neptune's priest by lot that year,
> With solemn pomp then sacrific'd a steer;
> When, dreadful to behold, from sea we spied
> Two serpents, rank'd abreast, the seas divide,
> And smoothly sweep along the swelling tide.
> Their flaming crests above the waves they show;
> Their bellies seem to burn the seas below;
> Their speckled tails advance to steer their course,
> And on the sounding shore the flying billows force.
> And now the strand, and now the plain they held;
> Their ardent eyes with bloody streaks were fill'd;
> Their nimble tongues they brandish'd as they came,
> And lick'd their hissing jaws, that sputter'd flame.
> We fled amaz'd; their destin'd way they take,
> And to Laocoon and his children make;
> And first around the tender boys they wind,
> Then with their sharpen'd fangs their limbs and bodies grind.
> The wretched father, running to their aid
> With pious haste, but vain, they next invade;
> Twice round his waist their winding volumes roll'd;
> And twice about his gasping throat they fold.
> The priest thus doubly chok'd, their crests divide,
> And tow'ring o'er his head in triumph ride.
> With both his hands he labors at the knots;
> His holy fillets the blue venom blots;
> His roaring fills the flitting air around.
> Thus, when an ox receives a glancing wound,
> He breaks his bands, the fatal altar flies,
> And with loud bellowings breaks the yielding skies.

In these lines the amassing and careful ordering of many details (or "building" to a climax to suggest again the relationship to architecture) enables the reader to fill in much that would be missing in the supposed music and dance, and is missing in the actual sculpture. But we can hear in the movement of the lines something of the rhythmical compulsion that we might find in the music, and, if we have active imaginations, we might well arrive at a picture in our minds that would not be incompatible with what we might see in a Laocoon ballet, or in the sculpture itself.

It becomes, then, not a question of either/or in the arts. Through an adequate understanding of the relative strengths of each, each becomes a supporting element in the full appreciation of the others. The fuller the knowledge we have of architecture, painting, sculpture, the dance, and music, the fuller will be our response to and enjoyment of poetry.[5] And the better aware we are of the nature of the creative personality and the creative process the better will we be able to share the creation of the poet, and to bring to it the best of our own capabilities; for when Shelley in *Adonais* wrote of the "quick dreams" (the poems) wandering "from kindling brain to brain" he recognized that every reader must be at least half a poet, and bring a creative response to the poet's creation.

We turn now to the artist behind the art.

[5] It should be emphasized that in this section we have been concerned with each art as an independent mode of expression, not with those unions in which, for example, the words of a poem are set to music, or a ballet is choreographed to an existing piece of music. Many times, of course, this will be done, and frequently to the enhancement of each art involved, but at the same time to the diminishment of each in the degree to which it must share.
Other examples of the kind dealt with in this chapter will be found in a comparison of Sibelius' incidental music for *As You Like It*, or Tchaikovsky's *Romeo and Juliet* (*Overture Fantasy*) with Shakespeare's plays; the latter's *Manfred Symphony* and *Francesca Da Rimini* (*Symphonic Fantasy*) with Byron's *Manfred* and Dante's *Inferno* (Canto V) respectively; Stéphane Mallarmé's poem *L'Après-Midi d'un Faune* with Debussy's music and the ballet of the same title; Dante Gabriel Rossetti's *The Blessed Damozel* with his own painting of the subject. Many others will come to mind or be recognized if the relationships between the arts are understood and watched for in the different areas of expression.

ᐊ 2 ᐅ

The Poet as Artist

THE CREATIVE personality is an essential attribute of every artist,[1] but it is also an attribute in which all human beings can share, for it is in a very real sense the human personality at its maximum effectiveness. Moreover, it is a quality that can be developed and strengthened even though the individual never intends to write a poem, compose music, or attempt to express himself in terms of the arts as such. And there is no better way for such development than through learning to appreciate one or more of the arts in some detail, thus sharing the experience of the artist.

It is natural that poets themselves, involved as they are in the creative life, should be called in as expert witnesses on this subject, even though we have seen in the preceding chapter

[1] In this sense any artist or idealist was, for Shelley, a poet: "But poets . . . are not only the authors of language and of music, of the dance and architecture, and statuary, and painting; they are the institutors of laws, and the founders of civil society, and the inventors of the arts of life, and the teachers, who draw into a certain propinquity with the beautiful and the true, that partial apprehension of the agencies of the invisible world which is called religion" (*Defence of Poetry*).

In this chapter the discussion will draw rather heavily on the Romantic poets. They were writing in a period when fresh insights were being brought to the art of poetry, when attempts at definition, evaluation, and self-analysis as artists were rich, suggestive, and less encumbered with the psychological and critical jargon (what has been called the "labored neologisms") that so frequently befuddles the introductory student of the art, than is much of our contemporary offering. Once grounded in these fundamentals, however, the student should turn for modern developments to collections such as Robert Wooster Stallman's *Critiques and Essays in Criticism, 1920–1948* (1949), Ray B. West, Jr.'s *Essays in Modern Literary Criticism* (1952), Irving Howe's *Modern Literary Criticism: An Anthology* (1958), or John Oliver Perry's *Approaches to the Poem: Modern Essays in the Analysis and Interpretation of Poetry* (1965).

[16]

that, despite a consistent awareness of its spirit, they have frequently fallen short of a satisfactory definition of poetry. We shall, therefore, give some of them a chance to indicate how they see themselves, first with respect to the essential nature of the poet, then with attention to the specific details that set him apart.

Sometimes, indeed, a clearly recognizable poet will deny the high seriousness of his art. When Robert Frost did so he had a twinkle in his eye and almost certainly his tongue in cheek; and when Robert Burns did so in the following lines from his *Epistle to J. Lapraik,* he used the denial largely to suggest the importance of inspiration over learning—claiming, indeed, to be a versifier rather than a poet since he dealt with "homely" subjects and simple form:

> I am nae poet, in a sense,
> But just a rhymer like by chance,
> An' hae to learning nae pretence;
> 　Yet, what the matter?
> Whene'er my Muse does on me glance,
> 　I jingle at her.
>
> Your critic-folk may cock their nose,
> And say, "How can you e'er propose,
> You, wha ken* hardly verse frae prose,　　　*know
> 　To make a sang?"
> But, by your leaves, my learned foes,
> 　Ye're maybe wrang.
>
> What's a' your jargon o' your schools,
> Your Latin names for horns an' stools?
> If honest Nature made you fools,
> 　What sairs* your grammars?　　　　　　　*serves
> Ye'd better ta'en up spades and shools,*　　*shovels
> 　Or knappin-hammers.*　　　　　　　　　*stone breakers
>
> A set o' dull, conceited hashes*　　　　　　*oafs
> Confuse their brains in college classes,
> They gang in stirks,* and come out asses,　　*go in oxes
> 　Plain truth to speak;
> An' syne* they think to climb Parnassus**　　*since **Muses'
> 　By dint o' Greek!　　　　　　　　　　　　mountain

Gie me ae* spark o' Nature's fire!   *one
That's a' the learning I desire;
Then, though I drudge through dub* an' mire   *puddle
  At pleugh* or cart,   *plough
My Muse, though hamely in attire,
  May touch the heart.

Burns, too, would appear to have tongue in cheek, but beneath the bantering spirit of his lines is the recognition that a
compulsion to write, a "spark o' Nature's fire," irrespective of the
learning that gives the poet something to write about, is an
essential part of the creative personality. Oliver Wendell Holmes
called it *Cacoethes Scribendi* ("The Disease of Writing"), which
he described as follows:

> If all the trees in all the woods were men;
> And each and every blade of grass a pen;
> If every leaf on every shrub and tree
> Turned to a sheet of foolscap; every sea
> Were changed to ink, and all earth's living tribes
> Had nothing else to do but act as scribes,
> And for ten thousand ages, day and night,
> The human race should write, and write, and write,
> Till all the pens and paper were used up,
> And the huge inkstand was an empty cup,
> Still would the scribblers clustered round its brink
> Call for more pens, more paper, and more ink.

It might appear at first sight from the following passage that
Shakespeare, like Burns, placed the poet slightly lower than the
angels, but the context of these lines from *A Midsummer Night's
Dream* should be kept in mind. It has been a strange night, a
"lunatic" night, what with magic potions that lead lovers to fly
to that from which they would flee, including "asses' heads in
fairyland." Duke Theseus (Act V, Scene 1) finds the lovers'
report of it:

> More strange than true. I never may believe
> These antique fables, nor these fairy toys.
> Lovers and madmen have such seething brains,
> Such shaping fantasies, that apprehend
> More than cool reason ever comprehends.
> The lunatic, the lover and the poet
> Are of imagination all compact:
> One sees more devils than vast hell can hold,

That is, the madman: the lover, all as frantic,
Sees Helen's beauty in a brow of Egypt:
The poet's eye, in a fine frenzy rolling,
Doth glance from heaven to earth, from earth to heaven;
And as imagination bodies forth
The forms of things unknown, the poet's pen
Turns them to shapes and gives to airy nothing
A local habitation and a name.
Such tricks hath strong imagination,
That, if it would but apprehend some joy,
It comprehends some bringer of that joy;
Or, in the night, imagining some fear,
How easy is a bush supposed a bear!

The poet might not appreciate the company in which he is placed here, but Shakespeare is simply reflecting the Elizabethan conception of the imagination as a faculty for calling up pictures, even of things unknown, and giving them a communicable form. Later writers were to view the imagination as a far more significant faculty of the mind, as we shall see (they would substitute the term "fancy" in the above passage), but Shakespeare is unquestionably correct in assigning to it the key position when the poet is considered, for the imaginative personality is synonymous with the creative personality as we have described it above.

Wordsworth had something in common with both Burns and Shakespeare. Like Burns he felt that the poet should be concerned with "incidents and situations from common life," and like Shakespeare he would call on imagination, "whereby ordinary things [are] presented to the mind in an unusual aspect." But he did not deny his high calling, and in lines from Book IV of his autobiographical poem, *The Prelude*, he described the moment of his dedication. He was home from college for the summer vacation, and had gone to a neighborhood party, which clearly lasted most of the night:

Ere we retired,
The cock had crowed, and now the eastern sky
Was kindling, not unseen, from humble copse
And open field, through which the pathway wound,
And homeward led my steps. Magnificent
The morning rose, in memorable pomp,

Glorious as e'er I had beheld—in front,
The sea lay laughing at a distance; near,
The solid mountains shone, bright as the clouds,
Grain-tinctured, drenched in empyrean light;
And in the meadows and the lower grounds
Was all the sweetness of the common dawn—
Dews, vapors, and the melody of birds,
And laborers going forth to till the fields.
Ah! need I say, dear Friend! that to the brim
My heart was full; I made no vows, but vows
Were then made for me; bond unknown to me
Was given, that I should be, else sinning greatly,
A dedicated Spirit. On I walked
In thankful blessedness, which yet survives.

There is a suggestion here, as in Burns's lines, that the dedication was in the nature of an inspiration, for "bond unknown to me / Was given . . ." And so it was for Shelley who, a few years later, described his own dedication in his *Hymn to Intellectual Beauty*. It is perhaps more than coincidence that both of these poets found their great moment in late spring or early summer, a time when the creative forces of the natural world were in evidence all around them. Shelley is more specific than is Wordsworth or Burns in identifying the source of his moving impulse: it is that essence of beauty (*intellectual* in contrast to *physical* beauty) which is in all beautiful things, the Platonic idea of a beauty that is universal and timeless; a loveliness (or the essence of love) which Shelley saw as the guiding force behind the universe. The poet, or any artist, must in some way find his kinship with this force, and once having done so he is powerless to turn aside; his way is determined, whether it be only to the foothills of versification, to the highest summits of poetry, or to that point in between where the rarefied atmosphere tells him he has found his farthest reach. Shelley, in the following lines from the *Hymn*, described his own experience thus:

While yet a boy I sought for ghosts, and sped
    Through many a listening chamber, cave and ruin,
    And starlight wood, with fearful steps pursuing
Hopes of high talk with the departed dead.

I called on poisonous names with which our youth is fed;
　I was not heard—I saw them not—
　When musing deeply on the lot
Of life, at that sweet time when winds are wooing
　All vital things that wake to bring
　News of birds and blossoming,—
　Sudden, thy shadow fell on me;
I shrieked, and clasped my hands in ecstasy!

I vowed that I would dedicate my powers
　To thee and thine—have I not kept the vow?
　With beating heart and streaming eyes, even now
I call the phantoms of a thousand hours
　Each from his voiceless grave: they have in visioned bowers
　Of studious zeal or love's delight
　Outwatched with me the envious night:
They know that never joy illumed my brow
　Unlinked with hope that thou wouldst free
　This world from its dark slavery,
　That thou, O awful Loveliness,
Wouldst give whate'er these words cannot express.

In the poems of Burns, Wordsworth and Shelley we have
listened to the poet speaking of his inspiration and his dedication. In each instance he has been in high spirits, whether in
the playful expression of Burns or in the elation of discovery
that marks the other two—restrained in Wordsworth, bursting
forth in an emotional flood in Shelley. But what of the poet who
has known this elation, this power, this joy, and lost it? If we
turn to a contemporary of these three we find our answer. Coleridge, ill and dulled by the drug through which he sought re-
lief from pain, has left us, in his *Dejection: An Ode,* a poignant
record of what the poet must have or, failing of it or losing it,
turn from poetry.

For Coleridge, as for Wordsworth, the imagination was not
merely the ability to call up and record pictures. It was, rather,
akin to the creative spirit of the universe, and in itself creative;
it was the faculty that brought reason and understanding into
harmony; it was the unifying (or *esemplastic,* which was Coleridge's word) power that *fused* or *synthesized* (again his words)
seemingly unlike things, instead of merely "aggregating and

associating" them, as did the fancy.[2] Through it, in the words of
this poem, "we receive but what we give," for it was to him a
"shaping spirit," or, in a word that for him was synonymous with
the life force, it was "joy." Coleridge knew that, without this
inner spirit of imagination, the artist in whatever field was
limited to working with counters, to perceiving instead of
creating.

Dejection: An Ode opens with a beautiful description of the
evening sky, but the tragedy for Coleridge is found in his comment: "I see these things so beautifully fair, / I see, not feel,
how beautiful they are."[3] Without the feeling that accompanies
imagination, without the ability to "half create," the mind to
him was but a passive receptor of external stimuli. He knew that
he would never again be the poet he once was, the poet of
The Rime of the Ancient Mariner, Christabel, and *Kubla Khan,*
but that he must turn to "abstruse research"—to philosophy and
literary criticism. Perhaps we can see most clearly what the essential poet is by reading, from the *Dejection: An Ode,* these
words of one who felt that he could no longer claim the title:

> My genial spirits fail;
> And what can these avail
> To lift the smothering weight from off my breast?
> It were a vain endeavor,
> Though I should gaze forever
> On that green light that lingers in the west:
> I may not hope from outward forms to win
> The passion and the life, whose fountains are within.
>
> O Lady! we receive but what we give,
> And in our life alone does Nature live:
> Ours is her wedding garment, ours her shroud!
> And would we ought behold, of higher worth,
> Than that inanimate cold world allowed
> To the poor loveless ever-anxious crowd,

[2] "The poet, described in *ideal* perfection, brings the whole soul of man
into activity, with the subordination of its faculties to each other, according to their relative worth and dignity. He diffuses a tone and spirit of
unity, that blends, and (as it were) *fuses,* each into each, by that syn-
thetic and magical power to which we have exclusively appropriated the
name of imagination." (*Biographia Literaria,* Chapter XIV.)

[3] Compare Wordsworth's *Lines Composed a Few Miles Above Tintern
Abbey*: ". . . the mighty world / Of eye, and ear,—both what they half
create, / And what perceive."

Ah! from the soul itself must issue forth
A light, a glory, a fair luminous cloud
 Enveloping the earth—
And from the soul itself must there be sent
 A sweet and potent voice, of its own birth,
Of all sweet sounds the life and element!

O pure of heart! thou need'st not ask of me
What this strong music in the soul may be!
What, and wherein it doth exist,
This light, this glory, this fair luminous mist,
This beautiful and beauty-making power.
 Joy, virtuous Lady! Joy that ne'er was given,
Save to the pure, and in their purest hour,
Life, and life's effluence, cloud at once and shower,
Joy, Lady, is the spirit and the power,
Which wedding Nature to us gives in dower
 A new earth and new heaven,
Undreamt of by the sensual and the proud—
Joy is the sweet voice, joy the luminous cloud—
 We in ourselves rejoice!
And thence flows all that charms or ear or sight,
 All melodies the echoes of that voice,
All colors a suffusion from that light.

There was a time when, though my path was rough,
 This joy within me dallied with distress,
And all misfortunes were but as the stuff
 Whence Fancy made me dreams of happiness:
For hope grew round me, like the twining vine,
And fruits, and foliage, not my own, seemed mine.
But now afflictions bow me down to earth:
Nor care I that they rob me of my mirth;
 But oh! each visitation
Suspends what nature gave me at my birth,
 My shaping spirit of Imagination.
For not to think of what I needs must feel,
 But to be still and patient, all I can;
And haply by abstruse research to steal
 From my own nature all the natural man—
 This was my sole resource, my only plan:
Till that which suits a part infects the whole,
And now is almost grown the habit of my soul.

The "shaping spirit," which Coleridge felt he had lost, the
ability to "half create" which was so important to Wordsworth,

are in fact the imaginative compulsion which urges the artist on; and if the expression has seemed to the reader somewhat idealized and "poetic" it will be rewarding to follow one of these poets as he attempts to delineate more specifically what he conceives the poet to be. It is Wordsworth, writing in his Preface to *Lyrical Ballads*:

What is a poet? . . . He is a man speaking to men: a man, it is true, endowed with more lively sensibility, more enthusiasm and tenderness, who has a greater knowledge of human nature, and a more comprehensive soul, than are supposed to be common among mankind; a man pleased with his own passions and volitions, and who rejoices more than other men in the spirit of life that is in him; delighting to contemplate similar volitions and passions as manifested in the goings-on of the Universe, and habitually impelled to create them where he does not find them. To these qualities he has added a disposition to be affected more than other men by absent things as if they were present; an ability of conjuring up in himself passions, which are indeed far from being the same as those produced by real events, yet . . . do more nearly resemble the passions produced by real events, than anything which . . . other men are accustomed to feel in themselves:—whence, and from practice, he has acquired a greater readiness and power in expressing what he thinks and feels, and especially those thoughts and feelings which, by his own choice, or from the structure of his own mind, arise in him without immediate external excitement. . . . It will be the wish of the Poet to bring his feelings near to those of the persons whose feelings he describes, nay, for short spaces of time, perhaps, to let himself slip into an entire delusion, and even confound and identify his own feelings with theirs. . . . The Man of science seeks truth as a remote and unknown benefactor; he cherishes and loves it in his solitude: the Poet, singing a song in which all human beings join with him, rejoices in the presence of truth as our visible friend and hourly companion.

It is important to note that in Wordsworth's view the poet differs from non-poets only in degree, and that, as was indicated at the beginning of this chapter, every human being has the potential of a full imaginative experience—that the creative personality is the human personality at its maximum effectiveness. It will be well now to summarize the details of this personality in its broadest application.

The first characteristic, then, is so elementary that there is some danger of its being passed by without adequate attention, although it has been stressed directly or by implication in the writers we have quoted. It is *sensitivity of perception*. Someone has suggested that "the world is full of walking vegetables," a statement designed, it is hoped, merely to startle his listeners; yet there is a serious point in the comment. We do tend to insulate ourselves from the fullest participation in the myriad appeals to our senses, and we lose greatly to the extent that we do so. Or we receive the impulse at the surface only, failing of its penetration to the depths of feeling. It is this that differentiates the ordinary man from the artist, and it was this of which Emerson wrote in *The Poet*:

Too feeble fall the impressions of nature on us to make us artists. Every touch should thrill. Every man should be so much an artist, that he could report in conversation what had befallen him. Yet, in our experience, the rays or appulses have sufficient force to arrive at the senses, but not enough to reach the quick, and compel the reproduction of themselves in speech. The poet is the person in whom these powers are in balance, the man without impediment, who sees and handles that which others dream of, traverses the whole scale of experience, and is representative of man, in virtue of being the largest power to receive and to impart.

But we may be sensitive in a limited area only, neglecting other areas that would widen our appreciation. This suggests that the second element should be *inclusiveness of perception*. The mind that finds great satisfaction in poetry, but little in painting, music, or the dance, is clearly denying itself the fullest response to an appreciation of poetry; for, as we have seen, the interrelationship of the arts means that any one of them has something to offer in support of any other.

Sensitivity and inclusiveness of perception, however, would be of comparatively little value without *retentiveness of perception*, the "emotion recollected in tranquillity" of Wordsworth's definition of poetry, or, more broadly, the ability to carry the intellectual or emotional impact of an experience into a related experience at a different time, thus permitting one experience to supplement and support the other. The poem read in childhood is recalled when another poem on a similar theme is read, and both are richer for the association. Acquaintance with a piece of music may form the basis for later recollection on hearing another piece of music, or on seeing a painting, or on reading a poem. Frequently these will not be detailed remembrances, nor need they be, but they form the fabric of our responses—of our sensitivity and its inclusiveness.

But these first three aspects of the creative personality are relatively passive, for the photographic film and the phonograph record are also, in their way, sensitive, inclusive, and retentive. The human mind, however, is capable of an active sharing in the aesthetic experience, and the fourth element can be described as *a sympathetic projection of the mind toward the object.* Many listeners to fine music in the concert hall feel themselves (in their concentration) "reaching" towards the stage lest they miss the more subtle nuances of the performance; many experience the same feeling in looking at a painting, or a beautiful building, or a ballet, or a sculpture, or in reading a poem.

In one sense this sympathetic projection represents an intermediate step toward the fifth and most significant element in the creative personality: what the psychologist calls *empathy* (a "feeling into"), a projection of the mind or personality into unity with, and so fully understanding, the object of contemplation. Although the word was not coined until 1912, we have seen the principle behind Wordsworth's suggestion that the poet must at times "confound and identify his own feelings" with those of the "persons whose feelings he describes." But empathy can go beyond identification with persons. Keats's friend Richard Woodhouse reported him to have "affirmed that he can conceive of a billiard ball that it may have a sense of delight from its own roundness, smoothness and volubility and the rapidity of its motion"; and Keats himself wrote that "If a sparrow come before my window, I take part in its existence and pick about the gravel," and again that "I lay awake last night listening to the rain with a sense of being drowned and rotted like a grain of wheat." But perhaps the most complete

suggestion of the empathic nature of the creative personality
is to be found in Keats's letter of October, 1818:

> As to the poetical character itself . . . it is not itself; it has no
> self; it is everything and nothing; it has no character; it enjoys light
> and shade; it lives in gusto, be it foul or fair, high or low, rich or
> poor, mean or elevated; it has as much delight in conceiving an
> Iago as an Imogen. What shocks the virtuous philosopher delights
> the chameleon poet. It does no harm from its relish of the dark side
> of things, any more than from its taste for the bright one, because
> they both end in speculation. A poet is the most unpoetical thing in
> existence, because he has no identity; he is continually in for and
> filling some other body.[4]

These five elements, then, form the basis of the creative per-
sonality, and they must, for most meaningful effect, be accompanied by a sixth: *individuality,* despite the overemphasis that
Keats placed on its denial. Thus Coleridge could write to
Wordsworth, who had sent him a new poem, *The Boy of
Winander* (see p. 67): "That 'uncertain heaven received /
Into the bosom of the steady lake' I should have recognized
anywhere; and had I met the lines running wild in the deserts
of Arabia, I should have instantly screamed out 'Wordsworth!' "
For though the artist or the sharer in the arts must be rich in
empathy, he does not literally "go out of himself"; rather he
interprets *through* himself, and, if he is a poet, the mark of his
individuality will be on his poem, even though (again in Keats's
words) it "strike the reader as a wording of his own highest
thoughts, and appear almost a remembrance."

And if individuality is the mark of the poet, so is it of the
true artist in any area, and so can it be of the devotee of the
arts, for there is individuality and imagination behind the in-
terpreter of the art as well as behind the creator.

---

[4] The ardent pinball addict frequently contorts himself into odd positions as he "becomes" the ball and tries to roll into the preferred hole;
or the audience watching a high-wire performer will manipulate its
shoulders as it "shares" the wire. A recent cartoon showed a painter who
had just finished a picture of a storm at sea; the painter was leaning out
of his window, "seasick" from his participation in his own work; and a
news picture of an athlete setting a new record as he went over the high-
jump bar showed, in the background, his coach and several teammates
with legs raised and bodies tensed as they "went over" with him. These
are grosser evidences of empathy to which many others can be added by
the observant reader.

Part Two: The Poet and His Craft

⤙ 3 ⤚

The Creative Process

THE CREATIVE personality, indispensable as it is, nevertheless produces no work of art, even though it may make us, in the terms of Wordsworth describing his brother John, "silent poets." There must follow the mastery of the tools of the art, the heartbreaking struggle to bring to fruition—through the perverse medium that seems determined to block the way—whatever it is we are seeking to create. Some of these tools as they relate to poetry will be considered in later chapters, but here we may concern ourselves briefly with the general nature of the creative process.

The first step in this process is *analysis*, although in practice it is not isolated from the others, but works simultaneously with them. It is the procedure whereby the painter considers every element of the scene before him, the musician every note of the keyboard, the poet every possible aspect and detail of the subject he wishes to treat. Experience, of course, in each instance enables the artist to do much of this unconsciously, but, in principle, analysis in some degree will always be present.

Since, however, economy demands the omission of many details, analysis in effect represents the survey of possibilities for choice, and even as it is taking place the second step in the creative process, *selection*, comes into play. The poet must include enough material so that his ideas are presented clearly rather than vaguely or ambiguously; but since his art is one of suggestion he must also use restraint, many times working by implication rather than specific statement, by figures of speech that carry overtones which in themselves say much in little space. The ideal is the poem which is neither overwritten nor

underwritten, but which leaves the reader with a sense of satisfaction rather than satiation. "Its touches," wrote Keats, "should
never be half-way, thereby making the reader breathless, instead of content. The rise, the progress, the setting of imagery
should, like the sun, come natural to him, shine over him, and
set soberly, although in magnificence, leaving him in the luxury
of twilight."

Selection is then followed, or accompanied, by the third step,
synthesis, which integrates the selected details into a unified
whole, which is the work of art. Synthesis is the end result of
the "shaping spirit," and, when successfully accomplished, it
gives what Coleridge called "such delight from the *whole,* as
is compatible with a distinct gratification from each component
part." For it is a creative force, not content with merely moving
bits about into interesting patterns, but demanding mastery of
every skill in order that a fresh light, a "coloring of the imagination," be thrown over that which may have become "flat, stale,
and unprofitable" to our jaded eyes.

Perhaps the best way to gain an understanding of the significance of the creative process is to observe what happens when
it fails and is then judiciously recovered. Since he has contributed so much of theory to the preceding chapter, it will be interesting to use a poem of Wordsworth as our example, for he
could, to modern eyes, seem far removed at times from the
nicely reasoned principles he developed.

One of the most famous, and justly famous, of this poet's
shorter works is the nearly perfect lyric:

> She dwelt among the untrodden ways
>   Beside the springs of Dove,
> A maid whom there were none to praise
>   And very few to love:
>
> A violet by a mossy stone
>   Half hidden from the eye!
> Fair as a star, when only one
>   Is shining in the sky.
>
> She lived unknown, and few could know
>   When Lucy ceased to be;
> But she is in her grave, and, oh!
>   The difference to me!

It is one of several poems dealing with the real or the assumed love of Wordsworth for a girl who has died, probably in her middle teens. "Lucy" has never been identified, and while it would be satisfying to a biographer to make the discovery, it is not necessary for the reader. Perhaps it was not necessary for the poet: he has recorded an experience and an emotion that were not unique to him, and he has exhibited every characteristic of the creative personality and of the creative process in doing so. His sensitivity of perception will be evident to all who read; his inclusiveness of perception is marked by the relationships he perceived between Lucy, violet, and star; his retentiveness of perception is implied in the assumption we may make that this poem, in terms of his definition of poetry, is an example of "emotion recollected in tranquillity" (the overwhelming sense of loss in the death of a loved one is not conducive to successful immediate expression), and that it was not necessary for him actually to observe a violet and a star afresh in order to have them for his comparison; his sympathetic projection of the mind is again self-evident, and shades quickly into empathy, either as he reenters the mood of the actual experience if it took place, or even more strongly if it is but an imagined situation in which he becomes one with the lover and through him shares an imagined loss.

The creative process is even more clearly defined. Taking only the three stanzas above, the reader will be aware of the careful analysis that preceded the selection of each detail that has gone into the poem—each detail contributing to the sense of isolation, beauty, and love which are the threads of the poem. Note that although "the springs of Dove" suggests a beautiful setting, the ways are "untrodden" because there are few living there who might praise or love Lucy. Then "a" violet and "a" star, both, in terms of the imagery, sharing their beauty with her, but both, like her, alone, the violet "half hidden," even as she is among the untrodden ways. And the isolation is reemphasized in the repetition, but repetition with a subtle difference, found in the first two lines of the last stanza, which lead into the finality of the isolation of the grave, from which not even his love can rescue her. With utmost restraint, but with powerful suggestion, he closes with the simple words of the last line. The nearly perfect progression of thought and imagery is the mark of skillful synthesis. If the poem is read with the second stanza first it loses the integration that comes from the early introduction of the girl.

Admittedly, then, one could scarcely ask more from a poet who is master of his art and his craft. But the first version of the poem was deficient in both respects. Here it is:

> My hope was one, from cities far
>   Nursed on a lonesome heath:
> Her lips were red as roses are,
>   Her hair a woodbine wreath.
>
> She lived among the untrodden ways
>   Beside the springs of Dove,
> A maid whom there were none to praise,
>   And very few to love:
>
> A violet by a mossy stone
>   Half-hidden from the eye!
> Fair as a star when only one
>   Is shining in the sky!
>
> And she was graceful as the broom
>   That flowers by Carron's side;
> But slow distemper checked her bloom,
>   And on the heath she died.
>
> Long time before her head lay low
>   Dead to the world was she:
> But now she's in her grave, and Oh!
>   The difference to me!

In this version the failure is largely that of the creative process rather than of the creative personality. As with so many weak poems, there can be no question of the sincerity of the writer's feelings. But sincerity is not enough to make a work of art. One might speculate, without evidence, that these lines were written too close to the time of Lucy's death, and thus lack the perspective that would come when the emotion was recollected in comparative tranquillity. Whatever the cause, the analysis present was undisciplined, untempered by adequate selection, and such synthesis as there is failed because of the details to be synthesized.

Consider, for a moment, what has happened here. The first two lines are superfluous, since they are but a weak attempt to say what is said so much better in the first line of the second stanza, a line (indeed, a stanza) that asked only the change of "lived" to "dwelt" in the final version. ("Dwelt" has more of a social than a biological connotation. It offers a softer transition from the concept of life to that of death.) The third line is trite, of course, and the fourth might prove to be ambiguous and somewhat unflattering to the girl, dependent on one's concept of a woodbine wreath. Then, with these weak details out of the way, Wordsworth caught the true spirit of what he was trying to say, and except for the one word we have noted he wrote two of the three perfectly conceived and synthesized stanzas of the final version, stanzas that bear the mark of his individuality and his genius. But the disturbing temptations of the first stanza returned as he picked up and continued its weaknesses. "That flower by Carron's side" would be quite good had we not in the meantime had the superior "Beside the springs of Dove," but "graceful as the broom" has its dangers, even assuming that most readers would relate it to the shrub rather than the household implement, for it carries no firm image to the mind. The next two lines of this stanza, however, together with the first two of the next, unfortunately carry far too firm and definite an image, but of an entirely unfortunate kind for a poem of this sort. The details of death intrude and break the spell of lost love: death is the victor; we need not be concerned with the instruments of his victory.[1] And it is now too late to save the poem, even with a sudden return in the last lines to the restraint which has been abrogated by the immediately preceding expression.

The sign of the true poet who is master of the creative process is found in the remarkable revision that reduced the five stanzas to three. Further selection pared away the weak lines that had

---

[1] Always, of course, there are the exceptions, as in John Crowe Ransom's *Here Lies a Lady*, where, in a context that makes it perfectly appropriate, we are told that "Of chills and fever she died, of fever and chills"; or in some of the realistic war poems, such as those by Siegfried Sassoon, Wilfred Owen, or Randall Jarrell. See also *To My Friend Whose Parachute Did Not Open*, p. 183f.

resulted from faulty analysis, and added one additional word change ("she is" for "now she's"). And then, with a clear sense of effective synthesis, the six disastrous lines were replaced by two lines: "She lived unknown, and few could know / When Lucy ceased to be;" which echoed the now opening stanza of the poem, but also pointed forward with a perfect transition to the poet's individual grief, which in itself echoes the isolation of Lucy, since he seems so nearly alone as a mourner.[2]

Analysis, selection, and synthesis are, then, important elements in bringing into most effective arrangement the materials of the poet's world. But the prose writer, too, is concerned with these matters, and in very much the same way: he must analyze (although the normally broader scope of his work will permit him a freer ranging); he must select (although his selection will usually not be as rigid as is that of the poet); and he must synthesize (although frequently his groupings will be in more broadly sweeping units). The poet's art is distinguished from that of the prose writer by the greater opportunity offered in the use of devices for rhythm and sound. We turn now to a consideration of these.

---

[2] For more detailed evidence of revision as it develops in a poet's drafts of his work, see pp. 159n, 183f, 212n, and the frontispiece of this book. See also (for another approach to the growth of a poem) p. 173n.

≺ 4 ≻

Poetic Tools: Devices for Rhythm and Sound

IN THE preceding chapters we have been reading poems, but our attention has been centered on the content of the verses, with a minimum of attention given to the structural elements, or *prosody* (other than the three steps in the creative process) resulting from the poet's use of his "tools." And "tools" in a very real sense they are—as much so as are the chisels and hammers of the sculptor, the pigments and brushes of the painter, the notes and harmonies and keys of the musician, the pirouettes of the ballet dancer. So, in his turn, the poet works with syllables, poetic feet, verses, stanzas, rimes, refrains, alliteration, assonance, and other devices in order that he may say what he has to say with maximum effectiveness.

That we may understand fully the nature of verse structure we will separate and analyze the principal steps in the process, but as we do so let us remember that the poem as poem is the result of all of these things working together at one and the same time. A full appreciation of the well-written poem must involve some understanding of these things, even though the reader of poetry may never intend to try his hand at writing, just as a full appreciation of music must involve some understanding of the elements of musical composition if the music is to be more than just a pleasant (or unpleasant) wash of sound.

Devices for Rhythm

Rhythm can be defined as the regularity of recurrence in time. We have learned that the arts of tempo (time) and

[37]

rhythm are the dance, music, and poetry, and each is distinguished by a recurring beat. In poetry, that which is repeated is the emphasized syllable, for the poem is made up of words which are in turn made up of syllables. But behind this seemingly obvious statement lies the magic of great poetry as well as the flatness of yesterday's headline. The difference lies in the recognition and use made of the potentials in this basic tool.

THE SYLLABLE

The *syllable* can be defined as a group of letters the sound of which can be uttered with a single vocal impulse or effort. Words may be of one or many syllables (*go*; *antidisestablishmentarianism*), but each time a syllable is uttered four characteristics come into play: loudness, pitch, duration, and timbre (or quality). *Loudness* may be used for emphasis (as when someone whispers during a lecture, "Wait for me in the hall," or shouts "Wait!" after a car that is pulling away from the curb); for contrast ("He won't *listen* to me" or "He won't listen to *me*"); or for separation of the syllables as a polysyllabic word is pronounced ("for sepa*ra*tion of the *syll*ables"). Changes in *pitch* prevent monotony (note the related word *monotone,* which is a failure to change pitch) and are the mark of the speaker who is interesting because he is on the alert to keep his audience alert by varying his expression. *Duration* offers another form of emphasis, which comes from giving more time to a word or syllable rather than more loudness or pitch change ("I will *never* do it again" as against "I will *neeeever* do it again," in which a louder volume and a heightened pitch will normally accompany the duration). And *timbre* or *quality* is the characteristic that makes the voices of different persons unlike, just as in music it is the characteristic that makes the cello different in sound from the violin or any other instrument although playing the same note. Varied timbre is also possible to the individual voice, however, so that a single reader may suggest different qualities of meaning, or take parts both masculine and feminine in reading dramatic poetry.

It will be noted that all of these characteristics assume the oral reading of the poem, and we can repeat here a point made earlier: *poetry is never truly poetry until it is read aloud.* Only then are the ideas, the images, or the characters projected in terms of the subtleties of rhythm upon which the poet has based them.

THE FOOT

Loudness and pitch combined make *accent* possible. The word "un*fold*," for example, is accented on the second syllable: x /; "immor*tal*ity" on the third: x x / x x. If, then, a pattern of repetition can be worked out and words found to fit the pattern, rhythm or *meter* (which is organized rhythm) will result. In English there are four basic patterns or *feet*: the *iambic* (x /) and the *anapestic* (x x /), also called *rising* meters because of movement to the higher pitch of the accent; and the *trochaic* (/ x) and *dactylic* (/ x x) or *falling* meters.[1] But strict adherence to these patterns would result in monotony, in the type of singsong reading which is too frequently heard. Some variety is necessary. Indeed, *the underlying principle of all art is variety within uniformity*: enough uniformity to maintain the rhythmical pattern, enough variety to prevent monotony. Variety may be gained by interchanging the four basic feet, as in

    x   /   x x   / x   x   / x   x /
    I sprang to the stirrup, and Joris, and he

[1] Two- and three-syllable feet are also called *duple* and *triple* *meters* respectively.

The names of these feet are inherently interesting. In Greek an *iambus* is a lame man, one who walks with a cane, with first a light (unaccented) step, then a heavier (accented) step; an *anapest* is a reversal, or a turning around (as the anapestic foot is a turning around of the dactyl); a *trochus* is a runner who, in a track meet, gives a strong thrust (accent) as he leaves the starting block, and bridges to the next strong thrust with a lighter (unaccented) step; a *dactyl* is a finger, made up of a long bone and two short bones. The latter illustrates an important difference between ancient and modern scansion, the former based on duration (long and short syllables), the latter on accent. When the accentual system (which retains some qualities of the other, since an accented syllable is normally held slightly longer than its unaccented counterpart) came in the earlier names of the feet were retained.

where an iamb is followed by three anapests; or

/ x   x   x /x /   x /   x / x
Fireside, the heroic wealth of hall and bower

in which a trochee and an anapest precede the three dominant iambs (the last iamb with an added unaccented syllable gives an effect known as *feminine ending*, to be discussed below). Or variety may be gained by the use of two principal variant feet: the *spondee* (/ /) and the *pyrrhic* (x x),[2] as in

/ / / /   x /   x /   x /x
O, Wild West Wind, thou breath of Autumn's being

where two spondees are followed by three iambs (the last again with feminine ending); or

x / x / / /   x / x x
And I, the last, go forth companionless

where the spondee in foot three and the pyrrhic in foot five give interesting variety to the line; or

/ x /   /   x /x   x / /
Milton! thou shouldst be living at this hour

in which the ringing challenge is initiated in the opening trochee, emphasized in the spondee of foot two, and returned to, after the pyrrhic of foot four, by another spondee in the final foot. If the last example is forced into the singsong monotony of a strict iambic pattern, the importance of a natural reading which profits from the variant feet and in which the emphasis is permitted to bring out the essential meaning will be clear. And if it is felt that this opening line of Wordsworth's sonnet is overly varied in the indicated reading it should be pointed out that the lines which follow resolve themselves into a dominantly iambic movement, but one rhythmically enhanced by the use of substitute feet (see p. 51). It is true, also, that the indicated marking represents only one possible reading;

---

[2] In Greek, a *pyrrhic* is an ancient martial dance (hence the lightness of the unaccented syllables); a *spondee* is a libation, and the libation service would be slow and dignified, as is the effect of the spondaic foot.

individuality is important to bring out shadings of interpretation. But the shadings will not violate the underlying structure unless a forced or distorted reading is given.[3]

Short poems illustrating each of the four principal foot types may be helpful here. If the reader will listen carefully as he reads the lines aloud naturally, he will be conscious of the dominant pattern and also of the spondees, pyrrhics, feminine endings, or other variants in the structure. Consider first the *iambic,* which represents the majority of English poetry since it lends itself so well to the natural movement of the language and offers a graceful, dignified expression, while blending most effectively with other devices for rhythm. The poem is Christina Rossetti's *Song:*

> When I am dead, my dearest,
>   Sing no sad songs for me;
> Plant thou no roses at my head,
>   Nor shady cypress tree:
> Be the green grass above me
>   With showers and dewdrops wet:
> And if thou wilt, remember,
>   And if thou wilt, forget.
>
> I shall not see the shadows,
>   I shall not feel the rain;
> I shall not hear the nightingale
>   Sing on as if in pain:
> And dreaming through the twilight
>   That doth not rise nor set,
> Haply I may remember,
>   And haply may forget.

In this lyric, the present writer's reading of the first stanza would give spondees at *sad songs* and *green grass;* a trochee at *Plant thou;* pyrrhics at *roses at* and *Be the;* and an anapest at *showers and dew;* with feminine endings at *dearest, remember, shadows, twilight,* and again at *remember.* The second stanza, with its increasing sense of acceptance and calm, is, except for

[3] Almost every possible combination of accented and unaccented syllables has been named, but most of those not given above (except possibly for the amphibrach and amphimacer) are seldom used today. Typical are the following: amphibrach (x / x), amphimacer (/ x /), tribrach (x x x), molossus (/ / /), bacchius (x / /), antibacchius (/ / x), etc.

a trochee at *Haply* in line seven, a strict pattern of iambs, although shadings for feeling will prevent a metronomic monotony in the reading, as will the feminine endings.

The *anapestic* foot is more limited in its scope because of the lightness of the added unaccented syllable. This gives it a tendency to "gallop," as it does most effectively in Byron's *The Destruction of Sennacherib*, which opens as follows:

> The Assyrian came down like a wolf on the fold,
> And his cohorts were gleaming in purple and gold,
> And the sheen of their spears was like stars on the sea
> When the blue wave rolls nightly on deep Galilee.[3]

The anapest must be handled with great care and skill if it is to be used in poems that are concerned more with emotion than they are with action. Such skill is evident in Tennyson's elegiac lines:

> Break, break, break,
>   On thy cold gray stones, O Sea!
> And I would that my tongue could utter
>   The thoughts that arise in me.
>
> O well for the fisherman's boy,
>   That he shouts with his sister at play!
> O well for the sailor lad,
>   That he sings in his boat on the bay!

[3] If iambs are substituted for anapests here, the greater effectiveness of the triple meter for this subject will be evident immediately:

> The foe came down like wolves upon the fold,
> With cohorts all agleam in brightest gold;
> The sheen of spears was like the stars at sea
> When waves roll through the night on Galilee.

Suddenly the action is slowed to a walk, the force and fire of the attack are diminished in our minds as we read.

Similarly, if we reverse the procedure and substitute anapests for the iambs of the first few lines of Rossetti's *Song* the quiet dignity and strength of the lyric will be crowded out in the incongruous rapidity of the meter:

> If the time ever comes, O my dearest,
>   That I die, sing no sad songs for me;
> Let no roses be planted above my fair head,
>   Nor a cypress: not one shady tree.

Note that "Sing no sad songs for me" is retained but completely changed in its effect because of the different rhythmical setting.

And the stately ships go on
To their haven under the hill;
But O for the touch of a vanish'd hand,
And the sound of a voice that is still!

Break, break, break,
At the foot of thy crags, O Sea!
But the tender grace of a day that is dead
Will never come back to me.

Here the anapest dominates the lines, with twenty-seven occurrences, but there are also sixteen iambs tempering the movement, and an opening line that appears at first sight to be simply three accents, but which in fact proves to be a subtly rhythmical balance to what follows. Each "break" of this line is followed by a pause, or what is known technically as a *metrical silence*, a pause compensating for the omission of an unaccented syllable. Thus the mind in effect hears three duple feet, and in the silence of the pause it is not difficult to imagine the sound of the breaking wave. In the second line this serious, impressive opening is modulated by the occurrence of the first anapest, but this is immediately followed by two spondees ("gray stones, O Sea!"), and the third and fourth lines are balanced equally between three anapests and three iambs.

The next stanza is predominantly anapestic, reflecting perfectly the lightness of spirit in the subject treated; the third is slowed by the reintroduction of the iambic variants; and the fourth returns to the solemn "Break, break, break," with which the poem opened, then ends on a balance between anapests and iambs for which the poem has prepared us, and which now offers no conflict with the mood of nostalgia in which the poem closes.

The *trochaic* and *dactylic* patterns are difficult to maintain in English poetry because the language itself is basically one in which the rising element predominates, even though it is not as evident in ordinary conversation or written prose as it is in the regularized rhythms of verse. The principal advantage of the falling patterns, then, is found in the emphasis that can be gained by starting each foot with an accent; the principal difficulty is found in maintaining the movement. Not many readers are able to read the following line in terms of its rhythmical intent:

```
/ x x  / x   x / x   x  /  x x   /
This is the forest primeval, the murmuring pines

       x   x   /  x
       and the hemlocks.
```

Most will start with a trochee, follow with an iamb ("the for—") and continue with the rising anapest, accounting for the last syllable by calling it a feminine ending. Thus the intended dactylic meter is denied. Similarly, readers will reverse intended trochees if the phrasing permits. But if most of the lines open with the strong beat the stanzas will normally not be mistaken for their opposites. In the following *Song* by John Suckling, for example, one would not likely confuse the movement with that of Christina Rossetti's *Song* given above:

> Why so pale and wan, fond lover?
>   Prithee, why so pale?
> Will, when looking well can't move her,
>   Looking ill prevail?
>   Prithee, why so pale?
>
> Why so dull and mute, young sinner?
>   Prithee, why so mute?
> Will, when speaking well can't win her,
>   Saying nothing do't?
>   Prithee, why so mute?
>
> Quit, quit for shame, this will not move,
>   This cannot take her.
> If of herself she will not love,
>   Nothing can make her.
>   The devil take her!

In Suckling's lines the trochees fit perfectly with his "needling" of the lover, and reflect (or help to establish) the tone of bantering cynicism of the speaker, who is not (at the moment at least) caught in the web of love. Many other poetic devices enter into the creation of this effect, of course, but the trochee proves an admirable medium through which they can work.

The dactylic movement, like the anapestic, is marked by the

added syllable in each basic foot. Thus there is the added force, as in the trochee, that comes from the initial accent, plus the added speed, or lightness, or action, as the case may be, that is possible to the triple meter. These characteristics are well illustrated in Byron's *Song of Saul Before His Last Battle*:

> Warriors and chiefs! should the shaft or the sword
> Pierce me in leading the host of the Lord,
> Heed not the corse, though the king's, in your path:
> Bury your steel in the bosoms of Gath.
>
> Thou who art bearing my buckler and bow,
> Should the soldiers of Saul look away from the foe,
> Stretch me that moment in blood at thy feet!
> Mine be the doom which they dared not to meet.
>
> Farewell to others, but never we part,
> Heir to my royalty, son of my heart!
> Bright is the diadem, boundless the sway,
> Or kingly the death, which awaits us today.

The purpose of Saul is clearly to inspire the troops and their leaders, and at the same time to suggest the king's own strength and fearlessness as he speaks. This could, of course, be done in iambs or trochees, but the dactyl increases the feeling of tension, of impending movement in battle, while the omission of the unaccented syllables in the last foot of each line, known technically as *catalexis*,[4] permits the lines to end on strong, accented beats that in their turn contribute to the intended mood.

THE VERSE

When a number of feet are grouped together they form the poetic line, or *verse* (not to be confused with *stanza*, which is a group of verses). The verses of a poem may be of the same length throughout, or may be arranged in balancing or free arrangements. The principal verse lengths, indicating lines of one to nine feet, are the monometer, dimeter, trimeter, tetram-

---

[4] From the Greek meaning "incomplete" or "to leave off." When an unaccented syllable is omitted at the beginning of a line the effect is called *truncation* ("to cut off"). If a syllable is added at the beginning of a line it is *anacrusis* ("to extend backward"), while if it is added at the end the result is, as we have seen, *feminine ending*.

eter, pentameter, hexameter, heptameter, octameter, and, rarely, the nonameter.

The *monometer* is normally used as a variant to longer lines because its brevity and its tendency towards an uneven or "jerky" movement are such that maintenance of a thought is difficult. Also, there is little opportunity for variety in so short a line. But occasionally an entire poem is written effectively in this pattern, as in Helen Finch's *Good Night* in which the monometer suggests the tolling of the bell:

> Good night,
> Fair one;
> The day
> Is done.
>
> The bell
> Rings clear;
> I seem
> To hear
>
> "Good night,
> Fair one;
> The day
> Is done."

The *dimeter* is less particularized than is the monometer, but contains the same limitations, if in lesser degree, and likewise finds its most frequent use as a variant to longer verses. In Carlyle's *To-Day*, however, the blending of iambs and anapests combines with the dimeter to gain the effect the poet desired (compare Blake's *The Fly*, p. 173):

> So here hath been dawning
>   Another blue day:
> Think, wilt thou let it
>   Slip useless away?
>
> Out of Eternity
>   This new day was born:
> Into Eternity
>   At night, will return.
>
> Behold it aforetime
>   No eye ever did;
> So soon it forever
>   From all eyes is hid.

Here hath been dawning
Another blue day:
Think, wilt thou let it
Slip useless away?

With the use of the *trimeter* there is introduced enough line length to remove the unevenness and mechanical regularity noted in the monometer and dimeter, and, as a result, many more poems will be found written in this form. Yet it is still fairly short and, like the others, finds its most popular use in connection with other verse lengths, especially the tetrameter, as we shall see when stanza forms are discussed. The trimeter is illustrated by Robert Herrick's *How Roses Came Red*, a poem of light, delicate compliment for which the pattern is ideally suited:

Roses at first were white,
Till they could not agree
Whether my Sappho's breast
Or they more white should be.

But being vanquished quite,
A blush their cheeks bespread;
Since which, believe the rest,
The roses first came red.

The *tetrameter* and the pentameter are the two most frequently used line lengths in English poetry, for they (frequently in combination with shorter verses) offer greater opportunities for variety, and hence are more readily adapted to the poet's needs. The tetrameter is more quickly read, and therefore better suited to rapidly moving material, especially when it is made up of anapests or dactyls with their added light syllables (see Byron's *Song of Saul* above, p. 45); but it may also be used for other types of expression, as in A. E. Housman's beautiful lyric:

Loveliest of trees, the cherry now
Is hung with bloom along the bough,
And stands about the woodland ride
Wearing white for Eastertide.

Now, of my threescore years and ten,
Twenty will not come again,
And take from seventy springs a score,
It only leaves me fifty more.

And since to look at things in bloom
Fifty springs are little room,
About the woodlands I will go
To see the cherry hung with snow.

But the *pentameter,* since its introduction in the late fourteenth century, has been the most important verse in English
poetry. It is an admirable length for easy, dignified reading, and,
whereas the tetrameter has a tendency to divide into sections
of two and two feet, the pentameter will normally divide into
uneven phrase lengths, permitting almost unlimited possibilities
for variations in rhythm. This makes for poetry that is more naturally spoken than in any other form, and accounts for the extensive use of the pentameter in poetic drama (see the passage
from *Macbeth,* p. 145). When this most natural of verse lengths
is combined with the iambic, the most natural of feet, the result
is an almost ideal unit for expression in English. Walter Savage
Landor's brief poem will illustrate a rimed use of the pattern:

Proud word you never spoke, but you will speak
Four not exempt from pride some future day.
Resting on one white hand a warm wet cheek
Over my open volume you will say,
"This man loved *me!*" then rise and trip away.[5]

Verses longer than the pentameter are used only rarely today,
and usually in combination with shorter lines to give rhythmical
variety. The *hexameter* tends to break into three and three, the
heptameter into four and three, the *octameter* into four and
four, with the *nonameter* almost too long for successful use.

In discussions of this kind there is a danger that we may fall
into the habit of assigning particular effects to particular feet
or line lengths. While it is true that within limits there are
possibilities better fulfilled by one measure than another—such
as speed from triple measures and short verses—the skillful
poet may, with slight variations, gain an almost opposite effect
from the same movement. Thus, we would expect the anapestic
trimeter to lend itself to light, gay, dancing material, but we

---

[5] Note how remarkably suggestive is the word "trip" in characterizing
the girl—as compared, for example, with "move," "turn," etc. See also
p. 10*n.*

have seen that, with a deft blending of iambs and a subtle use of phrasing, Tennyson employed the form for a poem of deep seriousness.[6]

MEDIAL PAUSES AND VERSE ENDINGS

It will be clear from what has been said above that verse is not a matter of metronomic regularity, but that the effects of rhythm come from a constantly shifting use of variation, always within the framework of an acceptable uniformity. The variants so far considered have been the different feet and the different verse lengths. Some attention should now be given to medial pauses and verse endings, which prevent an equally monotonous effect of filling each line with a single undivided unit of thought. Note, for example, the flatness and stiffness of the following Elizabethan translation of Vergil's *Aeneid* by Henry Howard, Earl of Surrey, an early attempt in the use of blank verse:

> Who can express the slaughter of that night?
> Or tell the number of the corpses slain?
> Or can in tears bewail them worthily?
> The ancient famous city falleth down,
> That many years did hold such seignory.

When, instead, the thought is permitted to pause naturally within the line, or to run freely from one line to another, the rhythm is not destroyed, but is enhanced in its effectiveness. For example: in the following lines from Browning's *My Last Duchess* (see p. 154 for the complete poem) the iambic pentameter becomes as natural as dignified conversation in Browning's hands, despite the use of riming couplets:

> Sir, 'twas all one! My favor at her breast,
> The dropping of the daylight in the west,
> The bough of cherries some officious fool
> Broke in the orchard for her, the white mule
> She rode with round the terrace—all and each
> Would draw from her alike the approving speech,

[6] See p. 42. For other poems which illustrate the different line lengths, see Index.

> Or blush, at least. She thanked men—good! but thanked
> Somehow—I know not how—as if she ranked
> My gift of a nine-hundred-years-old name
> With anybody's gift. Who'd stoop to blame
> This sort of trifling? Even had you skill
> In speech—which I have not—to make your will
> Quite clear to such an one . . .

Admittedly this offers an unusual array of medial and end variety, but it shows well what can be done. Note that the medial pauses fall irregularly within the lines, with as many as four pauses or as few as none. Some lines have end pauses, others run directly into the next (*run-on* or *enjambement*), giving a sense of urgency as the Duke speaks. But the *kind* of pause is important also: here there are exclamation points, dashes, question marks, commas, and periods. These keep the reader on the alert and give him clues to the thought processes of the speaker, leading to the vital relationship between form and content toward which all of these poetic tools contribute. And one other effect should be noted: the difference between the masculine and feminine pause or ending.

When the verse ends on the accented syllable, or when the syllable immediately preceding the medial pause is accented, the effect is described as *masculine* (suggesting strength). Thus all of the lines in the passage above have masculine endings, as compared with the opening lines of Keats's *Endymion*:

> A thing of beauty is a joy forever:
> Its loveliness increases; it will never
> Pass into nothingness . . .

in which the softness of effect sought is suggested by the *feminine* endings and medial pauses (or *caesural* pauses, from the Greek word meaning "to cut"—thus the pause cuts or divides the line). The nature of the Duke's speech in Browning's poem is such as to invite strong expression, and it will be noted that not only the endings, but the great majority of the caesuras are of the masculine type. The exceptions, which add to the variety, come at "terrace," and "trifling," and represent but two of the fifteen medial pauses present in these lines.

If the Browning passage is compared with the following Wordsworth sonnet, *London, 1802* (we have already met its first line in discussion of variant feet, p. 40), the varied use of masculine and feminine pauses and endings will be clearer. It will be recalled that the poet needed strength and challenge in his opening, which he gained by use of the opening trochee and the spondees of the first line.

> Milton! thou shouldst be living at this hour:
> England hath need of thee: she is a fen
> Of stagnant waters: altar, sword, and pen,
> Fireside, the heroic wealth of hall and bower,
> Have forfeited their ancient English dower
> Of inward happiness. We are selfish men;
> Oh! raise us up, return to us again;
> And give us manners, virtue, freedom, power.
> Thy soul was like a Star, and dwelt apart;
> Thou hadst a voice whose sound was like the sea:
> Pure as the naked heavens, majestic, free,
> So didst thou travel on life's common way,
> In cheerful godliness; and yet thy heart
> The lowliest duties on herself did lay.

It will be seen now that the opening strength is enhanced by the masculine ending of the first line, the repeated trochee in the opening of the second, and the immediately following masculine caesura at "thee." But this is Wordsworth, not the Duke, speaking: it is a poet who is concerned with his country's loss of those virtues that have made her culturally as well as militarily great. The cultural are, in a sense, the "softer" qualities of a nation. Appropriately, then, Wordsworth "softens" his lines by use of the feminine caesuras and endings,[7] and returns to the desired strength at the point where it is needed: "Oh! raise us up, return to us again," and "Thy soul was like a Star, and dwelt

[7] An interesting phonetic effect is present in this poem: the impact of the one-syllable *hour* (as it is usually pronounced) in its strong position in line one invites a correspondingly monosyllabic pronunciation of its rime words (*bower, dower, power*) even though they are disyllabic and hence feminine. The result is something of a compromise in their pronunciation. Some readers make them monosyllables, but clearly in this context there is no reason to force them into exact agreement with *hour* since the poet has used feminine caesuras so freely.

apart"; both lines, this time, in strict iambs (or with a possible opening spondee in each), with the strength suggested primarily through masculine pauses and endings.

Clearly, then, the poet has at his command the means not alone for keeping his poems interesting, but actually for heightening the content through appropriateness of form. This should never be done self-consciously, of course, any more than the accompanist should try to "steal the show" from the soloist at a concert, but whether in the more obvious types of form-content relationship or in the subtle rhythmical uses which frequently defy analysis, the poet as artist must be master of his technique. Just as a sculptor will select a certain tool for gaining an effect, or the musician a certain chord for his harmony, so must the poet select wisely the elements of form with which he works. All elements must work together to make the poem: the mood of the poet, the nature of the subject, the infinite variety of effects. And among these effects there remain to be considered those most important tools that add so much of oral beauty to the work of art: the poetic devices for sound.

Devices for Sound

The principle of recurrence has been stressed repeatedly in these pages: recurrence of stressed syllables, of type of feet, and of verse lengths. It follows that the principle can be extended to the other elements of the poet's craft, among them sound, of which the best known is certainly *rime*. But the average reader is scarcely aware of the variety of rime types possible in any given poem or group of poems, or of the uses that can be made of the other sound effects, such as refrain, alliteration, assonance, and onomatopoeia.

RIME

The type of rime with which we are most familiar is *exact rime*, the *June-croon, love-dove* sort of thing, which can be de-

fined as the recurrent sound between two or more words due
to the agreement of the stressed vowel sound and its succeeding
consonants or syllables (when present) and the differences in
the preceding consonants or syllables (when present). Thus
love-dove agree in identity of sound in the stressed vowel *o*
and the succeeding consonant *v*, and differ in the preceding consonants *l* and *d*; *owe-so* agree in vowel sound, differ in the preceding consonant of *so* (a preceding consonant in one of the
words satisfies the conditions), and have no succeeding consonants. Note that this is a matter of vowel and consonant *sounds*:
laugh-calf form exact rime, as do *go-sew*, even though the actual
letters may be quite different, for the sounds are the same in the
related positions. Moreover, the foregoing are all of the *single*
exact type, with the rime composed of words of one syllable.
Beauty-duty would thus be double exact, *beautiful-dutiful* triple
exact, etc. Also, the actual agreement is determined by the number of syllables riming, without respect to other syllables necessary to form one or both of the words. Thus *prism* when rimed
with *humanitarianism* forms a single rime despite the number of
syllables in the longer word: the rime is *prism-ism*.

But English is a language not especially rich in exact rime
sounds, as Pope realized as early as the eighteenth century. In
An Essay on Criticism, he was speaking, in couplets using single
exact rime,[8] of writers concerned only with the mechanical aspects of poetry:

> These equal syllables alone require,
> Though oft the ear the open vowels tire;
> While expletives their feeble aid do join;
> And ten low words oft creep in one dull line:
> While they ring round the same unvaried chimes,
> With sure returns of still expected rhymes;
> Where'er you find "the cooling western breeze,"
> In the next line it "whispers through the trees";
> If crystal streams "with pleasing murmurs creep,"
> The reader's threatened (not in vain) with "sleep."

[8] In Pope's day "join" was pronounced "jine." It may be noted that
Pope uses the spelling *rhyme*, a form that for many years was standard
and that still finds its champions. Etymologically, however (as well as in
the interest of preventing confusion with *rhythm*), the spelling *rime* seems
preferable for modern use.

Since Pope's day repeated use of the same rimes has made the situation even more serious, and writers have tended more and more to resort to words that are similar rather than exact in their sound relationships.

The first of these is *rime approximate in sound*.[9] If the exact pair *took-book* is changed to *took-bake* a sound relationship still exists, but it only approximates the closeness of the first pair. Whether aware of it or not, all children who have gone with Old Mother *Hubbard* to the *cupboard* have done so in double exact rime (at least as usually pronounced), but when there was no *bone* the dog not only ended up with *none* but the poet ended up with a rime single and approximate in sound. With the pressure for fresh sound relationships, the rime approximate in sound has been given increasing use in recent decades, but that it is no new discovery is suggested by its extensive use in the past century by Emily Dickinson and, before her, in lines such as the following from Shelley's *Ode to the West Wind*:

> Make me thy lyre, even as the forest is:
> What if my leaves are falling like its own!
> The tumult of thy mighty harmonies
>
> Will take from both a deep, autumnal tone,
> Sweet though in sadness. Be thou, Spirit fierce,
> My spirit! Be thou me, impetuous one!

Here *is-harmonies* and *tone-one*, as well as *fierce* and, in the line following this selection, *universe* illustrate this rime type, as do the following which appear earlier in the poem: *thou-low, everywhere-here, sepulchre-atmosphere, Thou-below, wear-fear,* and *even-heaven*.[10]

If the approximate rime, with its differing emphasized vowel sounds, is modified slightly, a rime type that has come to be used quite widely in this century results, the *consonantal rime*.

[9] Variously called also slant rime, oblique rime, near rime, half rime, para-rime, and consonance. *Consonance,* however, is broader in its implications, ranging from its suggestion simply of pleasing sounds to its rime effect as described here and finally to its more specialized effect in *consonantal rime* (see below) where the preceding consonants are the same.

[10] Compare also the two sonnets by Pauline Starkweather (p. 107) which employ this rime type most effectively.

For example, if instead of the exact *took-book,* or the approximate *took-bake,* the combination *took-take* is employed, the presence of the same consonant before the emphasized vowel gives this type of rime. Consonantal rime and rime approximate in sound open needed areas to the poet, and with them he can gain a freshness in his expression, once the reading public attunes its ear to the phenomenon. Note, for example, in the following anonymous lines, the haunting, otherworldly effect of consonantal rimes in a context that envisions the last man in a desolated world:

> Under the surface of the reaching lake,
> So deep, it was beyond my searching look,
> From its translucent hollows now there called
> To me the self-same force that surely killed
> The singing voice of every singing bird
> That flew these skies before the earth was bared.

The foregoing represent the principal rime types. Others might be listed, such as *rich rime* or *identical rime* (made up of two words that sound alike but have different meaning: *sea-see, fair-fare, way-weigh*); *rime approximate in accent* (in which the rime elements agree exactly or approximately in sound but

$$/ \; \text{xx} \quad /$$

not in accent: *immortality-be*); *composite* or *mosaic rime* (in which the rime, frequently for light or humorous effect, is made up of more than one word in each position, or one word balanced by more than one: *miss you-kiss you; prairie-where he*); and a special form of composite rime which the Germans call *scheutel* ("shaking") *rime,* an example of which the pianist Artur Schnabel composed while crossing the ocean:

> Every day the sailing rougher,
> People at the railing suffer.

In this the first letters of the two riming pairs must be interchangeable, and yet result in different words that fit the thought. So clearly is this based on an intellectual manipulation that it would be unlikely to find a place in serious verse.

Finally, any of the above types may be further qualified by their position. Normally we think of rime at the ends of verses, but it may be used very effectively within the lines also (*medial rime*) as Poe illustrated in *The Raven*:

Ah, distinctly I remember, it was in the bleak December;
And each separate dying ember wrought its ghost upon the floor.
Eagerly I wished the morrow;—vainly I had sought to borrow
From my books surcease of sorrow—sorrow for the lost Lenore—
For the rare and radiant maiden whom the angels name Lenore—
Nameless *here* for evermore.

While rime is admittedly effective as a poetic device, its use can present problems in the form of concessions to the thought when a second rime word is needed, for, as Samuel Butler wrote, rime

the rudder is of verses,
With which like ships they steer their courses,

and at times the rudder sticks and the writer finds himself on the shoals of forced expression. (In these lines Butler illustrates not only his idea but also double rime approximate in sound.) With these difficulties inherent in the tool, unrimed patterns and free verse innovations have been, in part at least, the result of a desire to avoid what Milton, defending blank verse, called "the troublesome and modern bondage of riming."

REFRAIN AND PARALLELISM

There are other types of repetition besides rime words. One of these is *refrain*, in which all or substantial parts of lines are repeated for effect. If the repetition is exact, or with only such slight change as does not modify the idea, the device is *normal refrain*, as in all of stanzas one and four and lines four and five of the following ballad. But in this same ballad there is also an *incremental refrain*, in which something is added to the thought in the repetition, in lines one and two of the second stanza:[11]

[11] See also *Lord Randal*, below, p. 126, in which the knight says four times, 'For I'm weary wi hunting, and fain wald lie down," giving normal refrain; while in the last line of the poem he says, "For I'm sick at the heart, and I fain wald lie down." There is clearly a difference between the two statements, and the difference not only gives incremental refrain but also some insight into Lord Randal's attitude toward the "true love" who has poisoned him.

O Bessie Bell and Mary Gray,
   They war twa bonnie lasses!
They bigget* a bower on yon burn-brae,   *built
   And theekit* it oer wi rashes.   *thatched

They theekit it oer wi rashes green,
   They theekit it oer wi heather;
But the pest* cam frae the burrows-town,   *epidemic
   And slew them baith thegither.

They thought to lie in Methven kirk-yard
   Amang their noble kin;
But they maun lie in Stronach-haugh,*   *river bank
   To biek forenent the sin.*   *bake in the sun

And Bessie Bell and Mary Gray,
   They war twa bonnie lasses;
They bigget a bower on yon burn-brae,
   And theekit it oer wi rashes.

An effect similar to refrain, but with greater opportunity for variety, is found in *parallelism*, with repetition limited to the opening word or words of certain lines, without enough duplication to form incremental refrain. The difference will be immediately apparent if the above ballad is compared with Swinburne's *Cor Cordium*, in which it will also be noted that this device has something of the effect at line beginnings that rime does at line ends, but without the patterning or the variety in sound that rime offers.

The poem, a tribute to Shelley, stems from the fact that after the poet's untimely death by drowning, the stone placed on his grave included the words Cor Cordium ("Heart of Hearts"). The musical quality of the sonnet is typical of Swinburne and not only illustrates our present subject but also anticipates admirably the repetitions of consonant and vowel sounds, to be considered next:

O Heart of hearts, the chalice of love's fire,
Hid round with flowers and all the bounty of bloom:
O wonderful and perfect heart, for whom
The lyrist liberty made life a lyre;
O heavenly heart, at whose most dear desire
Dead love, living and singing, cleft his tomb,
And with him risen and regent in death's room
All day thy choral pulses rang full choir;

O heart whose beating blood was running song,
O sole thing sweeter than thine own songs were,
Help us for thy free love's sake to be free,
True for thy truth's sake, for thy strength's sake strong,
Till very liberty make clean and fair
The nursing earth as the sepulchral air.

ALLITERATION, ASSONANCE, AND ONOMATOPOEIA

In addition to rime and refrain, or as a substitute for them, it is possible to have the repetitions rest on the sounds of letters. When the repetition is of consonant sounds *alliteration* results; when it is of vowel sounds we have *assonance*. It should be remembered that there are only twenty-six letters in the alphabet (although the many possibilities for vowel pronunciation increase the possible number of sounds) and inevitably these will constantly recur. Normally, therefore, the sounds will need to be in positions of stress or proximity so the ear of the reader will catch them, and they should be so used that emphasis is given to the words linked by them. Alliteration, to be effective, might therefore be defined as the purposeful repetition of consonant sounds in positions of stress or proximity, normally initial to the syllable; and assonance as the purposeful repetition of vowel sounds in positions of stress or proximity. With these limitations in mind, note how the alliteration and assonance supplement Poe's strong use of rime in the lines from *The Raven* given above:

vainly I had sought to borrow
From my books surcease of sorrow—sorrow for the lost Lenore—
For the rare and radiant maiden whom the angels name Lenore—
Nameless *here* for evermore.

The principal alliteration is found in the following syllables: *s*ought-*s*urcease-*s*orrow-*s*orrow; *b*orrow-*b*ooks; *f*rom-*f*or-*f*or; *l*ost-*L*enore; *r*are-*r*adiant; *m*aiden-*m*ore; *wh*om-*h*ere; *n*ame-*n*ore-*n*ameless; *L*enore-*l*ess. The assonance is found in *I*-m*y*; *f*or-*L*enore-*f*or-*L*enore-*e*vermore (which involves medial rime also); r*a*diant-m*a*iden-*a*ngels-n*a*me-n*a*meless; l*e*ss-*e*vermore.

It will be noted that, with as strong a concentration of sound as this poem possesses, many secondary sounds (to say nothing of repeated words) suddenly become evident through association.

Swinburne's *Cor Cordium* is similarly textured with sound, as the reader will discover if he reads the poem aloud. Indeed, so frequently was Swinburne parodied for his use of these devices that he finally out-parodied the parodists by writing *Nephelidia* ("Cloudlets"), a poem of twenty-eight lines of which the following are typical:

> From the depth of the dreamy decline of the dawn through a notable
>> nimbus of nebulous noonshine,
>> Pallid and pink as the palm of the flagflower that flickers with
>> fear of the flies as they float,
> Are the looks of our lovers that lustrously lean from a marvel of
>> mystic miraculous moonshine,
>> These that we feel in the blood of our blushes that thicken and
>> threaten with throbs through the throat?
> Thicken and thrill as a theater thronged at appeal of an actor's
>> appalled agitation,
>> Fainter with fear of the fires of the future than pale with the
>> promise of pride in the past;
> Flushed with the famishing fullness of fever that reddens with
>> radiance of rathe recreation,
>> Gaunt as the ghastliest of glimpses that gleam through the gloom
>> of the gloaming when ghosts go aghast?

From examples such as the foregoing, in which alliteration and assonance are perhaps overly obvious, it will be well to turn to a more restrained use of these devices, as in A. E. Housman's lyric:

> Far in a western brookland
> That bred me long ago
> The poplars stand and tremble
> By pools I used to know.
>
> There, in the windless night-time,
> The wanderer, marveling why,
> Halts on the bridge to hearken
> How soft the poplars sigh.

He hears; no more remembered
   In fields where I was known,
Here I lie down in London
   And turn to rest alone.

There, by the starlit fences,
   The wanderer halts and hears
My soul that lingers sighing
   About the glimmering weirs.

Finally, there is a device that, while it differs from alliteration and assonance, frequently makes use of them in creating its effect. This is *onomatopoeia*, through which the poet attempts to suggest the thing about which he is writing by choosing words whose sound is characteristic or at least suggestive of the thing itself. We are all familiar with this in single words such as "buzz," "crash," "bang," "whisper," etc., but the effect can be extended in poetry so that whole passages may suggest quietness, or noise, or particular feelings. It is obvious in such lines as the following from Poe's *The Bells*, in which the clanging becomes almost audible:

Hear the sledges with the bells—
   Silver bells!
What a world of merriment their melody foretells!
  How they tinkle, tinkle, tinkle,
   In the icy air of night!
  While the stars that oversprinkle
  All the heavens, seem to twinkle
   With a crystalline delight;
  Keeping time, time, time,
   In a sort of Runic rhyme,
To the tintinnabulation that so musically wells
  From the bells, bells, bells, bells,
   Bells, bells, bells,—
  From the jingling and the tinkling of the bells.

In this the effect is one of massed bells ringing together. How different is the effect gained by the irregular placement of the word "ring" in Tennyson's well-known section from *In Memoriam*, in which the cumulative repetition of the word is the important thing:

Ring out, wild bells, to the wild sky,
   The flying cloud, the frosty light;
   The year is dying in the night;
Ring out, wild bells, and let him die.

Ring out the old, ring in the new,
   Ring, happy bells, across the snow;
   The year is going, let him go;
Ring out the false, ring in the true.

Ring out the grief that saps the mind,
   For those that here we see no more;
   Ring out the feud of rich and poor;
Ring in redress to all mankind.

Ring out a slowly dying cause,
   And ancient forms of party strife;
   Ring in the nobler modes of life,
With sweeter manners, purer laws.

Ring out the want, the care, the sin,
   The faithless coldness of the times;
   Ring out, ring out my mournful rimes,
But ring the fuller minstrel in.

Ring out false pride in place and blood,
   The civic slander and the spite;
   Ring in the love of truth and right;
Ring in the common love of good.

Ring out old shapes of foul disease;
   Ring out the narrowing lust of gold;
   Ring out the thousand wars of old,
Ring in the thousand years of peace.

Ring in the valiant man and free,
   The larger heart, the kindlier hand;
   Ring out the darkness of the land,
Ring in the Christ that is to be.

Varied effects are found in the suggestive sounds and rhythms of the following lines from Dryden's *A Song for St. Cecilia's Day*:

   The trumpet's loud clangor
     Excites us to arms
   With shrill notes of anger
     And mortal alarms.

The double, double, double beat
Of the thundering drum
Cries, Hark! the foes come;
Charge, charge, 'tis too late to retreat!

The soft complaining flute,
In dying notes, discovers
The woes of hopeless lovers
Whose dirge is whisper'd by the warbling lute.

Sharp violins proclaim
Their jealous pangs and desperation,
Fury, frantic indignation,
Depth of pains, and height of passion,
For the fair, disdainful dame.

In all of the foregoing the impact is primarily audible. A kinesthetic response is called for in this stanza from Coleridge's *Rime of the Ancient Mariner*. Note how perfectly he has communicated the onomatopoetic effect in the last two lines, and invited an empathic participation by the reader. It is not easy to keep these sea creatures in their own domain, and many readers will shudder involuntarily as they "feel" contact with them:

The very deep did rot: O Christ!
That ever this should be!
Yea, slimy things did crawl with legs
Upon the slimy sea.

The line of demarcation between onomatopoeia and *connotation* is frequently quite thin. In the former the actual *sounds* of the words should be the determining factor, while in the latter the *suggestions* of the words may create a related response. In the following stanza from Keats's *The Eve of St. Agnes,* for example, one can well ask whether it is the connotation only, or something in the richness of the alliteration and assonance—a form of onomatopoeia indeed—that makes the reader's mouth water:

And still she slept an azure-lidded sleep,
In blanchèd linen, smooth, and lavendered,
While he from forth the closet brought a heap
Of candied apple, quince, and plum, and gourd,
With jellies soother than the creamy curd,

And lucent sirups, tinct with cinnamon,
Manna and dates, in argosy transferred
From Fez, and spicèd dainties, every one,
From silken Samarcand to cedared Lebanon.

Poetic devices for sound are, in a sense, the "embroidery" of poetry. On or into the cloth of language which the poet cuts into shape by the aid of patterns called stanzas (to be discussed in the next chapter) these sound devices are applied or woven. They give color, life, and often great beauty to the poems in which they are used; they go far to create the effect which we call "poetic." Prose may make use of some of them, but it can never do so with the same degree of skill that poetry does, for the patterns of prose are not so sharply defined, and the recurrence which distinguishes poetry also finds a place in the sounds which it uses. Whether it be the more obvious rime, alliteration and refrain, or the more subtle assonance and onomatopoeia, the sounds of poetry are its glory since (we must say it again) poetry is made to be read aloud. For this reason a poem should never be read rapidly except for a special effect; only care in reading can give full expression to the sounds and words which have been so skillfully worked into the lines; only in this way can its full meaning and beauty be recreated and understood.[12]

[12] More extended treatment of the devices for sound will be found in the extended analyses of Chapter 8.

⤙ 5 ⤚

Poetic Tools: Stanza and Poem Forms

W E HAVE, in the preceding discussions, been dealing
with the smaller units of poetic structure by means of
which the poet creates his effects. The next larger unit is the
stanza, or group of verses, which can be characterized in terms
of its four basic elements: dominant foot, number of feet to the
line, number of lines, and *rime scheme.* The latter is determined
by calling the last word of the first line *a,* the last word of the
next line *a* if it rimes with the first, *b* if it does not, and so on
through the stanza. Thus Walter Savage Landor's *Death,* complete in one stanza, would be described as four lines of iambic
tetrameter, riming *abab*:

> Death stands above me, whispering low
> I know not what into my ear;
> Of his strange language all I know
> Is, there is not a word of fear.

It will be evident that possibilities for stanza structure are
almost unlimited, for by combining lines of different length and
dominant foot, unified by different rime schemes, and more or
fewer lines per stanza, hundreds can be worked out. For our
purposes this number must be limited to representative stanza
forms that have had a reasonably wide use in English poetry.
These will illustrate the principles involved, and once these
principles are understood the reader will be able to analyze any
stanza in terms of its appropriateness for the ideas presented in
it; for each stanza has, within its limits, its own individuality,
arousing a particular type of response in the reader. The names
associated with these stanzas may be taken as shortcuts to their

description: since the word "heroic" in this context always means iambic pentameter in English poetry, the "heroic couplet" always represents two iambic pentameter verses riming in pairs, *aa*; "Spenserian stanza" always means a nine-verse stanza, the first eight lines iambic pentameter, the last iambic hexameter, or an "Alexandrine,"[1] and the rime scheme *ababbcbcc*.

Stanza Forms

BLANK VERSE

By definition *blank verse* is not a stanza form, since its basis is not a group of rimed verses but unrimed iambic pentameter lines without stanzaic separation. Yet it is the most important of the conventional patterns in English poetry, and the absence of rime and stanzaic groupings gives it its unique value. We have seen that the iamb is the most natural foot pattern in English, and that the pentameter is the most natural line length. In blank verse we have the two combined, but the naturalness is elevated and dignified beyond the scope of normal conversation by the presence of the regularizing foot and line. For this reason it is the form used most frequently in poetic drama (see pp. 144–47), or in long narrative or philosophical poems in which it is desired that the reader shall be chiefly concerned with the subject matter and as little as possible with the more obvious elements of mechanical structure. For although we have seen, in the discussion of rhythm, that early blank verse was quite stiff and end-stopped, the form is capable of beautifully subtle rhythms, involving run-on or enjambement lines, wherein the thought is permitted to move freely from verse to verse where

[1] So called either from its use by the French poet, Alexandre Paris, or from its use in poems about Alexander the Great. It is a basic line in French poetry, but in English the word refers to a hexameter used as a variant to pentameter verses. Pope wrote, in his *Essay on Criticism*:

A needless Alexandrine ends the song,
That, like a wounded snake, drags its slow length along,

in which the hexameter's length is exaggerated by the monosyllabic words (including *drags*, *slow*, and *length*), the long vowel sounds, and the final spondee. The result is an onomatopoetic effect.

this seems desirable to the poet. Three passages, each descriptive but quite different in tone, will illustrate (for others, see
pp. 96–106). The first is from Milton's *Paradise Lost,* and even
in these few lines describing Satan in Hell there is some hint in
their rolling strength of what Wordsworth meant in his sonnet
(see p. 51) when he wrote: "Thou hadst a voice whose sound
was like the sea":

> Nine times the space that measures day and night
> To mortal men, he, with his horrid crew,
> Lay vanquished, rolling in the fiery gulf,
> Confounded, though immortal. But his doom
> Reserved him to more wrath; for now the thought
> Both of lost happiness and lasting pain
> Torments him: round he throws his baleful eyes,
> That witnessed huge affliction and dismay,
> Mixed with obdurate pride and steadfast hate.
> At once, as far as Angel's ken, he views
> The dismal situation waste and wild.
> A dungeon horrible, on all sides round,
> As one great furnace flames; yet from those flames
> No light; but rather darkness visible
> Served only to discover sights of woe,
> Regions of sorrow, doleful shades, where peace
> And rest can never dwell, hope never comes
> That comes to all, but torture without end
> Still urges, and a fiery deluge, fed
> With ever-burning sulphur unconsumed.

The second illustration is in the softer voice of Shelley's
Prometheus Unbound, in which the blank verse is equally at
home, but modulated to suit the different scene described. Asia
(representing love and beauty) is the wife of Prometheus,
who has been bound for centuries by the tyranny of Jupiter but
who is about to be freed and reunited with her. Panthea, Asia's
sister, recalls Asia's birth (similar to that of Venus):

> *Panthea.* How thou art changed! I dare not look on thee;
> I feel, but see thee not. I scarce endure
> The radiance of thy beauty. Some good change
> Is working in the elements which suffer
> Thy presence thus unveiled.—The Nereids tell
> That on the day when the clear hyaline
> Was cloven at thine uprise, and thou didst stand

Within a veinèd shell, which floated on
Over the calm floor of the crystal sea,
Among the Ægean isles, and by the shores
Which bear thy name, love, like the atmosphere
Of the sun's fire filling the living world,
Burst from thee, and illumined Earth and Heaven
And the deep ocean and the sunless caves
And all that dwell within them; till grief cast
Eclipse upon the soul from which it came:
Such art thou now, nor is it I alone,
Thy sister, thy companion, thine own chosen one,
But the whole world which seeks thy sympathy. . . .
Asia. Thy words are sweeter than all else but his
Whose echoes they are—yet all love is sweet,
Given or returned; common as light is love,
And its familiar voice wearies not ever.
Like the wide Heaven, the all-sustaining air,
It makes the reptile equal to the god:
They who inspire it most are fortunate
As I am now; but those who feel it most
Are happier still, after long sufferings,
As I shall soon become.

The third illustration, *There Was a Boy*, is in the quietly re-
flective voice of Wordsworth, and is reminiscent of his own
childhood experiences in England's Lake District:

There was a Boy: ye knew him well, ye cliffs
And islands of Winander!*—many a time   *Lake Windermere
At evening, when the earliest stars began
To move along the edges of the hills,
Rising or setting, would he stand alone
Beneath the trees or by the glimmering lake,
And there, with fingers interwoven, both hands
Pressed closely palm to palm, and to his mouth
Uplifted, he, as through an instrument,
Blew mimic hootings to the silent owls,
That they might answer him; and they would shout
Across the watery vale, and shout again,
Responsive to his call, with quivering peals,
And long halloos and screams, and echoes loud,
Redoubled and redoubled, concourse wild
Of jocund din; and, when a lengthened pause
Of silence came and baffled his best skill,
Then sometimes, in that silence when he hung
Listening, a gentle shock of mild surprise

Has carried far into his heart the voice
Of mountain torrents; or the visible scene
Would enter unawares into his mind,
With all its solemn imagery, its rocks,
Its woods, and that uncertain heaven, received
Into the bosom of the steady lake.

HEROIC AND OCTOSYLLABIC COUPLETS

In English prosody the word *heroic*, as we have seen, means iambic pentameter. (Thus blank verse is also heroic verse.) The term *heroic couplet*, then, describes iambic pentameter lines riming in couplets, a form that has, in its history, swung between two extremes: the *open couplet*, in which the ideas follow a free movement and overlap the couplet endings, as in blank verse but with the added touch of rime, and the *closed couplet*, in which a unit of thought relatively complete in itself is contained in the two lines. The latter, especially popular in the early eighteenth century, is illustrated by the following lines from Pope's *An Essay on Criticism*:[2]

True ease in writing comes from art, not chance,
As those move easiest who have learned to dance.
'Tis not enough no harshness gives offense;
The sound must seem an echo to the sense:
Soft is the strain when Zephyr gently blows,
And the smooth stream in smoother numbers flows;
But when loud surges lash the sounding shore,
The hoarse, rough verse should like the torrent roar:
When Ajax strives some rock's vast weight to throw,
The line too labors, and the words move slow;
Not so when swift Camilla scours the plain,
Flies o'er th' unbending corn, and skims along the main.

The *open couplet* makes use of the run-on or enjambement line, and although the rime is often scarcely noticeable as the

[2] In this passage Pope both comments on and illustrates a number of the poetic devices with which we have been concerned. Note especially how the devices for rhythm and sound form "an echo to the sense" of the content; and note also the particular effectiveness of the closing hexameter, here given a maximum lightness of movement as compared with the opposite quality of the same poet's "That, like a wounded snake, drags its slow length along," quoted above. p. 65*n*.

lines are read, it has a definite effect on the reader, and adds
to the structural basis of the poem. In the following selection
from Keats's *Sleep and Poetry* the poet finds the writers of the
closed heroic couplet of Pope's day to be mere craftsmen, incap-
able of letting their imaginations range freely on the wings of
the creative spirit (represented in mythology by Pegasus, the
winged horse):

> With a puling infant's force
> They swayed about upon a rocking horse,
> And thought it Pegasus. Ah, dismal soul'd!
> The winds of heaven blew, the ocean roll'd
> Its gathering waves—ye felt it not. The blue
> Bared its eternal bosom, and the dew
> Of summer nights collected still to make
> The morning precious: Beauty was awake!
> Why were ye not awake? But ye were dead
> To things ye knew not of,—were closely wed
> To musty laws lined out with wretched rule
> And compass vile; so that ye taught a school
> Of dolts to smooth, inlay, and clip, and fit,
> Till, like the certain wands of Jacob's wit
> Their verses tallied. Easy was the task:
> A thousand handicraftsmen wore the mask
> Of poetry.

The *octosyllabic couplet* (so named because iambic or trochaic
tetrameter contains eight syllables to the line) offers a more
rapid, terse, and frequently less smooth movement than does the
heroic couplet, but it too will be subject to the same qualifica-
tions of end-stop or enjambement. Robert Herrick's *Delight in
Disorder* takes full advantage of the comparative lightness of
touch also suited to the form:

> A sweet disorder in the dress
> Kindles in clothes a wantonness.
> A lawn* about the shoulders thrown   *fine linen cloth
> Into a fine distraction;
> An erring lace, which here and there
> Enthralls the crimson stomacher*;   *ornamental covering
> A cuff neglectful, and thereby   for the bodice of a dress
> Ribbands to flow confusedly;
> A winning wave, deserving note,
> In the tempestuous petticoat;

A careless shoestring, in whose tie
I see a wild civility;—
Do more bewitch me, than when art
Is too precise in every part.[3]

TERZA RIMA

The *terza rima* ("triple riming"), famous as the form of
Dante's *Divine Comedy*, finds little use today, but from the
standpoint of its structure it is subtly complex. The first three
of its iambic pentameter verses rime *aba*; the next stanza then
picks up the *b* sound for its first and third lines, *bcb*, with *cdc*,
ded, *efe*, etc., following, until the forward-moving effect is finally stopped by use of a quatrain, either *xyxy* or *xyxx*. Shelley
based his *Ode to the West Wind* on this pattern, but varied it
by using five sections of fourteen lines each; Byron employed it,
appropriately, for *The Prophecy of Dante*; and William Morris
found it well suited for *The Defence of Guinevere*, in which
King Arthur's wife is on trial for her affair with Lancelot. The
terza rima structure suggests her nostalgic reaching back to her
memories, and at the same time forward to the outcome of her
trial. The closing lines of the poem (which Morris ends with
an alternating-rime quatrain) follow:

> "Nevertheless, you, O Sir Gauwaine, lie;
> Whatever may have happened these long years,
> God knows I speak truth, saying that you lie!
>
> "All I have said is truth, by Christ's dear tears."
> She would not speak another word, but stood
> Turned sideways, listening, like a man who hears
>
> His brother's trumpet sounding through the wood
> Of his foes' lances. She leaned eagerly,
> And gave a slight spring sometimes, as she could
>
> At last hear something really; joyfully
> Her cheek grew crimson, as the headlong speed
> Of the roan charger drew all men to see,
> The knight who came was Launcelot at good need.

[3] For a long narrative poem in this form, in which medial pauses have
been used most effectively for variety in phrasing, see William Morris's
The Haystack in the Floods, p. 139.

QUATRAINS

Of the standard patterns, the *quatrain* offers a wider range of possibilities than does any one of the others. Blank verse and the couplets, as we have seen, normally run without break down the page (although couplets might be separated at any time should the poet wish to do so), and the terza rima stanzas are uniquely interlinked. With four lines, however, more opportunities for varying the rime scheme or the line lengths are available, and at the same time the stanza is sufficiently short that it can be easily grasped by the reader. The more important of the combinations resulting from these possibilities can be described and illustrated briefly.

Common meter takes its name from its frequent use in all periods of English poetry, and its alternate name, *ballad stanza,* from its many appearances in the structure of ballads. In this form alternating rime is used, balancing the 4343 (tetrameter-trimeter-tetrameter-trimeter) line lengths with an *abcb* or *abab* scheme and, in doing so, satisfying the reader's expectation as he proceeds through the stanzas. By lengthening the short lines, *long meter* (4444) results, and by shortening one or both of the long lines, *short meter* (3343 or 3333) is formed. (In all of these the iambic is usually but [especially in long meter] not exclusively employed.) Consider for a moment the following three versions of the same stanza. Burns himself made the change from common meter (1) to long meter (2), with the short meter (3) adapted from the original for this illustration. If the three are read aloud the changes in effect will be evident:

(1) Ye flowery banks o' bonnie Doon	4
How can ye blume sae fair?	3
How can ye chant, ye little birds,	4
And I sae fu' o' care?	3
(2) Ye banks and braes o' bonnie Doon,	4
How can ye bloom sae fresh and fair?	4
How can ye chant, ye little birds,	4
And I sae weary fu' o' care?	4

(3) Ye banks o' bonnie Doon   3
     How can ye blume sae fair?   3
     How can ye chant, ye little birds,   4
     And I sae fu' o' care?   3

The effectiveness of the common meter stanza with its economy
of expression is clearly exhibited in the following delightful
lyric by A. E. Housman:

> Oh, when I was in love with you,
>   Then I was clean and brave,
> And miles around the wonder grew
>   How well did I behave.
>
> And now the fancy passes by,
>   And nothing will remain,
> And miles around they'll say that I
>   Am quite myself again.

Of the other conventional four-line stanzas two take their
names from famous poems, Tennyson's *In Memoriam* (although
the form was not invented by Tennyson) and Edward Fitzgerald's translation of Omar Khayyám's *The Rubáiyát*. The *In
Memoriam stanza* is in tetrameters riming *abba* (a *brace-rime
quatrain,* since the *bb* "braces" the center of the stanza and
offers an interesting departure from our normally expected alternate rime schemes) and has been illustrated above (p. 61),
but the following offers a different context and incorporates an
approximate rime:

> I hold it true, whate'er befall;
> I feel it when I sorrow most;
> 'Tis better to have loved and lost
> Than never to have loved at all.

The *Rubáiyát stanza* is in pentameters riming *aaba* (or *quatrain with rime skip* since all lines have the same rime sound
except one which is "skipped"). This pattern offers a surprising
lack of the expected couplet in lines three and four, yet satisfies the ear by the echo of the opening rime pair in the last line:

> Myself when young did eagerly frequent
> Doctor and saint, and heard great argument
>   About it and about; but evermore
> Came out by the same door wherein I went.[4]

---

[4] It should be noted how, in these and certain other stanzas, the appearance on the page guides the reader to the corresponding rimes.

The third of the remaining four-line stanzas is the *heroic quatrain,* which takes its name from its four iambic pentameter lines, and has a rime scheme *abab.* The dignified movement offered by the pentameter makes the stanza ideal for serious thought (in specialized use it is called the *elegiac stanza* for this reason), as the following complete poem in this form, Ethelyn Miller Hartwich's *What Shall Endure,* illustrates:

> Great roads the Romans built, that men might meet,
> And walls to keep strong men apart—secure;
> Now centuries have passed, and in defeat
> The walls are fallen, but the roads endure.

STANZAS OF SIX TO EIGHT VERSES

The foregoing considerations and illustrations will indicate to the reader the process of analysis involved in determining the effectiveness of the different forms. Further analysis will be reserved for the Spenserian stanza, the sonnet, and free verse, but a brief example of each of these intervening patterns may be of interest.

The *stave of six* (iambic pentameter or tetrameter, *ababcc*) has a closing couplet after what is, in effect, a heroic quatrain opening. Carlin Aden's *Early Fishermen* makes distinctive use of the form (with an *abcb* variant in the first two stanzas):

> How long they have been there I cannot tell.
> They came when it was dark and lowered stones
> To anchor them securely in the night.
> How long? I know their hooks were carved of bones
> When first they slid with hardly splash or wake
> Over the still waters of this lake.
>
> The time to see them best is when the sun
> Has cleared the sky of all but one last star.
> When each dim form resembles all the rest,
> The parting darkness prints them as they are—
> Each with a line that ties him to his place
> Upon his lake, his planet and his race.
>
> Nothing is more enduring than this line
> That goes so deeply in so many seas—
> The last star tires as day outdoes its shine,

The herons flap among the willow trees,
A whistle shakes the world; the ancient men
Row back across the centuries again.

The *rime royal stanza,* or *Chaucerian heptastich* (iambic pentameter, *ababbcc*), introduced by Chaucer and named from its use by King James I of Scotland in the fifteenth century, delays the closing couplet but anticipates it with line five, which rimes with line four. It is illustrated here by a stanza from William Morris's *The Earthly Paradise*:

> Dreamer of dreams, born out of my due time,
> Why should I strive to set the crooked straight?
> Let it suffice me that my murmuring rhyme
> Beats with light wing against the ivory gate,—
> Telling a tale not too importunate
> To those who in the sleepy region stay,
> Lulled by the singer of an empty day.

The *ottava rima* (iambic pentameter, *abababcc*) also delays the closing couplet by permitting the *ab* progression to continue through six lines. Its flexibility is shown by its adaptability to (1) the light, conversational mood and composite rimes of Byron's satirical dedication of his *Don Juan* to Robert Southey (who, like Wordsworth and Coleridge, lived in the Lake District of England), but also (2) to the serious description in Keats's *Isabella, or the Pot of Basil*:

> (1) Bob Southey! you're a poet—Poet laureate,
>   And representative of all the race;
> Although 'tis true that you turned out a Tory at
>   Last,—yours has lately been a common case;
> And now, my epic Renegade! what are ye at
>   With all the Lakers, in and out of place?
> A nest of tuneful persons, to my eye
> Like "four and twenty Blackbirds in a pye."

> (2) In the mid days of autumn, on their eves
>   The breath of Winter comes from far away,
> And the sick west continually bereaves
>   Of some gold tinge, and plays a roundelay
> Of death among the bushes and the leaves,
>   To make all bare before he dares to stray
> From his north cavern. So sweet Isabel
> By gradual decay from beauty fell.

SPENSERIAN STANZA

The *Spenserian stanza,* so named from Edmund Spenser, author of the *Faerie Queene,* who invented it for use in that poem, resulted from the poet's need of a medium for extended description. The rime scheme is *ababbcbcc,* with the *b* rime used partly as a brace rime and partly as an interlinking device to unify the whole stanza. Then there seems to be a normal close (prepared for in line six) on the *cc* couplet. But the close is not normal, since another distinctive element is added: the hexameter, or Alexandrine, for the last verse. This is most effective. The reader, after making the necessary effort asked by the longer line, pauses to rest, and as he does so the full beauty of the stanzaic unity is impressed on his mind. The stanza is thus long enough for carefully detailed elements of description or narration, and the movement determined by the rime scheme is such that a minor climax is reached in the middle of the stanza, where the brace rime occurs, with a major climax at the end, through use of the lengthened line. These characteristics are well displayed in two stanzas from Keats's *Eve of St. Agnes,* already considered in another connection (pp. 9 and 62), and in the following well-known lines from the fourth canto of Byron's *Childe Harold's Pilgrimage*:

> Roll on, thou deep and dark blue Ocean—roll!
> Ten thousand fleets sweep over thee in vain;
> Man marks the earth with ruin—his control
> Stops with the shore; upon the watery plain
> The wrecks are all thy deed, nor doth remain
> A shadow of man's ravage, save his own,
> When, for a moment, like a drop of rain,
> He sinks into thy depths with bubbling groan,
> Without a grave, unknell'd, uncoffin'd, and unknown.

LONGER STANZAS

There are no widely used patterns in the ten-to-thirteen-verse stanzas, but Keats's famous odes indicate how richly those of ten and eleven lines can be employed. In the ten-line form

Keats appears to have blended the best elements of the two principal sonnet forms (see below), by use of a heroic quatrain as in the Shakespearean sonnet opening, to which is added a six-verse close that parallels the sestet of the Petrarchan pattern. In *To Autumn,* where he uses an eleven-line stanza, the same principle holds, but with an added line just before the close, giving the effect of a musical sostenuto as he leads into the cadence of the final line. The pattern of this ode is *ababcdedcce*:

> Season of mists and mellow fruitfulness,
>   Close bosom-friend of the maturing sun;
> Conspiring with him how to load and bless
>   With fruit the vines that round the thatch-eves run;
> To bend with apples the mossed cottage-trees,
>   And fill all fruit with ripeness to the core;
>   To swell the gourd, and plump the hazel shells
> With a sweet kernel; to set budding more,
>   And still more, later flowers for the bees,
>   Until they think warm days will never cease,
>   For Summer has o'er-brimmed their clammy cells.
>
> Who hath not seen thee oft amid thy store?
>   Sometimes whoever seeks abroad may find
> Thee sitting careless on a granary floor,
>   Thy hair soft-lifted by the winnowing wind;
> Or on a half-reaped furrow sound asleep,
>   Drowsed with the fume of poppies, while thy hook
>   Spares the next swath and all its twinèd flowers:
> And sometimes like a gleaner thou dost keep
>   Steady thy laden head across a brook;
>   Or by a cider-press, with patient look,
>   Thou watchest the last oozings hours by hours.
>
> Where are the songs of Spring? Ay, where are they?
>   Think not of them, thou hast thy music too.—
> While barrèd clouds bloom the soft-dying day,
>   And touch the stubble-plains with rosy hue;
> Then in a wailful choir the small gnats mourn
>   Among the river sallows, borne aloft
>   Or sinking as the light wind lives or dies;
> And full-grown lambs loud bleat from hilly bourn,
>   Hedge-crickets sing; and now with treble soft
>   The red-breast whistles from a garden-croft;
>   And gathering swallows twitter in the skies.

Poem Forms

To Autumn forms a transition to certain types of poems—the sonnet, the ode, free verse, the limerick, and the French and Japanese forms—that are units in themselves. The most important of these is the sonnet, which takes on something of the nature of a stanza when it is used in *sequences* or *cycles,* wherein a number of sonnets are written on a given theme. But even here, each sonnet can be taken out of its sequence and read as an independent poem.

THE SONNET

There are three basic forms of the *sonnet,* with many experimental modifications which have had but temporary interest. Traditionally, the sonnet has always been fourteen lines of iambic pentameter, with the rime scheme determining the subtype. The *Italian* (or *Petrarchan* from its important use by the fourteenth-century Italian poet Francesco Petrarch) is divided between an octave (eight lines) and a sestet (six lines), with the former riming *abbaabba* and the latter, permitting more variety, *cdecde* or *cdcdcd,* or some combination of two or three sounds that does not end in a couplet (since the couplet may, unless carefully controlled, destroy the close unity of expression aimed at in this form). Milton's *On His Being Arrived to the Age of Twenty-Three,* one of the earliest sonnets written in England in the strict Petrarchan form, is a good example of the pattern with a *cdedce* sestet. (Milton appeared younger than he was, and he felt that his talent was slow in maturing, but as a strict Puritan he left his future in God's hands):[5]

> How soon hath Time, the subtle thief of youth,
> Stolen on his wing my three and twentieth year!
> My hasting days fly on with full career,
> But my late spring no bud or blossom shew'th.

[5] For Wordsworth's tribute to Milton, also written in the Italian pattern, with *abbaabbacddece,* see p. 51. For an extended discussion of sonnet usage, with explications, see Chapter 8.

Perhaps my semblance might deceive the truth,
That I to manhood am arrived so near,
And inward ripeness doth much less appear,
That some more timely-happy spirits indu'th.
Yet be it less or more, or soon or slow,
It shall be still in strictest measure even
To that same lot, however mean or high,
Toward which Time leads me, and the will of Heaven,
All is, if I have grace to use it so,
As ever in my great Task-master's eye.

Although the true Italian pattern did not find its way into England until the time of Milton, sonnets based on the Petrarchan form had been introduced a century earlier. Some of these missed being the true form only by the presence of the closing couplet; others were more experimental, and out of these experiments came the two principal English forms. The *Spenserian sonnet,* named for, although not invented by, Edmund Spenser, broke away from the octave-sestet division and substituted three interlinked quatrains[6] and a closing couplet, all in iambic pentameter. The rime scheme is *abab bcbc cdcd ee,* which does away with the difficult *abbaabba* of the Italian pattern and permits a more normal progression through use of alternating rime. It also offers more opportunity than does the Italian for different rime sounds, an advantage in a language such as English, limited as it is in this regard. In the following, note how closely the thought follows the quatrain and couplet development:

One day I wrote her name upon the strand,
But came the waves and washed it away:
Again I wrote it with a second hand,
But came the tide, and made my pains his prey.
Vain man, said she, that dost in vain assay
A mortal thing so to immortalize!
For I myself shall like to this decay,
And eek* my name be wiped out likewise.   *also
Not so (quoth I) let baser things devise
To die in dust, but you shall live by fame:
My verse your virtues fair shall eternize,
And in the heavens write your glorious name.
Where, whenas death shall all the world subdue,
Our love shall live, and later life renew.

[6] Compare the interlinking of rimes in the Spenserian stanza (p. 75) and note that the first nine lines of the sonnet agree with the stanza exactly in rime scheme, although no hexameter is involved in the sonnet.

The difference in movement between the Italian and Spenserian sonnets will be clear if the two are read aloud consecutively.

The *Shakespearean sonnet,* like the Spenserian, is divided into quatrains plus couplet but does not make use of the interlinking rimes, for the scheme is *abab cdcd efef gg.* This permits even wider variety in choice of rime words and results in the greater popularity of the form. (When the *English sonnet* is referred to, it is normally the Shakespearean that is meant.) In the following example from Shakespeare, numbered XVIII, note how the same theme as that treated by Spenser (a conventional one in their day) has been adapted, and how the thought is made to conform to the three independently rimed quatrains plus couplet:

> Shall I compare thee to a summer's day?
> Thou art more lovely and more temperate.
> Rough winds do shake the darling buds of May,
> And summer's lease hath all too short a date.
> Sometime too hot the eye of heaven shines,
> And often is his gold complexion dimm'd;
> And every fair from fair sometime declines,
> By chance or nature's changing course untrimm'd;
> But thy eternal summer shall not fade,
> Nor lose possession of that fair thou ow'st;
> Nor shall Death brag thou wand'rest in his shade
> When in eternal lines to time thou grow'st.
> > So long as men can breathe or eyes can see,
> > So long lives this, and this gives life to thee.

THE ODE

Although quite limited in use today, there are enough important odes in the body of English poetry to justify some comment on their structure. The earliest of these is the *Regular Pindaric* (so named from its use by the Greek poet of the fifth century B.C., Pindar), a form which found its way into England during the Elizabethan period. The various "movements" (rather than stanzas) of which it is composed have led to the suggestion that it is related to the pattern of classical drama, in which a chorus chanted lines as it moved or made its turn (or *strophe*) across the stage, following this with a counter-turn (or *antistrophe*) which brought it back to the original position, where a final section of the chant was recited while standing (the *epode*, or "singing after"). From this the names of the units of the Regular Pindaric ode derived.

The writer may use for his strophe any number of lines, usually iambic, of any length or variety of length, and with any rime pattern, that he wishes. For the antistrophe he must then follow his strophe exactly with respect to these details, while in the epode opportunity is given for variety, usually with more and shorter lines and a different rime arrangement. If the poem is not finished in these three units of the first section, one or more additional sections can be used, but these must be built on the patterns already established. The closing section of Thomas Gray's *The Progress of Poesy* will illustrate these characteristics as well as the highly dignified and formal diction associated with the ode. A careful reading will reveal that the strophe refers to Shakespeare, the antistrophe to Milton and Dryden, and the epode to the "daring spirit" who is Gray himself, while the "Theban Eagle" is, appropriately, Pindar:

III

Strophe

Far from the sun and summer gale,
In thy green lap was Nature's darling laid,
What time, where lucid Avon strayed,
   To him the mighty mother did unveil
Her awful face: the dauntless child
Stretched forth his little arms, and smiled.
This pencil take (she said), whose colors clear
Richly paint the vernal year:
Thine too these golden keys, immortal boy!
This can unlock the gates of joy;
Of horror that, and thrilling fears,
Or ope the sacred source of sympathetic tears.

Antistrophe

Nor second he, that rode sublime
Upon the seraph-wings of Ecstasy,
The secrets of the abyss to spy:
   He passed the flaming bounds of place and time:
The living Throne, the sapphire-blaze,
Where Angels tremble while they gaze,
He saw; but, blasted with excess of light,
Closed his eyes in endless night.

Behold, where Dryden's less presumptuous car,
Wide o'er the fields of glory bear
Two coursers of ethereal race,
With necks in thunder clothed, and long-resounding pace.

Epode

Hark, his hands the lyre explore!
Bright-eyed Fancy, hovering o'er,
   Scatters from her pictured urn
   Thoughts that breathe, and words that burn.
But ah, 'tis heard no more!—
   O Lyre divine! what daring Spirit
   Wakes thee now? Though he inherit
Nor the pride, nor ample pinion,
   That the Theban Eagle bear,
Sailing with supreme dominion
   Through the azure deep of air:
Yet oft before his infant eyes would run
   Such forms as glitter in the Muse's ray,
With orient hues, unborrowed from the Sun:
   Yet shall he mount, and keep his distant way
Beyond the limits of a vulgar fate,
Beneath the Good how far—but far above the Great.

The *Irregular Pindaric ode* was introduced to England from
France by Abraham Cowley in the seventeenth century, and is
sometimes called the *Cowleian ode* as a result. This form takes
as its starting point the freedom of structure found in the
strophe of the Regular Pindaric, but carries this freedom into
each unit, where the line lengths and rime placement are independent for each group of lines and are usually determined by
phrasing demands or by form-content relationships. There are
thus no formal strophes, antistrophes, or epodes, and the thought
can be even more perfectly housed in an appropriate structure
than it can in the regular form. The skill with which this can
be accomplished is illustrated by the passages from Dryden's
A Song for St. Cecilia's Day already quoted (p. 61), and by the
following from Wordsworth's *Ode: Intimations of Immortality*,
in which the gaiety and lightness of mood are suddenly reversed
with "But there's a Tree, of many, one":

   Ye blessed Creatures, I have heard the call
      Ye to each other make; I see
   The heavens laugh with you in your jubilee;

My heart is at your festival,
My head hath its coronal,
The fulness of your bliss, I feel—I feel it all.
Oh evil day! if I were sullen
While Earth herself is adorning,
    This sweet May-morning,
And the Children are culling
    On every side,
In a thousand valleys far and wide,
Fresh flowers; while the sun shines warm,
And the Babe leaps up on his Mother's arm:—
I hear, I hear, with joy I hear!
—But there's a Tree, of many, one,
A single Field which I have looked upon,
Both of them speak of something that is gone:
    The Pansy at my feet
    Doth the same tale repeat:
Whither is fled the visionary gleam?
Where is it now, the glory and the dream?

The *stanzaic* (or *homostrophic*) *ode* differs from the foregoing in that, as the name suggests, a regular stanza structure is used throughout the poem. Clearly, such an ode will be distinguished from other stanzaic poems only by the highly dignified mood, direct address or apostrophe, and nobility of sentiment; and very often these characteristics will be muted as compared with the larger sweep of the two Pindaric types. There is, for example, the simple dignity of William Collins' *Ode Written in the Beginning of the Year 1746*, which is actually in two stanzas made up of tetrameter couplets:

How sleep the brave who sink to rest,
By all their country's wishes blest!
When Spring, with dewy fingers cold,
Returns to deck their hallowed mould,
She there shall dress a sweeter sod
Than Fancy's feet have ever trod.

By fairy hands their knell is rung;
By forms unseen their dirge is sung;
There Honour comes, a pilgrim grey,
To bless the turf that wraps their clay;
And Freedom shall awhile repair,
To dwell, a weeping hermit, there!

But the historical forerunner of the stanzaic ode is the *Horatian,* so called from its use by the classical poet Horace. In this form the stanza is of four verses, either rimed or unrimed, with the pattern *aabb* in the former case. The first two verses of each stanza are one or two feet longer than the last two, and the dominant foot is iambic. William Collins again offers an admirable example, in his *Ode to Evening:*[7]

> If aught of oaten stop, or pastoral song
> May hope, chaste Eve, to soothe thy modest ear,
>   Like thy own solemn springs,
>   Thy springs, and dying gales,
>
> O nymph reserved, while now the bright-haired sun
> Sits in yon western tent, whose cloudy skirts,
>   With brede ethereal wove,
>   O'erhang his wavy bed:
>
> Now air is hushed, save where the weak-eyed bat
> With short, shrill shriek, flits by on leathern wing;
>   Or where the beetle winds
>   His small but sullen horn,
>
> As oft he rises 'midst the twilight path,
> Against the pilgrim borne in heedless hum:
>   Now teach me, maid composed,
>   To breathe some softened strain,
>
> Whose numbers, stealing through thy darkening vale,
> May, not unseemly, with its stillness suit,
>   As, musing slow, I hail
>   Thy genial loved return.
>
> For when thy folding star arising shows
> His paly circlet, at his warning lamp
>   The fragrant Hours, and elves
>   Who slept in buds the day,
>
> And many a nymph who wreathes her brows with sedge,
> And sheds the freshening dew, and, lovelier still,
>   The pensive Pleasures sweet
>   Prepare thy shadowy car.

[7] For a freer structure in the stanzaic ode see Keats's *To Autumn,* p. 76.

Then lead, calm votaress, where some sheety lake
Cheers the lone heath, or some time-hallowed pile,
    Or upland fallows grey
    Reflect its last cool gleam.

But when chill blustering winds, or driving rain,
Forbid my willing feet, be mine the hut
    That from the mountain's side
    Views wilds, and swelling floods,

And hamlets brown, and dim-discovered spires;
And hears their simple bell, and marks o'er all
    Thy dewy fingers draw
    The gradual dusky veil.

While Spring shall pour his showers, as oft he wont,
And bathe thy breathing tresses, meekest Eve!
    While Summer loves to sport
    Beneath thy lingering light;

While sallow Autumn fills thy lap with leaves;
Or Winter, yelling through the troublous air,
    Affrights thy shrinking train,
    And rudely rends thy robes:

So long, sure-found beneath the sylvan shed,
Shall Fancy, Friendship, Science, rose-lipped Health,
    Thy gentlest influence own,
    And hymn thy favorite name!

FREE VERSE

Writers who turn to *free verse* so that they may avoid the difficulties inherent in the formal structures described above are frequently surprised to learn that it is in fact one of the most difficult forms to use successfully. Merely breaking up lines into different lengths has never made poetry and it will never do so. The writer of free verse must be extremely sensitive to rhythm, phrasing, and cadence; he must exert an unusual amount of self-criticism and discipline to prevent his lines becoming mere jottings of ideas; and he must keep constantly in mind the basic principle of recurrence in order that his material may not be prosaic. Recurrence is more subtle in free verse than in stanzaic verse, because the artificial elements are absent, but it is none the less present.[8]

The *Arnold type of free verse*, so called from its use by Matthew Arnold, is characterized by its use of a norm line of five feet, and a dominant iambic foot. Shorter lines are grouped around the pentameters. This tendency to pentameter gives a fairly even rhythmical pattern to the lines, while at the same time the poet employs freedom from a regular rime scheme and constant line length. In Arnold's *Philomela* (based on the Greek myth of Philomela and Procne) it will be noted that eleven iambic pentameter verses unify the whole:

> Hark! Ah, the Nightingale!
> The tawny-throated!
> Hark! from that moonlit cedar what a burst!
> What triumph! hark—what pain!
>
> O Wanderer from a Grecian shore,
> Still, after many years, in distant lands,
> Still nourishing in thy bewilder'd brain
> That wild, unquench'd, deep-sunken, old-world pain—
> Say, will it never heal?
> And can this fragrant lawn
> With its cool trees, and night,
> And the sweet tranquil Thames,
> And moonshine, and the dew,
> To thy rack'd heart and brain
> Afford no balm?
> Dost thou to-night behold
> Here, through the moonlight on this English grass,
> The unfriendly palace in the Thracian wild?
> Dost thou again peruse
> With hot cheeks and sear'd eyes,
> The too clear web, and thy dumb Sister's shame?
> Dost thou once more assay
> Thy flight, and feel come over thee,

---

[8] Compare the Irregular Pindaric ode, above, but note that rime is normally used in the ode, whereas it is optional in free verse, and the mood of the ode is always dignified and elevated, while that of free verse may be more varied. It would, of course, be possible to write an ode in free verse, in which case the classification would depend on the subject matter.

Poor fugitive, the feathery change
Once more, and once more seem to make resound
With love and hate, triumph and agony,
Lone Daulis, and the high Cephissian vale?
Listen, Eugenia—
How thick the bursts come crowding through the leaves!
Again—thou hearest!
Eternal passion!
Eternal pain!

The *Whitman type of free verse* uses freedom from rime, from regular metrical pattern and from regular rhythmical pattern. There is no basic norm line, as in the Arnold type, and the feeling of appropriate rhythmical relationship between form and content largely determines the shortness or length of verses. Yet it is not as "free" as this might suggest, for a technique involving parallelism, phonetic recurrence, reiteration and other devices gives Whitman's verse actually more elements of form than are generally conceded to it. Many striking effects can be obtained by this comparative freedom, however, including strong climaxes gained by lengthening the lines as the sections of the poem progress. The reader must be sensitive to movement in order to catch the full beauty of such lines, but their final appreciation is ample reward for the effort required to gain such feeling and understanding. Since the cumulative effect is an integral part of this type of free verse, longer examples than can be analyzed here should be read, especially Whitman's powerful *Out of the Cradle Endlessly Rocking* and *When Lilacs Last in the Dooryard Bloomed*. A brief Whitman poem, however, will illustrate certain characteristics inherent in the form:

When I heard the learn'd astronomer;
When the proofs, the figures, were ranged in columns
    before me;
When I was shown the charts and diagrams, to add, divide,
    and measure them;
When I, sitting, heard the astronomer, where he lectured
    with much applause in the lecture-room,
How soon, unaccountable, I became tired and sick;
Till, rising and gliding out, I wander'd off by myself,
In the mystical moist night-air, and from time to time,
Look'd up in perfect silence at the stars.

Even a cursory examination of these lines will show devices such as parallelism, phonetic recurrence, reiteration, and, in the present instance, a predominance of iambs and anapests. But the phrase patterns take precedence over the foot patterns, and if the reader will listen carefully he will hear x / x x occurring no less than six times in the first five lines (*astronomer, and diagrams, and measure them, astronomer, the lecture-room,* [un] *accountable*). This phrase pattern is woven through these lines, and it serves even as does a figure in music to unify the whole. The last three lines of the poem then become more regular and controlled, in keeping with the subject matter, employing blended iambs and anapests that lead to masculine endings, whereas in the first four lines the feminine ending had been used.

A third type that may be described as *modern free verse* represents something of a compromise between the other types: not as regular as the Arnold, not as free as the Whitman. Rime is used freely or omitted, at the discretion of the poet, and the infinite variety in rhythm and phrasing has been adapted to the needs of a wide range of subjects and moods. To illustrate how this technique differs from a prose statement the following should be read aloud:

> In the hospital I find a world of half reality almost like a waking sleep, thick fog separating me from things that are; and through the dimness someone moves across the room. Long corridors echo with footsteps through the dark night; echoes of doors closing and the hushed tone of voices.

This bit of prose creates a mood and communicates an impression effectively; but I believe most readers would agree that the following *Hospital Impressions* when read aloud is more effective. Note that each phrase takes on added significance and dignity because it is separated from the others, and that the cumulative force of the emotion is intensified accordingly:[9]

---

[9] For other free verse poems in this book see the Twenty-third Psalm (p. 175), in a format that results in modern free verse; Coventry Patmore's *Departure* (p. 182), of the Arnold type; Marianne Moore's *Poetry* (p. 7), where the modern type with longer lines balanced by shorter in roughly stanzaic groupings, and a freer use of idiom set off by line-end breaks that are reminiscent of some of Hopkins' sprung rhythm

The world of half reality,
Almost like a waking sleep.
A thick fog
Separating me
From things that really are.
And through the dimness
Someone moves across the room . . .

Long corridors
That echo with footsteps
Through the dark night.
Doors softly closing
And the hushed tones of voices . . .

SPRUNG RHYTHM

Related to free verse in the sense that it seeks a different impact from that normally associated with the more regular patterns, *sprung rhythm* has, since its development by Gerard Manley Hopkins in the late nineteenth century and its first publication in 1918, exercised considerable influence on contemporary writers.

Hopkins defined "sprung" as "something like abrupt," and in this technique (related to Anglo-Saxon poetry [see the passage from *Beowulf*, p. 134]), the *stress* is substituted for the foot; indeed, one stress makes one foot, regardless of the number of unstressed syllables. Thus a pair of lines will balance if one has only five syllables, provided all are stressed, and the other ten or more, provided the reader feels five stresses in the latter also. Strong use is made of alliteration and assonance, as well as medial rime, repetition, or any device that can contribute to the impact sought.

To concentrate on stresses is, clearly, to gain force, energy, even a sense of shock. Compare, for example, the conventional heroic quatrain which follows with the same theme (the beauty

---

innovations (see p. 226), will be observed; Villa's *The Way My Ideas* (p. 179) in a more restrained modern form; Arnold's *Dover Beach* (p. 118); and Whitman's *Song of Myself* (p. 112).

of the force of the sea plus the sense of its power for destruction) in sprung rhythm:[10]

> The salt spray swings itself with shining flash,
> And breaks in beauty to a foaming breath;
> It finds me on the shore and with its lash
> The wind cries to me of a retching death.

By sprung rhythm scansion the following is still a heroic quatrain, even though the iambic foot has disappeared and five stresses per line substituted for it. (There will not always be agreement as to placement of the accents, but the writer and the reader should be able to indicate where they feel the key syllables to be):

> Salt spray, swinging to fling, flash,
> Breaking in beauty's beauty of foam's breath;
> Chasing the cut of chill-swept sand, lash
> Of wind-whispering whimper of worn torn death.

THE FRENCH FORMS

In the Middle Ages, when literature was in need of new forms, it was customary to imitate the patterns of other countries, especially France, substituting English words. Some of the *French forms* came in at this time, but it was in the late nineteenth century that their use became something of a fad, especially with writers such as Austin Dobson, Edmund Gosse, Andrew Lang, and Swinburne.

These poems are more interesting than they are important, and demand adherence to set patterns in which a limited number of rime sounds carry through an entire poem, with refrains (which must come in naturally) at determined points. Thus they are, in effect, puzzles to be solved, especially for a language as lacking in rime sounds as is English, and there is always the

---

[10] This illustration has been devised to point up the contrast between two treatments of the same theme. For an example of sprung rhythm by Hopkins, see the explication of *The Windhover*, pp. 214–33.

danger of artificiality in expression, a feeling that the author has been mastered by the form rather than the reverse. But they can be pleasantly graceful, especially when used for light or delicate compliment; and many writers have succeeded in incorporating serious moods or themes (especially of reverie or nostalgia) despite these handicaps.

Any meter and line length (so long as it is consistent throughout the poem) may be used, and a special system of notation indicates the manner of repeating refrains and rime sounds. A capital letter indicates the same rime sound as that letter in lower case, and also indicates that this particular verse, in the sequence shown, is repeated *verbatim* in all stanzas. A capital *R* indicates a shorter refrain, made up of the first part of an opening verse. A few of the many French forms will serve to illustrate these characteristics.[11]

The *ballade* (*3ababbcbC* plus envoy *bcbC*), not to be confused with the ballad (a narrative type to be discussed in Chapter 7), is illustrated by Andrew Lang's *To Theocritus in Winter*, in which a nostalgic mood is developed most skillfully:

Ah, leave the smoke, the wealth, the roar	a
Of London, and the bustling street,	b
For still, by the Sicilian shore	a
The murmur of the Muse is sweet.	b
Still, still, the suns of summer greet	b
The mountain-grave of Helikê,	c
And shepherds still their songs repeat	b
Where breaks the blue Sicilian sea.	C
What though they worship Pan no more	a
That guarded once the shepherd's seat,	b
They chatter of their rustic lore,	a
They watch the wind among the wheat:	b
Cicalas chirp, the young lambs bleat,	b
Where whispers pine to cypress tree;	c
They count the waves that idly beat	b
Where breaks the blue Sicilian sea.	C

[11] Since invention plays so large a part in these poems, it is not surprising that many other forms have been devised, among them the double and triple ballade, ballade with double refrain, double rondeau, roundel (invented by Swinburne), chant royal, and sestina. Most of these are extremely complex in their structure, and appeal more to the craftsman than to the artist.

Theocritus! Thou canst restore	a
The pleasant years, and over-fleet;	b
With Thee we live as men of yore,	a
We rest where running waters meet:	b
And then we turn unwilling feet	b
And seek the world—so must it be—	c
We may not linger in the heat	b
Where breaks the blue Sicilian sea.	C

Envoy

Master, when rain, and snow, and sleet	b
And northern winds are wild, to thee	c
We come, we rest in thy retreat,	b
Where breaks the blue Sicilian sea.	C

The *rondel* (*ABba abAB abbaAB*, or, as here, *ABab baAB ababAB*, with the final *B* optional in each case) is perfectly illustrated by Austin Dobson's *Vitas Hinnuleo,* the title of which, interestingly in the light of our previous discussion, is the opening of an ode by Horace ("You shun me, Chloe, like a fawn") on which this rondel is based. The slight change of wording in the refrain at line thirteen is consistent with the use of the French forms, although exact adherence to wording is normally sought:

You shun me, Chloe, wild and shy	A
As some stray fawn that seeks its mother	B
Through trackless woods. If spring winds sigh,	a
It vainly strives its fears to smother;—	b
Its trembling knees assail each other	b
When lizards stir the bramble dry:—	a
You shun me, Chloe, wild and shy	A
As some stray fawn that seeks its mother.	B
And yet no Libyan lion I,—	a
No ravening thing to rend another;	b
Lay by your tears, your tremors by—	a
A Husband's better than a brother;	b
Nor shun me, Chloe, wild and shy	A
As some stray fawn that seeks its mother.	B

The *rondeau* (*aabba aabR aabbaR*) is itself described delightfully by Dobson's *You Bid Me Try,* in which the playful mood of the French forms is illustrated. Note how the changed

emphasis on *"You"* and the tense shift of "bid" permit the exact
words of the refrain to carry modified meaning:

You bid me try, Blue Eyes, to write	a
A Rondeau. What!—forthwith?—to-night?	a
Reflect. Some skill I have, 'tis true;	b
But thirteen lines!—and rimed on two!	b
"Refrain," as well. Ah, hapless plight!	a
Still, there are five lines—ranged aright.	a
These Gallic bonds, I feared, would fright	a
My easy Muse. They did, till you—	b
You bid me try!	R
That makes them eight. The port's in sight—	a
'Tis all because your eyes are bright!	a
Now just a pair to end in "oo"—	b
When maids command, what can't we do?	b
Behold!—the Rondeau, tasteful, light,	a
You bid me try!	R

The *triolet* (*ABaAabAB*, with the *b* rimes usually on feminine
endings) is the "jewel" of the French forms. To be successful
it must be written with the greatest delicacy, the refrains must
come in naturally, even inevitably (not simply be tacked on at
the end), and a lightness of mood must prevail. Andrew Lang
has hinted at the problem in *Easy is the Triolet*:

Easy is the Triolet,	A
If you really learn to make it!	B
Once a neat refrain you get,	a
Easy is the Triolet.	A
As you see!—I pay my debt	a
With another rhyme. Deuce take it,	b
Easy is the Triolet,	A
If you really learn to make it!	B

But again it is Austin Dobson who shows his mastery of the
pattern in *A Kiss*, from a series in different French forms en-
titled, for reasons that will be evident, *Rose Leaves*. Note again
the changed emphasis gained through italics and punctuation
changes:

Rose kissed me to-day.	A
Will she kiss me to-morrow?	B
Let it be as it may,	a
Rose kissed me to-day.	A

But the pleasure gives way	a
To a savor of sorrow;—	b
Rose kissed me to-day,—	A
Will she kiss me to-morrow?	B

The *villanelle* (*AbA′ abA abA′ abA abA′ abAA′*) can best be illustrated by another of the *Rose Leaves* series, whose title is its first line. In this poem the naturalness of the repeated refrain lines is achieved largely through the skillful manipulation of punctuation:

When I saw you last, Rose,	A
You were only so high;—	b
How fast the time goes!	A′

Like a bud ere it blows,	a
You just peeped at the sky,	b
When I saw you last, Rose!	A

Now your petals unclose,	a
Now your May-time is nigh;—	b
How fast the time goes!	A′

And a life,—how it grows!	a
You were scarcely so shy	b
When I saw you last, Rose!	A

In your bosom it shows	a
There's a guest on the sly;	b
(How fast the time goes!)	A′

Is it Cupid? Who knows!	a
Yet you used not to sigh	b
When I saw you last, Rose;—	A
How fast the time goes!	A′

THE LIMERICK

The *limerick* (anapestic 33223, *aabba*) is the "clown" of the light verse family, and is frequently anonymous, as is the following:

There was a faith healer of Deal,
Who said, "Although pain isn't real,
    If I sit on a pin
    And I puncture my skin,
I dislike what I *fancy* I feel."

THE JAPANESE FORMS

If the power of suggestion is basic to poetry, it is nowhere better illustrated than in the miniatures of the *Japanese forms*. For here one is not concerned with metrical feet, rime,[12] or contrived stanzas. In the two basic patterns everything that is to be said must be said in either thirty-one or seventeen *syllables*. Thus the *tanka*, the longer structure, is made up of five lines, of 5-7-5-7-7 syllables respectively; while the *haiku* ("beginning phrase" or "head piece") limits itself to the first three of these lines, or 5-7-5 syllables.[13]

It will be noted that the tanka offers a balanced structure (5-7-5 / 7-7) reminiscent of the Italian sonnet with its octave and sestet, but here concentrated to such an extent that only a minimal imagery can be used. Yet even this limitation gave way in time to the challenge of making the first unit, 5-7-5, so complete and suggestive in itself that it would become like a seed in the reader's mind, a seed that would come to full growth as the reader permitted the nourishing spirit of his imagination to act upon it. We have said elsewhere that every reader should be at least half a poet, and the Japanese forms invite this kind of participation; for even though they have been described as "pictures to create a mood without interpretation," many will be so subtle as to entice the reader into increasing awareness of their insights.

[12] Some translators have chosen to use rime in order to adapt the forms to English, but usually with a loss of two important elements in the originals: the naturalness of the image and the subtlety of its overtones.

[13] Related to the Japanese forms is the *cinquain*, invented by the American poet Adelaide Crapsey. Its development is through 2-4-6-8-2 syllables, the five lines involved giving it its name. In this, as in the tanka and haiku, more is involved than merely counting words and syllables to fit a pattern. There must be a balanced relationship between the lines, and as the numbers of syllables increase, a sense of building to a climax should be felt; and the short last line must, for full effect, drop neatly off from the high point of the preceding line. Occasionally rime is used to enhance the effect, as in the second illustration below, but normally the cinquain is unrimed, as in the first (descriptive of the pattern), by Catherine Baker:

Five lines	Time, stop!
To make a sketch	Why hurry so?
In words—of sunlit grass	Can't you give back one day
Or city streets at twilight hour	Of joy I lost along the way—
Or star.	*Then* go?

The following typical examples, translated by Glenn Hughes, make no attempt to force a syllabic pattern on the translations. As Mr. Hughes has written: "Free verse poems, as brief as possible, not too musical nor yet too prosaic, seem best to convey to Western ears the sense and effect of the original." The first four are tankas by Akiko Yosano, the others are haikus by "White Lotus" (Akiko Yanagiwara), two of the most gifted women poets of modern Japan:

i

Feeling that you were waiting for me,
I went out into the flowering fields
And found—the new moon.

ii

There is another
Besides myself
To weep for him—
That is my bitterness.

iii

Five piles standing in the river,
Five crows sitting on the piles—
It is maddening!

iv

This evening
A mad wind blows in the sky.
The wind in the sea-grass
Whispers to my hair.

v

By what right did I pick these flowers
That were the bed of butterflies?

vi

If I could break the hearts of a hundred men
I might forget these sorrows.

vii

My heart has melted into the sea.
Let it go where the waves go.

viii

Today I met a stranger—
Though for ten years I have lived with him.

An Interlude:
The Heroic Couplet, Blank Verse, and the Sonnet—
A Historical View

In addition to a study of the types and tools of poetry, it is helpful to consider the manner in which poetry as an art has moved through different cultural periods and reflected elements in the cultural attitudes of the times. A historical view of three significant verse forms will illustrate this approach.

Of the three forms under consideration the *heroic couplet* was introduced first into English poetry, by Chaucer about the year 1387. It forms the basis of much of his *Canterbury Tales*, and in his use it is moderately open in structure: not as restricted to end-stopping as were to be the couplets of Pope in the eighteenth century, nor as free in run-on as would be those of Leigh Hunt or Keats in the early nineteenth. The famous opening lines of the Prologue to the *Canterbury Tales* will illustrate:

Whan that Aprille with his shoures soote*	*sweet
The droghte of Marche hath perced to the roote,	
And bathed every veyne in swich licour,*	*liquid
Of which vertu* engendred is the flour;	*power
Whan Zephirus eek* with his swete breeth	*also
Inspired hath in every holt* and heeth	*wood
The tendre croppes, and the yonge sonne	
Hath in the Ram* his halfe cours y-ronne,	*zodiac reference
And smale fowles* maken melodye,	*birds
That slepen al the night with open ye,	
(So priketh hem* Nature in hir corages*);	*stirs them *hearts
Than longen* folk to goon on pilgrimages	*then long
(And palmers* for to seken straunge strondes*)	*pilgrims *shores
To ferne halwes, couthe* in sondry londes;	*distant shrines,
And specially, from every shires ende	known
Of Engelond, to Caunterbury they wende,	
The holy blisful martir for to seke,	
That hem hath holpen, whan that they were	
seke.*	*sick

During the sixteenth century there was comparatively little use of the heroic couplet, and before it reappeared *blank verse* was introduced by Henry Howard, the Earl of Surrey, in a translation of Books II and IV of Vergil's *Aeneid*. Surrey's use of the heroic pattern was frequently quite stiff, possibly because he was translating or because blank verse was an unaccustomed instrument in his hands. We have met earlier with this lack of flexibility in his use:

> Who can express the slaughter of that night?
> Or tell the numbers of the corpses slain?
> Or can in tears bewail them worthily?
> The ancient famous city falleth down,
> That many years did hold such seignory.

Surrey's translation dates to about 1540, with the next important appearance of blank verse being in Sackville and Norton's drama, *Gorboduc*. In this first "regular" English tragedy (1561) the verse was still comparatively stiff, and it was not until 1587, in Christopher Marlowe's *Tamburlaine*, that a notable improvement in this respect was evidenced. The growth of flexibility is even more demonstrable in the transition (1591–1611) from the early to the later plays of Shakespeare, wherein development to full mastery is found. (See below and the scene from *Macbeth*, p. 145.)

During the Elizabethan period the heroic couplet was used principally as a variant to the blank verse of the drama, especially in those passages bringing a scene or a significant part of a scene to a close. The following selection from Act IV of Shakespeare's *Antony and Cleopatra* illustrates this and also offers us another evidence of the natural quality of the blank verse in Shakespeare's hands. Antony has died and Cleopatra has fainted. As she recovers she speaks, half apologizing for her feminine weakness:

> *Cleopatra.* No more, but e'en a woman, and commanded
> By such poor passion as the maid that milks
> And does the meanest chares.* It were for me   *chores
> To throw my sceptre at the injurious gods,
> To tell them that this world did equal theirs
> Till they had stol'n our jewel. All's but naught;
> Patience is sottish, and impatience does
> Become a dog that's mad: then is it sin
> To rush into the secret house of death,

Ere death dare come to us? How do you, women?
What, what! good cheer! Why, how now, Charmian!
My noble girls! Ah, women, women, look,
Our lamp is spent, it's out! Good sirs, take heart:
We'll bury him; and then, what's brave, what's noble,
Let's do it after the high Roman fashion,
And make death proud to take us. Come, away:
This case of that huge spirit now is cold:
Ah, women, women! Come; we have no friend
But resolution and the briefest end.

Even as blank verse was becoming established as the norm for dramatic literature, and the heroic couplet barely holding its own in any independent way, the most famous of the English patterns, the *sonnet,* was growing in popularity. Introduced from Italy by Sir Thomas Wyatt about 1530, Wyatt and Surrey did much to start this form on its way. Their sonnets were modeled frequently on Italian usage, and especially on the poems of Petrarch; but, as we have seen, the tendency in England was to end the sonnet with a couplet (in effect sustaining the heroic couplet quality in another limited way). This became the pattern for the Elizabethan period and into the middle of the seventeenth century. Many of the sonnet sequences or cycles of this time employed the theme of Platonic love (inherited from Italy), among them Spenser's *Amoretti* (1595; see p. 78), and Shakespeare's *Sonnets* (published 1609, although many were written during the 1590s; see pp. 79, 111, 186). Shakespeare's sonnets were unusual in that the first 125 were based on Platonic friendship for a young man, with the remainder addressed to the so-called "Dark Lady" of the sonnets. (Unlike the usual Platonic heroine she is presented as dark complexioned [see p. 168]; also, she is "dark" in the sense that her identity is unknown.)

Thus by the turn into the seventeenth century the three forms were well established, although the heroic couplet must wait for its principal revival. In the early part of the century blank verse continued in the drama, until the theaters were closed in 1642 because of civil wars. The sonnet, especially in the pseudo-Petrarchan form, continued, with John Donne's *Holy Sonnets* (see p. 114) marking a shift from love to other themes. This shift became even more evident when, in the 1630s, Milton turned to the form. In his hands the true Italian pattern appeared for the first time in England, with the closing couplet scrupulously avoided. Unlike his predecessors, who quite consistently wrote in sequences, Milton used the form for occasional poems only, with no love poems in the traditional sense, and with only seventeen in English (he wrote some in Italian also) over a span of some thirty years. These were on such subjects as his arrival at the age of twenty-three (see p. 77), a massacre, his blindness (see below and p. 196), a nightingale, his friends, the death of his wife, etc. In about half of his sonnets Milton permitted the octave and sestet to blend by use of a run-on at line eight. This gave greater unity to the fourteen lines as a whole, and emphasized his use of rhythmical variety within the lines. If the following poem is compared with the examples from Spenser and Shakespeare already given (pp. 78–79), the effect of these contributions to the sonnet in England will be evident. Milton, in *To Cyriack Skinner*, is writing of the blindness that resulted from his overwork in the cause of his country (he was Latin Secretary to Cromwell during the Puritan regime):

> Cyriack, this three years' day these eyes, though clear
> To outward view, of blemish or of spot,
> Bereft of light, their seeing have forgot;
> Nor to their idle orbs doth sight appear
> Of sun or moon or star throughout the year,
> Or man or woman. Yet I argue not
> Against Heaven's hand or will, nor bate a jot
> Of heart or hope, but still bear up and steer
> Right onward. What supports me, dost thou ask?
> The conscience, friend, to have lost them overplied
> In liberty's defence, my noble task,
> Of which all Europe talks from side to side.
> This thought might lead me through the world's vain mask
> Content, though blind, had I no better guide.

But Milton's contribution to English prosody was not limited to the sonnet, for he made equally important individual use of blank verse as he carried that pattern outside the drama in his *Paradise Lost* (see pp. 66, 136). This poem was started in 1658 and published in 1667, but between these two dates a most important historical event took place that was to influence poetic matters for nearly a hundred years: the restoration of Charles II to the throne of England.

The civil wars of the 1640s had eventuated in the beheading of Charles I in 1649, when the Puritans under Cromwell took over the rule of England. The man who was to be Charles II, together with many court followers, made his way to France. There, at the court of Louis XIV, they found a culture dominated by formalism, wit, and the other qualities that are summed up in the term Neoclassic. In literature this meant adherence to the "rules," with such literary lawgivers as Boileau in his *L'Art Poétique* pointing the way. The ideal was a rationally controlled, balanced, harmonized, and proportioned expression, and with the return of Charles and his followers in 1660 England was ready for the change. Almost immediately the heroic couplet returned to favor, for it, in its closed form, offered the ideal medium for the pointed, epigrammatic, succinct phrase or comment. It had been anticipated as early as 1645 by Edmund Waller in *Poems*, but it was after 1660, with Dryden and Pope leading the way, that it reached its full stature and dominated the field for almost a century. In the following description of Belinda in *The Rape of the Lock* (Canto II) Pope illustrates the use of the form for social satire:

> Not with more glories, in the ethereal plain,
> The sun first rises o'er the purpled main,
> Than, issuing forth, the rival of his beams
> Launched on the bosom of the silver Thames.
> Fair nymphs and well-dressed youths around her shone,
> But every eye was fixed on her alone.
> On her white breast a sparkling cross she wore,
> Which Jews might kiss, and infidels adore.
> Her lively looks a sprightly mind disclose,
> Quick as her eyes, and as unfixed as those:
> Favours to none, to all she smiles extends;
> Oft she rejects, but never once offends.
> Bright as the sun, her eyes the gazers strike,
> And, like the sun, they shine on all alike.
> Yet graceful ease, and sweetness void of pride,
> Might hide her faults, if belles had faults to hide:
> If to her share some female errors fall,
> Look on her face, and you'll forget 'em all.

With closed heroic couplets sweeping the field and even re-placing blank verse in the drama, Milton, even with the broadly moving, vigorous, organ-like harmonies of his epic, and the strongly personal and emotional subjectivity of his sonnets, was unable to stem the tide. Blank verse and sonnets were to lose their position of importance for many years, but before they did so Milton was to speak his mind with respect to the use of rime in longer poems. There is much of the debater's technique in the paragraph he wrote for the copies of *Paradise Lost* remaining in 1668, but there is also much of his theory as to what the true measure of rhythmical effectiveness in a poem can be:

> The measure is English heroic verse without rime, as that of Homer in Greek, and Virgil in Latin—rime being no necessary adjunct or true ornament of poem or good verse, in longer works especially, but the invention of a barbarous age, to set off wretched matter and lame metre; graced indeed since by the use of some famous modern poets, carried away by custom, but much to their own vexation, hindrance, and constraint to express many things otherwise, and for the most part worse, than else they would have expressed them. Not without cause therefore some both Italian and Spanish poets of prime note have rejected rime both in longer and shorter works, as have also long since our best English tragedies, as a thing of itself, to all judicious ears, trivial and of no true musical delight; which consists only in apt numbers, fit quantity of sylla-bles, and the sense variously drawn out from one verse into another, not in the jingling sound of like endings—a fault avoided by the learned ancients both in poetry and all good oratory. This neglect then of rime so little is to be taken for a defect, though it may seem so perhaps to vulgar readers, that it rather is to be esteemed an example set, the first in English, of ancient liberty recovered to heroic poem from the troublesome and modern bondage of riming.

Milton's paragraph is in effect an answer to Dryden's *Essay of Dramatic Poesy*, an extended defense of rimed couplets for the drama, also published in 1668.

The poetry and plays of Dryden and the poems of Pope and others made the closed heroic couplet the dominant form in the late seventeenth and first half of the eighteenth century. But no pattern, especially one as demanding of the reader as is the closed couplet, can hold its place without opposition, just as no cultural attitude as formally constituted as was that of Neoclassicism can deny for long the warmer, more individualistic, more emotional spirit that is suggested by the term Romanticism. And although the Romantic Period is usually considered to be the early nineteenth century, the preromantic tendencies leading up to it began to appear as early as 1725. These tendencies are to be found in early nature poetry, in expression of the emotions through the "graveyard school" and the Gothic novel as well as in less dramatic areas of interest, and in the revival of earlier poetic forms to break the hold of the couplet. It was Milton's influence that gave the strongest impetus to the latter expression of dissatisfaction.

The first evidence of this influence is to be found in James Thomson's *The Seasons*, a long poem in four sections written between 1726 and 1730, in blank verse of a strongly Miltonic cast. Thomson's poem, which evidenced a genuine feeling for nature and the common man (in contrast to the aristocratic, urban emphasis of the Neoclassic school) found its natural outlet in the "apt numbers, fit quantity of syllables, and the sense variously drawn out from one verse into another" of Milton's paragraph. The influence continued in Edward Young's *Night Thoughts* (1742), Robert Blair's *The Grave* (1743), and Mark Akenside's *The Pleasures of the Imagination* (1744)—a period marked also by critical defenses of Milton as superior to Pope. With William Cowper's *The Task* (1785) and Wordsworth's *Lines Composed a Few Miles Above Tintern Abbey* (1798) and *The Prelude* (1799–1805), a more original idiom entered blank verse poetry, with fewer of the Miltonic overtones, an idiom reflecting the style and personality of the individual poet, as in these lines (see also p. 19) from *The Prelude* (Book I):

> Fair seed-time had my soul, and I grew up
> Fostered alike by beauty and by fear:
> Much favoured in my birth-place, and no less
> In that beloved Vale to which erelong
> We were transplanted;—there were we let loose
> For sports of wider range. Ere I had told
> Ten birthdays, when among the mountain slopes
> Frost, and the breath of frosty wind, had snapped
> The last autumnal crocus, 'twas my joy
> With store of springes* o'er my shoulder hung   *traps

To range the open heights where woodcocks run
Along the smooth green turf. Through half the night,
Scudding away from snare to snare, I plied
That anxious visitation;—moon and stars
Were shining o'er my head. I was alone,
And seemed to be a trouble to the peace
That dwelt among them. Sometimes it befell
In these night wanderings, that a strong desire
O'erpowered my better reason, and the bird
Which was the captive of another's toil
Became my prey; and when the deed was done
I heard among the solitary hills
Low breathings coming after me, and sounds
Of undistinguishable motion, steps
Almost as silent as the turf they trod.

Also beginning about 1740 there was a gradual return of the sonnet to importance, again largely under Milton's influence (although there was little evidence of awareness of the theory behind the uses of the form). Some 2,500 examples written between 1740 and 1800 were found by R. D. Havens, most of them irregular in rime scheme but with clear indications that where regularity was approximated or achieved it was regularity of the Miltonic type. Occasional subject matter continued to prevail, and the new interest in nature found its way into many of the poems.[14]

The last important use of the Popean couplet was in Oliver Goldsmith's *The Deserted Village* (1766), after which there was

[14] During this period, also, the Spenserian stanza, which had not been used since its introduction by Spenser in the late sixteenth century, was revived. This was natural since it was so completely different from the Neoclassic couplet. William Shenstone's *The Schoolmistress* (1742) was almost a burlesque of the characteristics of the pattern, but James Thomson's *The Castle of Indolence* (1748) caught the spirit of the original effectively, including the use of archaisms by which Spenser had sought to infuse the content with a feeling of the past. Archaisms were also used by Shenstone, and by James Beattie in *The Minstrel* (1771), although the latter poem was not a strong representative of the form. Robert Burns avoided the archaisms but gained something of the same effect by substitution of Scotch idiom in some stanzas of *The Cotter's Saturday Night* (1785). In the early nineteenth century Byron, in Cantos I and II of *Childe Harold's Pilgrimage* (1812) was the last to make any significant use of the archaic touch, for in Cantos III and IV (1818; see p. 75) he used the stanza in his own idiom and style, as did Keats in *The Eve of St. Agnes* (1820; see pp. 9, 62), Shelley in *Adonais* (1821), and Tennyson in part of *The Lotos-Eaters* (1833). Since that time little use has been made of the pattern.

a drawing away from the closed stiffness, by William Cowper
and George Crabbe; and by the early nineteenth century the
couplet had been adapted to an open texture that went far
beyond even the moderate enjambement of its initial use by
Chaucer. Only Byron, in an obvious imitation of the satires of
Pope, made any use of the closed form, in *English Bards and
Scotch Reviewers* (1809). Leigh Hunt in *The Story of Rimini*
(1816) turned the form into an exaggeratedly loose structure,
and this influenced Keats in his *Endymion* (1818; see below).
When Keats came to write *Lamia* (1820) his reading of Dryden
resulted in more restraint, with nicely controlled enjambement
that went to neither extreme. Of the Victorians only William
Morris appeared to prefer couplets, as in *The Earthly Paradise*
(1868). Since that time, when the couplet has been used it has
been customary to employ the fairly open form unless some
special effect is sought in imitating the Popean model, as in
Robert Hillyer's *A Letter to Robert Frost*. The following opening lines from Keats's *Endymion* will illustrate the freer early
nineteenth-century use (see also p. 69), as Browning's *My
Last Duchess* (p. 154) does for the later nineteenth century:

> A thing of beauty is a joy forever:
> Its loveliness increases; it will never
> Pass into nothingness; but still will keep
> A bower quiet for us, and a sleep
> Full of sweet dreams, and health, and quiet breathing.
> Therefore, on every morrow, are we wreathing
> A flowery band to bind us to the earth,
> Spite of despondence, of the inhuman dearth
> Of noble natures, of the gloomy days,
> Of all the unhealthy and o'er-darkened ways
> Made for our searching: yes, in spite of all,
> Some shape of beauty moves away the pall
> From our dark spirits. Such the sun, the moon,
> Trees old and young, sprouting a shady boon
> For simple sheep: and such are daffodils
> With the green world they live in; and clear rills
> That for themselves a cooling covert make
> 'Gainst the hot season; the mid-forest brake,
> Rich with a sprinkling of fair musk-rose blooms:
> And such too is the grandeur of the dooms
> We have imagined for the mighty dead;
> All lovely tales that we have heard or read:

An endless fountain of immortal drink,
Pouring unto us from the heaven's brink.

The early nineteenth century saw wide use of blank verse, with a freshness and individuality of rhythm and phrasing that set the pattern for later use that continues into our own day, despite the many who have turned for much or some of their work to free verse. The influence of free verse has worked to give greater freedom to blank verse itself, even while the basic iambic pentameter is held to as the norm, by inviting greater metrical freedom within the dominant structure. Of the nineteenth- and twentieth-century examples of blank verse particular interest attaches to Wordsworth's *The Prelude* (see pp. 19, 102) and *Michael*; Shelley's *Alastor*, *The Cenci* (poetic drama), and *Prometheus Unbound* (see p. 66); Keats's *Hyperion*; Tennyson's *Morte d'Arthur*; Browning's *Fra Lippo Lippi*, *Andrea del Sarto*, and *The Bishop Orders His Tomb*; E. A. Robinson's *Tristram*; Robert Frost's *Mending Wall* and *The Death of the Hired Man*; and W. H. Auden's *To a Writer*. The following, from Tennyson's *Morte d'Arthur*, will illustrate the late nineteenth-century use, while the second selection, Stephen Spender's *The Express*, will indicate the tone and idiom of recent twentieth-century usage, in which an influence from sprung rhythm leads to a comparative freedom from regular metrical structure, but without loss of a strong rhythmical movement:

(1) And slowly answer'd Arthur from the barge:
"The old order changeth, yielding place to new,
And God fulfills himself in many ways,
Lest one good custom should corrupt the world.
Comfort thyself; what comfort is in me?
I have lived my life, and that which I have done
May He within himself make pure! but thou,
If thou shouldst never see my face again,
Pray for my soul. More things are wrought by prayer
Than this world dreams of. Wherefore, let thy voice
Rise like a fountain for me night and day.
For what are men better than sheep or goats
That nourish a blind life within the brain,
If, knowing God, they lift not hands of prayer
Both for themselves and those who call them friend?
For so the whole round earth is every way
Bound by gold chains about the feet of God."

(2) After the first powerful plain manifesto
The black statement of pistons, without more fuss
But gliding like a queen, she leaves the station.
Without bowing and with restrained unconcern
She passes the houses which humbly crowd outside,
The gasworks and at last the heavy page
Of death, printed by gravestones in the cemetery.
Beyond the town there lies the open country
Where, gathering speed, she acquires mystery,
The luminous self-possession of ships on ocean.
It is now she begins to sing—at first quite low
Then loud, and at last with jazzy madness—
The song of her whistle screaming at curves,
Of deafening tunnels, brakes, innumerable bolts.
And always light, aerial, underneath
Goes the elate meter of her wheels.
Steaming through metal landscape on her lines
She plunges new eras of wild happiness
Where speed throws up strange shapes, broad curves
And parallels clean like the steel of guns.
At last, further than Edinburgh or Rome,
Beyond the crest of the world, she reaches night
Where only a low streamline brightness
Of phosphorous on the tossing hills is white.
Ah, like a comet through flames she moves entranced
Wrapt in her music no bird song, no, nor bough
Breaking with honey buds, shall ever equal.

Finally, the eighteenth-century revival of the sonnet led it to become one of the most diversely used of the lyric forms in the next two centuries. Wordsworth wrote 523, on a wide range of subjects including nature (see p. 165), religion, and politics (see below and p. 51); Leigh Hunt was one of the first important theorists of the form; Keats used not only the Italian pattern (see p. 204), but reaffirmed the effectiveness of the Shakespearean and wrote a number of experimental sonnets in an effort to discover a more congenial rime scheme (see below); Elizabeth Barrett Browning wrote the *Sonnets from the Portuguese* and Dante Gabriel Rossetti *The House of Life* sequences; while in America, from many who might be named, E. A. Robinson, George Sterling, and Edna St. Vincent Millay hold an especially distinguished place. The following examples will illustrate, respectively, use of the sonnet (1) for a political

subject (Wordsworth's *Thoughts of a Briton on the Subjugation of Switzerland*); (2) for consideration of the theory of its
structure (Keats's *On the Sonnet*); and (3) for reflection, in a
current idiom, on our modern concern with a space age, but
with this concern placed in salutary perspective (Pauline Starkweather's *Two Mountains Men Have Climbed*):[15]

(1) Two voices are there; one is of the sea,
　　One of the mountains; each a mighty Voice.
　　In both from age to age thou didst rejoice;
　　They were thy chosen music, Liberty!
　　There came a Tyrant, and with holy glee
　　Thou fought'st against him; but hast vainly striven.
　　Thou from thy Alpine holds at length art driven,
　　Where not a torrent murmurs heard by thee.
　　Of one deep bliss thine ear hath been bereft;
　　Then cleave, O cleave to that which still is left;
　　For, high-souled Maid, what sorrow would it be
　　That mountain floods should thunder as before,
　　And ocean bellow from its rocky shore,
　　And neither awful voice be heard by thee!

(2) If by dull rhymes our English must be chain'd,
　　And, like Andromeda, the Sonnet sweet
　　Fetter'd, in spite of pained loveliness,
　　Let us find out, if we must be constrain'd,
　　Sandals more interwoven and complete
　　To fit the naked foot of Poesy:
　　Let us inspect the Lyre, and weigh the stress
　　Of every chord, and see what may be gain'd
　　By ear industrious, and attention meet;
　　Misers of sound and syllable, no less
　　Than Midas of his coinage, let us be
　　Jealous of dead leaves in the bay wreath crown;
　　So, if we may not let the Muse be free,
　　She will be bound with garlands of her own.

(3) *Sinai*
　　The good flat earth . . . and not so very high
　　above it, heaven fitting like a dome,

[15] Note, in the Starkweather sonnets, the effective use of approximate
rime. For an example typical of the greater metrical freedom of the sonnet in the mid-twentieth century (compare Spender's *The Express*, above,
and Schwartz's *In the Naked Bed*, p. 166, for similar freedom in blank
verse), as well as of contemporary rime use, see the explication of George
Barker's *Sonnet to My Mother*, pp. 243–57.

hole-pricked and set with stars . . . from time to time
a new star blazing forth to prophesy
of royal birth or that a king must die—
all this men knew. They knew and feared to name
that holy mountain that was Yahveh's home.
They knew enough to hide when He walked by.

All this men knew—had they not eyes for proof?
Could they not hear great Yahveh in the storm?
But someone dared to climb His holy place;
Somebody stuck a finger through the roof.
Lo, he that climbed the mountain knew no harm,
and he that pierced the dome found only space.

Palomar
A billion light years . . . if an ant could see
each mote that drifts above the canyon, still
with but an ant's eyes, would he see it whole?
Could he conceive a canyon? Nor do we,
O Palomar, find in your nebulae
one thread of meaning if there is no call,
no footstep echoing there; but can you tell
if there are voices in eternity?

"And Enoch walked with God, and he was not" . . .
Enoch is all that matters, Palomar.
If at long last, you peer beyond the brink,
beyond the shining of the farthest mote,
will you then find where God and Enoch are?
The answer may be nearer than we think.

It is hoped that this brief and necessarily superficial survey
may have offered some perspective on the manner in which
poetic form and idiom reflect the periods in which certain structures come into prominence—possibly because of limited states
of mind, as in the Neoclassic period, or because there is a fresh
outpouring of revived patterns or experimental innovations, as
in the Romantic and modern periods. Little attention has been
given here to a detailed analysis of the manner in which the
content of the poems involved reflects a corresponding expression of ideas and attitudes. These considerations will be left
for later discussion in Part Three.

⤙ 6 ⤚

Poetic Tools: Imagery and Figures of Speech

FOR THE serious student of poetry as an art, the frequently
held idea that imagery is merely the calling up of pictures
must give way to an understanding of the subtleties that can
be involved in this process, and of the shadings of emphasis
that can be given to any theme by the figures of speech used
by the poet.

Imagery is indeed the very heart of poetry. Robert Frost once
said: "Imagery and after-imagery; that is all there is to poetry."
Frost's statement is suggestive of music, formed of tones and
overtones (or "after-tones") which may be explained rationally
by the physics of sound, but which to the listener become
harmonies of moving impact, invitations to emotional responses.
As Browning wrote of music in his *Abt Vogler*:

And I know not if, save in this, such gift be allowed to man,
That out of three sounds he frame, not a fourth sound, but a star.

So in poetry something happens in the association of words and
the images built of words which seems to carry us beyond the
words; and Browning's lines illustrate this perfectly in his use
of the word (and image) "star."

Imagery, as the word suggests, is an outgrowth of the imagination which, as we have noted in an earlier chapter, is the
essence of the creative personality. Without the creative personality there can be no poetry (nor any other work of art),
and imagery is the expression of the creative mind. Through it
we know "the light that never was, on sea or land"; through it
"ordinary things [can] be presented to the mind in an unusual
aspect." (Both quotations are from Wordsworth.) And since the

[109]

creative personality is shared by the reader, he responds to the imagery and shares likewise in the emotional effectiveness of the poem. But meaningful participation can come only if the imagery is fresh, vital, and within the scope of acceptable comparison. Trite, commonplace, or exaggerated imagery will leave the reader either unmoved or merely amused by its incongruity.

From this point of view it will be clear that imagery can be in the form of direct description, as in Tennyson's lines from *The Lady of Shalott*:

> On either side the river lie
> Long fields of barley and of rye,
> That clothe the wold* and meet the sky;   * upland plain
> And through the field the road runs by
>   To many-towered Camelot;
> And up and down the people go,
> Gazing where the lilies blow
> Round an island there below,
>   The island of Shalott.

Of course this is more than mere description, for the rime, alliteration, assonance, and metrical devices all contribute to the haunting effect sought by the poet. But even beyond these devices there is in the third line a comparison and poetic exaggeration: the fields do not literally "clothe the wold," nor do they literally "meet the sky." They do so figuratively, and introduce us to the poetic tool known as *figures of speech*. Let us examine the most important of these.

Simile

Best known is probably the *simile*, normally introduced by *like* or *as*, in which one thing is compared to something else. But though the two objects are different it is essential that they have some characteristic in common (or in contrast, as when the child told her father: "I love you more than I hate skunks") in order that the figure may be valid. Thus Browning has

> The wild tulip, at the end of its tube, blows out its great red bell
> Like a thin clear bubble of blood.

Clearly this too is more than mere description: it is description that adds an extra dimension to the subject, the common links being shape and color. Milton has

> A dungeon horrible, on all sides round,
> As one great furnace flamed,

in which, speaking of Hell, heat is the link. And Wordsworth writes

> It is a beauteous evening, calm and free,
> The holy time is quiet as a Nun
> Breathless with adoration,

where the simile of reverent peace is in marked contrast to T. S. Eliot's likening the evening to "a patient etherized upon a table," in which the link is the sickness of the patient and of the society in which the speaker lives.

But these are similes incidental to longer poems. At times the entire poem may be, or grow out of, this figure, as in the following Shakespeare sonnet in which the various aspects of winter become the illustrations of his feelings during absence from his friend. The link which dominates the opening eight lines is the lack of warmth (friendship) even though the season is summer. Then a second simile ("widowed wombs") is introduced and developed to further the comparison:

> How like a winter hath my absence been
> From thee, the pleasure of the fleeting year!
> What freezings have I felt, what dark days seen!
> What old December's bareness every where!
> And yet this time removed was summer's time,
> The teeming autumn, big with rich increase,
> Bearing the wanton burthen of the prime,
> Like widow'd wombs after their lords' decease:
> Yet this abundant issue seem'd to me
> But hope of orphans and unfather'd fruit;
> For summer and his pleasures wait on thee,
> And thou away, the very birds are mute;
>   Or, if they sing, 'tis with so dull a cheer
>   That leaves look pale, dreading the winter's near.

Metaphor

In many respects stronger than the simile is the *metaphor*, in which one thing is said to be another. Thus, in Milton's line above, "dungeon" is used in place of "Hell." From the context there is no question about what Milton means, but the metaphor intensifies the significance of the description. Likewise, Shakespeare's sonnet, although using similes in its over-all development, is rich in metaphors as well: the friend is "the pleasure of the fleeting year," the poet has "frozen," etc.

Metaphors are common in everyday speech; indeed, most of them are notably trite: "You rat!" "You son of a gun!" "You dream!" "You angel!" etc.; but for poetic purposes the vivid metaphor can be a most effective part of the poem only when it is fresh and carefully devised to bring out the desired shade of emphasis, as in Whitman's lines from *Song of Myself*:

A child said *What is the grass?* fetching it to me with full hands;
How could I answer the child? I do not know what it is any more
     than he.

I guess it must be the flag of my disposition, out of hopeful green
     stuff woven.

Or I guess it is the handkerchief of the Lord,
A scented gift and remembrancer designedly dropt,
Bearing the owner's name someway in the corners, that we may see
     and remark, and say *Whose?*

Or I guess the grass is itself a child, the produced babe of the
     vegetation.

Like the simile, the metaphor is most often used incidentally (as it is in the larger context of the Whitman passage above) but Robert Herrick found it (except for one simile) appropriate for his entire poem, *A Meditation for His Mistress*:

> You are a tulip seen to-day,
> But, dearest, of so short a stay
> That where you grew scarce man can say.
>
> You are a lovely July-flower,
> Yet one rude wind or ruffling shower
> Will force you hence, and in an hour.

You are a full-spread, fair-set vine,
And can with tendrils love entwine,
Yet dried ere you distil your wine.

You are like balm enclosed well
In amber or some crystal shell,
Yet lost ere you transfuse your smell.

You are a dainty violet,
Yet wither'd ere you can be set
Within the virgin's coronet.

You are the queen all flowers among;
But die you must, fair maid, ere long,
As he, the maker of this song.

Conceit

The *conceit* is related to the foregoing, for it is an involved, frequently farfetched simile or metaphor. It is in the conceit that there is danger of carrying the exaggeration beyond the point of meaningful comparison, as when John Donne wrote *The Ecstasy*, the first lines of which follow (note also the more conventional simile of the first line and metaphor of the second):

Where, like a pillow on a bed,
    A pregnant bank swelled up, to rest
The violet's reclining head,
    Sat we two, one another's best.
Our hands were firmly cemented
    With a fast balm, which thence did spring,
Our eye-beams twisted, and did thread
    Our eyes, upon one double string.

Personification

Personification is another figure of speech encountered frequently in poetry. Here, too, there is a danger, described by John Ruskin as *pathetic fallacy*, or the ascription of human thoughts, feelings, and actions to nonhuman things. Ruskin drew certain meaningful distinctions with respect to this phenomenon, but today the phrase is normally applied to those weak applications of personification, such as Donne's description of the violet's head resting on a bed pillow. Personification in its stronger use is the treatment of inanimate objects as if human, but with a clear indication that it is done to bring out certain qualities in the object. Thus Shakespeare, in the sonnet above, personified autumn and, in the last line, leaves. Likewise, when Wordsworth wished to indicate his belief that nature was capable of influencing the individual, he wrote:

> Three years she grew in sun and shower,
> Then Nature said, "A lovelier flower
> On earth was never sown;
> This Child I to myself will take;
> She shall be mine, and I will make
> A lady of my own."

(Note also the metaphor of "lovelier flower" referring to the child, a metaphor perfectly chosen for Nature as the speaker.)

Apostrophe

Related to personification, but not necessarily involving it, is the *apostrophe*, or direct address to person or thing, as in Shelley's

> O Wild West Wind, thou breath of Autumn's being,
> Thou, from whose unseen presence the leaves dead
> Are driven, like ghosts from an enchanter fleeing,

in which apostrophe, personification, and simile all combine to create the desired mood. Apostrophe and personification also dominate the following, from John Donne's *Holy Sonnets*:

> Death, be not proud, though some have called thee
> Mighty and dreadful, for thou art not so;
> For those whom thou think'st thou dost overthrow
> Die not, poor Death; nor yet canst thou kill me.
> From rest and sleep, which but thy pictures be,
> Much pleasure, then from thee much more must flow:
> And soonest our best men with thee do go,
> Rest of their bones, and souls' delivery.

Thou art slave to Fate, Chance, kings, and desperate men,
And dost with poison, war, and sickness dwell,
And poppy or charms can make us sleep as well,
And better than thy stroke; why swell'st thou then?
One short sleep past, we wake eternally,
And Death shall be no more: Death thou shalt die.

Hyperbole

Unlike the conceit, *hyperbole* is simple exaggeration for emphasis or for some other special poetic effect. Emerson's famous
Concord Hymn uses this device with telling effect in the first
stanza, with others of the figures so far described to be found
in the remaining lines:

> By the rude bridge that arched the flood,
>   Their flag to April's breeze unfurled,
> Here once the embattled farmers stood
>   And fired the shot heard round the world.
>
> The foe long since in silence slept;
>   Alike the conqueror silent sleeps;
> And Time the ruined bridge has swept
>   Down the dark stream that seaward creeps.
>
> On this green bank, by this soft stream,
>   We set to-day a votive stone;
> That memory may their deed redeem,
>   When, like our sires, our sons are gone.
>
> Spirit, that made those heroes dare
>   To die, and leave their children free,
> Bid Time and Nature gently spare
>   The shaft we raise to them and thee.

Antithesis

Another figure of speech is *antithesis,* especially popular in
the Neoclassic period. The aim of antithesis is to balance one
idea against another, or one part of an idea against another part,
to the mutual intensification of both. The heroic couplet, as we

have seen, is particularly suitable for this, as the following separate couplets from Pope's *An Essay on Criticism* will indicate:

> A little learning is a dang'rous thing;
> Drink deep, or taste not the Pierian spring . . .

> Be not the first by whom the new are tried,
> Nor yet the last to lay the old aside . . .

> Good nature and good sense must ever join;
> To err is human, to forgive divine.

Synecdoche

The *synecdoche* occurs when a part is referred to as representative of the whole. "A hundred wings flashed by" would
thus use "wings" to stand for "birds" or "planes" or whatever
winged object was in the writer's mind. Clearly this is related
to metaphor, but it is a very specialized form of that device
and one extremely important to poetry, for it lends much of
the suggestive value to the lines and invites the reader to participate in the imaginative process by his realization of the
implied object. The detail chosen for the synecdoche should be
important to the object, a distinguishing feature that will emphasize the quality to be stressed. We have already had an illustration of synecdoche in Tennyson's

> Break, break, break,
>   On thy cold gray stones, O Sea!
> And I would that my tongue could utter
>   The thoughts that arise in me;

in which "tongue" is clearly intended to represent the poet himself. (Note also the presence of the apostrophe in the first two
lines.)

Metonymy

Metonymy is related to and sometimes confused with synecdoche, for it too is the substitution of one word for another, or
of a closely related idea for the idea itself. Perhaps it will be

well to consider the word in terms of its principal differentiating characteristic: whereas synecdoche is the substitution of the part for the whole, metonymy is the substitution of the whole for the part. "I am reading Tennyson" would thus be understood to mean that a poem of Tennyson is being read; "The camera is broken" would indicate that the shutter or some other part has been damaged. Such statements occur frequently in conversation, and the poet refines upon the device to enhance his poetic communication. Thus Keats uses metonymy in his well-known line:

> Till I heard Chapman speak out loud and bold,

when he is actually referring to the fact that he has read Chapman's translation of Homer.

The foregoing are but a few of the many figures of speech encountered, usually unknowingly, in the reading of poetry. It is not so important that the reader be aware of each as it occurs, or that he be able to name it, but some understanding of the poet's uses of such devices can broaden immeasurably the appreciation of his art. To the high school student with a very unimaginative mind Keats's

> Heard melodies are sweet, but those unheard
> Are sweeter

may have meant "It's nice to listen to music, but it's nicer not to." But to the reader who has become sensitive to the uses of language the "after-imagery" of such lines endows them with the richest possible suggestion and, in their context, makes them, in Keats's phrase, "the wording of our own highest thoughts." This will be clear if the following poem, Arnold's *Dover Beach*, is read with careful attention to the poet's command both of general imagery and specific figures of speech as he considers the decline of religious faith in mid-nineteenth-century England. The reference to Sophocles is an *allusion*, not technically a figure of speech but related to the simile since it invites a comparison. To the reader who knows Sophocles' *Antigone* with its powerful simile comparing man's life to a

stormy sea,[1] Arnold's lines at that point take on an added dimension, and the timelessness of Arnold's theme suddenly reaches
from the nineteenth century back to the fifth century before
Christ:

> The sea is calm to-night,
> The tide is full, the moon lies fair
> Upon the Straits;—on the French coast, the light
> Gleams, and is gone; the cliffs of England stand,
> Glimmering and vast, out in the tranquil bay.
> Come to the window, sweet is the night air!
> Only, from the long line of spray
> Where the ebb meets the moon-blanch'd land,
> Listen! you hear the grating roar
> Of pebbles which the waves suck back, and fling,
> At their return, up the high strand,
> Begin, and cease, and then again begin,
> With tremulous cadence slow, and bring
> The eternal note of sadness in.
>
> Sophocles long ago
> Heard it on the Ægean, and it brought
> Into his mind the turbid ebb and flow
> Of human misery; we
> Find also in the sound a thought,
> Hearing it by this distant northern sea.
>
> The sea of faith
> Was once, too, at the full, and round earth's shore
> Lay like the folds of a bright girdle furl'd;
> But now I only hear
> Its melancholy, long, withdrawing roar,
> Retreating to the breath
> Of the night-wind down the vast edges drear
> And naked shingles of the world.

[1] Happy indeed is the life of the man who tastes not of trouble!
For when from the gods a house is shaken,
Fails nevermore the curse,
On most and on least of the race descending:
Like to a rolling wave,
By furious blasts from the Thraceward driven—
Out of the nethermost deeps, out of the fathomless gloom,
Casting up mire and blackness and storm-vexed wrack of the sea—
And back, with a moan like thunder, from the cliffs the sea is hurled.

Note the free verse structure of this translation, and compare the discussion of the relationship between ode, free verse, and Greek drama above,
pp. 79, 85n.

Ah, love, let us be true
To one another! for the world, which seems
To lie before us like a land of dreams,
So various, so beautiful, so new,
Hath really neither joy, nor love, nor light,
Nor certitude, nor peace, nor help for pain;
And we are here as on a darkling plain
Swept with confused alarms of struggle and flight,
Where ignorant armies clash by night.

Part Three: The Poet and His Poem

≺ 7 ≻

The Range of Poetry

IN PART TWO we have reviewed the principal elements in the craft of the poet—the tools by which he shapes his creation and brings it into manageable and communicable form. With the help of foot, verse, stanza, devices for sound, and figures of speech he works through the creative process of analysis, selection, and synthesis; and the result, dependent on his imaginative strength, is either poetry or verse. This survey has brought us now to our final consideration: the poem as a whole with respect to its content, as opposed to the poem as form considered above. For there are different types or kinds of poetry, making different approaches to their themes, and expressing different moods or manners. These can be divided into three general categories: narrative, dramatic, and lyric; and an understanding of their principal differences will be helpful in the development of our appreciation. The characteristics as here given must be suggestive only, for there is much overlapping, but the separation into more or less distinct types will serve to guide the reader.

Narrative Poetry

Narrative poetry is that in which the chief interest is in the telling of a story. Usually, therefore (except in the case of ballads) a poem of this type will be fairly long, since "story" implies the development of characters, setting, and plot in such a way that interest is maintained until the end. At times, however, we may find that we are reading an *implied narrative*, a fairly short poem in which selection is more rigid than might otherwise be the case, and in which attention is focused on the high point, or climax, of the story, with the beginning and the end merely hinted at, or implied. To illustrate the difference, consider the following suggestive diagram of what is known as the "narrative triangle," or "dramatic triangle." It indicates the possible structure of a complete narrative, together with a general indication of how selected details will be arranged or synthesized for maximum effect:

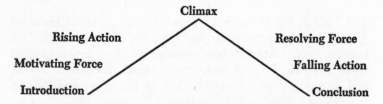

In this structure the *introduction* presents the setting and one or more characters; the *motivating force* will be that specific bit of action, situation, or character which makes a particular story develop as it does; the *rising action*, which stems from the motivating force, brings in complications; the *climax* represents the point at which the complications are so tightly knotted that it seems the story can progress no farther without a *resolving force*: that specific bit of action, situation, or character which makes a particular story work out as it does; the *falling action* then represents the unwinding of the knotted complications, leading to the *conclusion*. Admittedly this is an oversimplified formula, but it will prove useful.

THE BALLAD

If we turn to the first of the important narrative subtypes, the *ballad*,[1] the relationship of the narrative triangle to the content of the poem can be demonstrated. Here is what Coleridge

---

[1] From the Provençal *balada*, a "dancing song." Not to be confused with the French form, the *ballade* (see pp. 90–91).

called "The grand old ballad of Sir Patrick Spence" (or "Spens"
in the original spelling which has been retained here):

> The king sits in Dumferling toune,
>   Drinking the blude-reid wine:
> "O whar will I get a guid sailor,
>   To sail this schip of mine?"
>
> Up and spak an eldern knicht,
>   Sat at the kings richt kne:
> "Sir Patrick Spens is the best sailor,
>   That sails upon the se."
>
> The king has written a braid* letter,   *plain, clear
>   And signd it wi his hand,
> And sent it to Sir Patrick Spens,
>   Was walking on the sand.
>
> The first line that Sir Patrick red,
>   A loud lauch lauched he;
> The next line that Sir Patrick red,
>   The teir blinded his ee.
>
> "O wha is this has don this deid,
>   This il deid don to me,
> To send me out this time o' the year,
>   To sail upon the se!
>
> "Mak haste, mak haste, my mirry men all,
>   Our guid schip sails the morne."
> "O say na sae, my master deir,
>   For I feir a deadlie storme.
>
> "Late, late yestreen I saw the new moone,
>   Wi the auld moone in hir arme,
> And I feir, I feir, my deir master,
>   That we will cum to harme."
>
> O our Scots nobles wer richt laith*   *loath, unwilling
>   To weet their cork-heild schoone;
> Bot lang owre a' the play wer playd,
>   Thair hats they swam aboone.
>
> O lang, lang may their ladies sit,
>   Wi thair fans into their hand,
> Or eir they se Sir Patrick Spens
>   Cum sailing to the land.

O lang, lang may the ladies stand,
   Wi thair gold kems in their hair,
Waiting for thair ain dear lords,
   For they'll see thame na mair.

Haf owre, haf owre to Aberdour,
   It's fiftie fadom deip,
And thair lies guid Sir Patrick Spens,
   Wi the Scots lords at his feit.

In this famous old ballad (employing the 4343 *abcb* ballad stanza form) the introduction is given in stanza one, as we meet the king, locate him in Dumferling town, and hear him ask about a sailor. Whether the motivating force is also there will depend on the reader's interpretation: If the need for a sailor is sufficient, then the king's question is sufficient. But the question is quite general, and in the light of Sir Patrick's reaction in stanza five it would probably be wiser to take as the motivating force the speech of the elderly knight, since this points directly to Sir Patrick. The rising action then involves the sending of the letter, Sir Patrick's initial laughter of disbelief, his serious response (probably as "the next line" reveals the king's signature), his question, in stanza five, which makes us wonder if the elderly knight is the villain in the piece, and his unhesitating response to duty, which is emphasized by the sailor's expression of fear. These details lead to the climax, which is given by suggestion in stanza eight. A climax can frequently be framed in the form of a question: here, will he or won't he succeed in getting the ship through? The resolving force will then be the storm itself (so far as we know from the lines of the poem) which leads to the sailors' deaths and results in the actions of the ladies (falling action) as they wait for the final word, the conclusion.

Now let us consider another old ballad, *Lord Randal*, written this time in long meter:

"O where hae ye been, Lord Randal, my son?
O where hae ye been, my handsome young man?"
"I hae been to the wild wood; mother, make my bed soon,
For I'm weary wi hunting, and fain wald lie down."

"Where gat ye your dinner, Lord Randal, my son?
Where gat ye your dinner, my handsome young man?"
"I dined wi my true-love; mother, make my bed soon,
For I'm weary wi hunting, and fain wald lie down."

"What gat ye to your dinner, Lord Randal, my son?
What gat ye to your dinner, my handsome young man?"
"I gat eels boiled in broo; mother, make my bed soon,
For I'm weary wi hunting, and fain wald lie down."

"What became of your bloodhounds, Lord Randal, my son?
What became of your bloodhounds, my handsome young man?"
"O they swelld and they died; mother, make my bed soon,
For I'm weary wi hunting, and fain wald lie down."

"O I fear ye are poisoned, Lord Randal, my son!
O I fear ye are poisoned, my handsome young man!"
"O yes, I am poisoned; mother, make my bed soon,
For I'm sick at the heart, and I fain wald lie down."

Here, at first reading, we may feel that we have an introduction (mother and son talking), and a motivating force (his weariness), although we should be suspicious of the latter, since it offers little to suggest a development of tension. After completing the poem, however, it becomes clear that everything that we have read represents but the high point of a larger story that is only hinted at, or *implied*. We have accepted without initial question the fact that Lord Randal dined with his "true love," but after stanzas three and four our growing fears are confirmed in his admission that he has been poisoned, and there can be no question that it was his "true love" who did so.[2] We ask: Why? We assume that Lord Randal's sweetheart now

---

[2] The reference to his "true love," when he knows that she was anything but true, is a form of *irony*, in which a statement means the opposite of what it says, or an outcome of action becomes the opposite of what was indicated. If I shout "I'm not afraid of you" even as I am running away, my statement is ironic. If I pay high prices for tickets to a show, only to arrive with great anticipation at the theater and find that I have lost the tickets, the situation is ironic. Sometimes a distinction is drawn between *dramatic irony* in which, as above, the speaker is aware of the significance of what he is saying, and *tragic irony*, in which he is not— as if I should say, colloquially and figuratively "I'll see you in church," only to do so literally as I attend the unanticipated funeral of the one to whom I spoke. See *Proud Maisie* (p. 130) for a highly ironic poem, both from the point of view of the situation and the answers to Maisie's questions.

hated him, or for some reason felt it desirable to dispatch him; but somewhere in that assumption lies the real introduction and motivating force of this story. Is the true climax this meeting between mother and son, or did it come at the point where the girl carried out the killing? If the latter, the resolving force preceded the lines of our poem and led to them; if not, then this is the climax and the resolving force is the knight's ability or the lack thereof to throw off the effects of the poison. Clearly, the anonymous author has given us hints for the full story, but we must rest satisfied in the power of an implied narrative, for we are not even sure that the story does in fact end as it is implied it will: we do not see Randal die.

This is but one of many versions of the Lord Randal ballad. In others the poisonous eels are served in a pie or are fried in butter; or fish, snakes, or lizards are substituted as the main course. The poisoner, as might be expected, is usually a sweetheart, but the role has been filled by a stepmother, grandmother, grandfather, sister, wife, even the dying man himself. In an American version of the poem the story is told more bluntly and directly, with a different idiom, and the identity of the poisoner may come as a surprise:

"Where was you last night, Johnny Randall, my son?
Where was you last night, my heart's loving one?"
"A-fishing, a-fowling; mother, make my bed soon,
For I'm sick at my heart, and I fain would lie down."

"What had you for breakfast, my own pretty boy?
What had you for breakfast, my heart's loving joy?"
"Fresh trout and slow poison; mother, make my bed soon,
For I'm sick at my heart, and I fain would lie down."

"What will you will your brother, my own pretty boy?
What will you will your brother, my heart's loving joy?"
"My horse and my saddle; mother, make my bed soon,
For I'm sick at my heart, and I fain would lie down."

"What will you will your sister, my own pretty boy?
What will you will your sister, my heart's loving joy?"
"My watch and my fiddle; mother, make my bed soon,
For I'm sick at my heart, and I fain would lie down."

"What will you will your mother, my own pretty boy?
What will you will your mother, my heart's loving joy?"
"A twisted hemp rope, for to hang her up high;
Mother, make my bed easy till I lie down and die."

All three of these poems are *traditional ballads,* a part of that rich body of folk literature that has come down to us from the fifteenth century or possibly earlier. The ballad is really a cross-type, having elements of lyric and dramatic poetry as well as narrative. But in general it can be described as a short song-story (it was normally sung) which comes to the point immediately, uses little detail, and often suggests rather than treats large portions of the material. The dramatic question-answer, or dialogue, is often used for developing the story, and the cue to its solution is frequently withheld until near the end (as in *Lord Randal*). If the chivalric age forms the setting, the point of view is often that of the common man, and the themes, at times based on history or legend, are usually serious (but with some interesting exceptions), tend toward love as tragic passion or human conflict, and may involve the supernatural or current superstitions. The ballads were not printed or written down at first, but were sung by minstrels and passed down orally from generation to generation. As a result there are many versions of some of the more famous, appearing in widely ranging areas of England and the Continent, as well as in America, where, as we have seen, the backgrounds and idiom are different, and where more humor, more first person approaches, and a wider range of subject matter are likely to be found. Traditional ballads are compact in style, frequently somewhat rough in structure (the music would tend to overcome this), and make extensive use of repetitions, refrains, dialogue, stock phrases, etc. The authors are unknown.

The *literary ballad,* on the other hand, is the work of a single author writing in imitation of the earlier form. Since these stem from later centuries they represent greater sophistication, more conscious artistry in the poetic devices used, and are usually not written for musical presentation (although there is nothing to prevent this if it is desired). At times they will catch the traditional ballad spirit with remarkable fidelity, as in Sir Walter Scott's *Proud Maisie*, but without losing the feeling of having been written by a later poet:

> Proud Maisie is in the wood,
>   Walking so early;
> Sweet Robin sits on the bush,
>   Singing so rarely.
>
> "Tell me, thou bonny bird,
>   When shall I marry me?"
> "When six braw gentlemen,
>   Kirkward* shall carry ye."   *churchward
>
> "Who makes the bridal bed,
>   Birdie, say truly?"—
> "The gray-headed sexton
>   That delves* the grave duly.   *digs
>
> "The glow-worm o'er grave and stone
>   Shall light thee steady;
> The owl from the steeple sing,
>   'Welcome, proud lady!' "

Scott has used a 3232 *abcb* pattern, a slight modification of the ballad stanza, and one that in a natural reading tends to become 2222 with many light syllables. The effect is admirably suited to the content: the lightness of Maisie's feelings is echoed in the dialogue of the robin, with the foreboding suggestion of the bird's lines intensified by the casual tone of the irony in which they are given. The skillfully employed economy, typical of traditional ballads as well, also serves to drive home the point that finally pride will find its proper home in the grave. At the risk of burdening a fine poem, let us consider its organization. The introduction in the first stanza gives us the girl, the setting, and the second character of the dialogue. Since it is not a poem of action, the motivating force must be found either in the girl's pride, which we finally realize inspires the answers of the bird, or in her first question, which starts the dialogue. The rising action is then the progression of the questions and answers. "Six braw gentlemen" is innocent enough (but charged with irony) since they could be carrying her to church in a golden chair rather than, as we soon learn, in a casket.[3] With the next question and answer we are suddenly confronted with the fact that this bridal bed is indeed the bed of death, and the lights and welcome are to the graveyard. The penultimate word "proud" then drains all of the associations we might have had when we met the word originally at the beginning of the first line, and suggests how meaningless pride can be in a world where, in Gray's famous line, "The paths of glory lead but to the grave." We are left, then, with an introduction, a motivating force, and some rising action. The rest is implied, yet in the implication there is a sense of conclusion, for the only resolving force possible is one that will provide a falling action to end in death.

An equally successful literary ballad, of recent origin, has been written by the contemporary poet, John Manifold. It is *The Griesly Wife*, in which the medieval werewolf superstition, according to which a person could turn into a wolf with the appetite of the animal, has been adapted to the theme:

> "Lie still, my newly married wife,
>   Lie easy as you can.
> You're young and ill accustomed yet
>   To sleeping with a man."
>
> The snow lay thick, the moon was full
>   And shone across the floor.
> The young wife went with never a word
>   Barefooted to the door.

[3] Two poetic devices not previously discussed, and which contribute to the effectiveness of this poem, should be mentioned here. The first is *ambiguity*, which, when purposefully used, adds to rather than detracts from the statement. Thus the answers of the bird are ambiguous, since they can be taken in two senses: one in which the hopeful Maisie can find some assurance; the other through which the reader, aware of the irony, comes closer to the true meaning than the girl with her pride and heedlessness of death is able to do.

The second device is *symbolism*, in which a concrete reference calls up in the reader's mind an abstract concept or idea: a flag is symbolic of the country, a serpent of evil, a rose of beauty, etc. In poetry, symbolism may be extremely subtle and ambivalent, but if poems are read with the careful attention they merit, the reader will soon learn to respond to its effectiveness. In the present poem, the sexton is symbolic of the grave with which he is associated, and the owl is traditionally connected with and symbolic of the graveyard. Also, as the irony becomes clear, the six men become symbolic of the pallbearers at a funeral.

He up and followed sure and fast,
  The moon shone clear and white.
But before his coat was on his back
  His wife was out of sight.

He trod the trail wherever it turned
  By many a mound and scree,*   *rocky debris
And still the barefoot track led on,
  And an angry man was he.

He followed fast, he followed slow,
  And still he called her name,
But only the dingoes* of the hills   *wild dogs
  Yowled back at him again.

His hair stood up along his neck,
  His angry mind was gone,
For the track of the two bare feet gave out
  And a four-foot track went on.

Her nightgown lay upon the snow
  As it might upon the sheet,
But the track that led from where it lay
  Was never of human feet.

His heart turned over in his chest,
  · He looked from side to side,
And he thought more of his gumwood fire
  Than he did of his griesly bride.

And first he started walking back
  And then began to run,
And his quarry wheeled at the end of her track
  And hunted him in turn.

Oh, long the fire may burn for him
  And open stand the door,
And long the bed may wait empty:
  He'll not be back any more.

It will be observed that something of the horror of the subject has been mitigated by the haunting otherworld atmosphere in which the full moon seems to be the motivating force for what happens. We follow Coleridge's dictum of exercising "that willing suspension of disbelief for the moment which constitutes poetic faith" and agree that this never happened, it never could happen, but if it ever *should* happen it would probably happen this way. This is the magic of *The Rime of the Ancient Mariner,* an element of which Manifold has caught. The triangle is fairly clear. We are introduced to a newly married couple, one of whom, apparently drawn by the full moon, leaves the bed and the house. The climactic question is: Will the husband overtake his wife and bring her back? The question is answered by the resolving force in which the two-foot track gives way to the four. If we are not acquainted with the werewolf superstition we may think that an animal has seized her, but there is something about the subsequent details (the falling action) that disabuses us of this, and when the "quarry" wheels at the end of "her" track there can be no further doubt as to what has happened.[4] The conclusion is straightforward: "He'll not be back any more," but it follows three lines that are interestingly reminiscent of the ladies' waiting for Sir Patrick Spens.

THE EPIC

The *epic* (a much older genre than the ballad, with its name derived from the Greek *epos*, a speech, tale, or song) is found in both traditional and literary examples. The *traditional epic*, normally cumulative in its growth over the many decades or centuries before it was written down, is characterized by its heroic style, elaborate detail, great hero, supernatural characters and actions, and national or racial themes, with little stress on social distinctions or love elements. It stems from a heroic age, with the ideals of life of the time evident in the story; and the actions, which are based on high achievement, lead to a long, highly serious, well unified narrative in which the reader is only slightly aware of the narrator (who is, in the traditional form, unknown). The style is frequently unpolished, and makes use of much detail, long formal speeches, invocations, extended or epic similes, and cataloguing. Examples, with their countries of origin, are the *Iliad* and the *Odyssey* (Greece),[5] *Beowulf* (Eng-

[4] To read this poem, as has been done, as an allegory of married life, is to lose all of its magic and show a complete ignorance of, or inability to participate in, the great body of ballad literature of which it is a part.
[5] We need not enter here into the debate on Homer's identity. If he as an individual in fact wrote the poems they would technically be literary epics, discussed below.

land by way of Denmark), the *Nibelungenlied* (Germany), and the *Chanson de Roland* (France). Although their length precludes more than a suggestion of their quality here, the following passage from *Beowulf* (translated from the Old English by Francis B. Gummere), with its strong alliterative technique and its four-accent line (compare sprung rhythm) will give some hint of its spirit. A monster, Grendel, has been raiding the hall in which King Hrothgar's warriors sleep:

> Unhallowed wight,
> grim and greedy, he grasped betimes,
> wrathful, reckless, from resting-places,
> thirty of the thanes, and thence he rushed
> fain of his fell spoil, faring homeward,
> laden with slaughter, his lair to seek.

Word of the attack reaches Beowulf; he volunteers his help and, after a welcoming feast, is escorted to the hall by Hrothgar, where Beowulf delivers a formal speech unhampered by the modesty that was to develop only in later centuries with the growth of Christianity, and prepares to face Grendel in the night:

> Then Hrothgar went with his hero-train,
> defence-of-Scyldings, forth from hall;
> fain would the war-lord Wealhtheow seek,
> couch of his queen. The King-of-Glory
> against this Grendel a guard had set,
> so heroes heard, a hall-defender,
> who warded the monarch and watched for the monster.
> In truth, the Geats' prince gladly trusted
> his mettle, his might, the mercy of God!
> Cast off then his corselet of iron,
> helmet from head; to his henchman gave,—
> choicest of weapons,—the well-chased sword,
> bidding him guard the gear in battle.
> Spake then his Vaunt the valiant man,
> Beowulf Geat, ere the bed he sought:—
> "Of force in fight no feebler I count me,
> in grim war-deeds, than Grendel deems him.
> Not with the sword, then, to sleep of death
> his life will I give, though it lie in my power.
> No skill is his to strike against me,
> my shield to hew though he hardy be,
> bold in battle; we both, this night,

shall spurn the sword, if he seeks me here,
unweaponed, for war. Let wisest God,
sacred Lord, on which side soever
doom decree as he deemeth right."
Reclined then the chieftain, and cheek-pillows held
the head of the earl, while all about him
seamen hardy on hall-beds sank.
None of them thought that thence their steps
to the folk and fastness that fostered them,
to the land they loved, would lead them back!
Full well they wist that on warriors many
battle-death seized, in the banquet-hall,
of Danish clan. But comfort and help,
war-weal weaving, to Weder folk
the Master gave, that, by might of one,
over their enemy all prevailed,
by single strength. In sooth 'tis told
that highest God o'er human kind
hath wielded ever!—Thro' wan night striding,
came the walker-in-shadow. Warriors slept
whose hest was to guard the gabled hall,—
all save one. 'Twas widely known
that against God's will the ghostly ravager
him* could not hurl to haunts of darkness;   *Beowulf
wakeful, ready, with warrior's wrath,
bold he bided the battle's issue.

The *literary epic*, with its single known author, may continue the national themes, as in Vergil's *Aeneid*, or, in later periods, may introduce a religious or moral emphasis, with Biblical, knightly, or allegorical characters and less glorification of the hero. There will, as in the case of the literary ballad, be more conscious artistry. Such poems as Dante's *Divine Comedy*, Spenser's *Faerie Queene*,[6] and Milton's *Paradise Lost* are rep-

[6] *The Faerie Queene* is also an *allegory*, which is, in effect, an extended metaphor. Thus there is a story which is interesting in itself, but whose characters and actions represent moral, religious, political, or other concepts. *The Faerie Queene* reflects all three of the named concepts. On the moral level, for example, in Book I the Red Cross Knight (Holiness) goes with Una (Truth) to rescue her parents (Mankind) from a dragon (Sin) which holds them prisoner. Political and religious allegories are also present.

Spenser's poem, while a true literary epic fragment (only six and part of a seventh of the planned twelve books were completed) contains a great deal of metrical romance material (see below). Indeed, if taken out of the context of the entire poem, Book I in its entirety is a unified metrical romance.

resentative of the literary epic, while Pope's *The Rape of the Lock* is a *mock* or *burlesque epic* in which a trivial theme is treated with much of the grandeur of the more serious forms. A comparison of the openings of Milton's and Pope's poems will indicate the difference in tone, contributed to in part at least by the sweeping blank verse of Milton and the epigrammatic closed couplets of Pope:

(1) Of Man's first disobedience, and the fruit
Of that forbidden tree whose mortal taste
Brought death into the World, and all our woe,
With loss of Eden, till one greater Man
Restore us, and regain the blissful Seat,
Sing, Heavenly Muse, that, on the secret top
Of Oreb, or of Sinai, didst inspire
That Shepherd who first taught the chosen seed
In the beginning how the heavens and earth
Rose out of Chaos: or, if Sion hill
Delight thee more, and Siloa's brook that flowed
Fast by the oracle of God, I thence
Invoke thy aid to my adventurous song,
That with no middle flight intends to soar
Above the Aonian mount, while it pursues
Things unattempted yet in prose or rhyme.
And chiefly Thou, O Spirit, that dost prefer
Before all temples the upright heart and pure,
Instruct me, for Thou know'st; Thou from the first
Wast present, and, with mighty wings outspread,
Dove-like sat'st brooding on the vast Abyss,
And mad'st it pregnant: what in me is dark
Illumine, what is low raise and support;
That, to the highth of this great argument,
I may assert Eternal Providence,
And justify the ways of God to men.
    Say first—for Heaven hides nothing from thy view,
Nor the deep tract of Hell—say first what cause
Moved our grand Parents, in that happy state,
Favoured of Heaven so highly, to fall off
From their Creator, and transgress his will
For one restraint, lords of the World besides.
Who first seduced them to that foul revolt?

(2) What dire offense from am'rous causes springs,
What mighty contests rise from trivial things,

I sing. This verse to CARYL,[7] Muse! is due:
This, ev'n Belinda may vouchsafe to view:
Slight is the subject, but not so the praise,
If she inspire, and he approve my lays.
  Say what strange motive, Goddess! could compel
A well-bred lord t' assault a gentle belle?
O say what stranger cause, yet unexplor'd,
Could make a gentle belle reject a lord?
In tasks so bold, can little men engage,
And in soft bosoms dwells such mighty rage?
  Sol through white curtains shot a tim'rous ray,
And op'd those eyes that must eclipse the day;
Now lap-dogs give themselves a rousing shake,
And sleepless lovers just at twelve awake;
Thrice rung the bell, the slipper knock'd the ground,
And the press'd watch return'd a silver sound.
Belinda still her downy pillow prest,
Her guardian Sylph prolong'd the balmy rest:
'Twas he had summon'd to her silent bed
The morning dream that hover'd o'er her head;
A youth more glitt'ring than a Birth-night Beau,*   *birthday suitor
(That ev'n in slumber caused her cheek to glow),
Seem'd to her ear his winning lips to lay,
And thus in whispers said, or seemed to say . . .

THE METRICAL ROMANCE

The third principal narrative type is the *metrical romance*, especially popular in the middle ages although imitated by later writers. The name derives from poems written in the former period in the romance languages (Italian, Spanish, French, etc.). It is characterized by its aristocratic themes in which knights and ladies play their parts against a background of

----

[7] The poem is based on an actual incident. Lord Petre (the "well-bred Lord") cut off a lock of Arabella Fermor's ("Belinda") hair, leading to a quarrel. Pope's friend, John Caryll, suggested that he write a poem to smooth out the difficulty.

The Rape of the Lock, in addition to being a mock epic, is a *satire*, a mode of writing fundamentally intended to correct or reform, which employs a biting wit since it is dependent for its effect not on forcing reform, but on pointing out the evil by exaggerating it, or making it appear ridiculous. In this poem Pope is attacking the artificiality and vanity of one level of society in his day.

love, war, and adventure. A spirit of idealism is usually found in the romance, and the ideals of chivalry and knighthood dominate. In length, these poems are between the short ballad and the long, detailed epic; and because adventure is frequently brought in for itself the narrative action may be looser than in the epic. Moreover, the metrical romance is frequently light-hearted in tone as compared with the more serious quality of the other forms discussed. The narrator will be very much in evidence, for every effort is made to write a highly polished, skillfully devised poem with vivid imagery and the richness offered by the poetic devices for rhythm and sound. Two most enjoyable examples of this type of poetry are the fourteenth-century *Sir Gawain and the Green Knight* and Chaucer's *Knight's Tale*, while Spenser's *Faerie Queene*, as we have seen, incorporates much metrical romance material although it is a literary epic.

Of the later metrical romances, or poems making use of metrical romance materials or themes, Coleridge in his *Christabel* fragment held close to the originals, Keats offered an especially rich and exotic treatment in *The Eve of St. Agnes*, and Tennyson tended to moralize in his *Idylls of the King*. On the other hand, Browning in *Childe Roland to the Dark Tower Came* and William Morris in *The Haystack in the Floods* offered more serious and more realistic treatments, whereas Alfred Noyes in his well-known *The Highwayman* shifted the setting from the middle ages to the eighteenth century and made his hero a romantic outlaw in love with an innkeeper's daughter who gives her life in a vain attempt to save him from King George's soldiers—after which their spirits return to the scene as love conquers death.

Since the Coleridge, Keats, Tennyson, Browning and Noyes poems are so well known, it may be of greater interest here to illustrate the metrical romance with Morris's *The Haystack in the Floods*, published in 1858. While the poem is thus relatively modern, William Morris was a writer who was thoroughly imbued with a feeling for the spirit of the middle ages. He succeeded in infusing his writings dealing with that period, both in prose and verse, with a sense of actuality unsurpassed by any writer since his time. But he also knew the middle ages well enough to know that life was not always moonlight-and-roses for the knights and ladies who lived then. So in this poem we find the adventure, the color, the heroism of virtue in conflict with villainy, and the technical skill that we have come to expect of the metrical romance—but with a difference; for here villainy wins out and counters the easy victories of virtue so often made a part of the genre. It is, however, no less a metrical romance for that; indeed, it may be a stronger example of the type since it is more lifelike and more believable, and the "romantic" victory comes in the manner in which the two lovers meet their fate.

The story is set in the fourteenth century, shortly after the English, although outnumbered five to one, gained the victory over the French in the Battle of Poictiers (1356) in the Hundred Years' War. It is clear from the poem that the hero, Sir Robert de Marny, an English knight, had fought in that battle, but now he is riding with his French mistress, Jehane, through the south of France toward Gascony. Gascony is held by the English, and if the lovers succeed, with the small band of Robert's followers, in reaching the border they will be safe and free. But they are ambushed by the villainous French knight Godmar, who is waiting to slay Robert and carry off Jehane either to his castle or to Paris, where she will be tried on false charges, probably as a witch, by the "ordeal by water." In this medieval form of trial she would be thrown into the River Seine. If she drowned it would be a sign that she was innocent and God had taken her. But if the water "refused" her because she swam or floated and did not drown, she would be judged guilty and would be burned. The poem begins as Jehane and Robert ride into the ambush.

Had she come all the way for this,
To part at last without a kiss?
Yea, had she borne the dirt and rain
That her own eyes might see him slain
Beside the haystack in the floods?

Along the dripping leafless woods,
The stirrup touching either shoe,
She rode astride as troopers do;
With kirtle kilted* to her knee,   *skirt tucked up
To which the mud splash'd wretchedly;
And the wet dripp'd from every tree
Upon her head and heavy hair,
And on her eyelids broad and fair;
The tears and rain ran down her face.
By fits and starts they rode apace,
And very often was his place
Far off from her; he had to ride
Ahead, to see what might betide
When the roads cross'd; and sometimes, **when**
There rose a murmuring from his men,
Had to turn back with promises;
Ah me! she had but little ease;
And often for pure doubt and dread
She sobb'd, made giddy in the head
By the swift riding; while, for cold,
Her slender fingers scarce could hold
The wet reins; yea, and scarcely, too,
She felt the foot within her shoe
Against the stirrup: all for this,
To part at last without a kiss
Beside the haystack in the floods.

For when they near'd that old soak'd hay,
They saw across the only way
That Judas, Godmar, and the three
Red running lions dismally
Grinn'd from his pennon,* under which,   *banner with coat of
In one straight line along the ditch,   arms
They counted thirty heads.

                    So then,
While Robert turn'd round to his men,
She saw at once the wretched end,
And, stooping down, tried hard to rend
Her coif* the wrong way from her head,   *tight-fitting cap tied
And hid her eyes; while Robert said: under chin, which
"Nay, love, 'tis scarcely two to one,   she turned around
At Poictiers where we made them run   to hide her eyes
So fast—why, sweet my love, good cheer.   from the scene
The Gascon frontier is so near,
Nought after this."

But "O" she said,
"My God! my God! I have to tread
The long way back without you; then
The court at Paris; those six men*;   *her judges
The gratings at the Chatelet*;   *Paris prison
The swift Seine on some rainy day
Like this, and people standing by,
And laughing, while my weak hands try
To recollect how strong men swim.*   *the ordeal by water
All this, or else a life with him,
For which I should be damned at last,
Would God that this next hour were past!"

He answer'd not, but cried his cry,
"St. George* for Marny!" cheerily;   *patron saint of
And laid his hand upon her rein.   England
Alas! no man of all his train
Gave back that cheery cry again;
And, while for rage his thumb beat fast
Upon his sword-hilts, someone cast
About his neck a kerchief long,
And bound him.

        Then they went along
To Godmar; who said: "Now, Jehane,
Your lover's life is on the wane
So fast, that, if this very hour
You yield not as my paramour,
He will not see the rain leave off—
Nay, keep your tongue from gibe and scoff,
Sir Robert, or I slay you now."

She laid her hand upon her brow,
Then gazed upon the palm, as though
She thought her forehead bled, and—"No."
She said, and turn'd her head away,
As there were nothing else to say,
And everything were settled: red
Grew Godmar's face from chin to head:
"Jehane, on yonder hill there stands
My castle, guarding well my lands:
What hinders me from taking you,
And doing that I list to do
To your fair willful body, while
Your knight lies dead?"

                    A wicked smile
Wrinkled her face, her lips grew thin,
A long way out she thrust her chin:
"You know that I should strangle you
While you were sleeping; or bite through
Your throat, by God's help—ah!" she said,
"Lord Jesus, pity your poor maid!
For in such wise they hem me in,
I cannot choose but sin and sin,
Whatever happens: yet I think
They could not make me eat or drink,
And so should I just reach my rest."
"Nay, if you do not my behest,
O Jehane! though I love you well,"
Said Godmar, "would I fail to tell
All that I know?" "Foul lies," she said.
"Eh? lies, my Jehane? by God's head,
At Paris folks would deem them true!
Do you know, Jehane, they cry for you,
'Jehane the brown! Jehane the brown!
Give us Jehane to burn or drown!'—
Eh—gag me Robert!*—sweet my friend,   *gag Robert for me
This were indeed a piteous end
For those long fingers, and long feet,
And long neck, and smooth shoulders sweet;
An end that few men would forget
That saw it—So, an hour yet:
Consider, Jehane, which to take
Of life or death!"

                    So, scarce awake,
Dismounting, did she leave that place,
And totter some yards: with her face
Turn'd upward to the sky she lay,
Her head on a wet heap of hay,
And fell asleep: and while she slept,
And did not dream, the minutes crept
Round to the twelve again; but she,
Being waked at last, sigh'd quietly,
And strangely childlike came, and said:
"I will not." Straightway Godmar's head,
As though it hung on strong wires, turn'd
Most sharply round, and his face burn'd.

For Robert—both his eyes were dry,
He could not weep, but gloomily
He seemed to watch the rain; yea, too,

His lips were firm; he tried once more
To touch her lips; she reach'd out, sore
And vain desire so tortured them,
The poor grey lips, and now the hem
Of his sleeve brush'd them.

              With a start
Up Godmar rose, thrust them apart;
From Robert's throat he loosed the bands
Of silk and mail; with empty hands
Held out, she stood and gazed, and saw
The long bright blade without a flaw
Glide out from Godmar's sheath, his hand
In Robert's hair; she saw him bend
Back Robert's head; she saw him send
The thin steel down; the blow told well,
Right backward the knight Robert fell,
And moan'd as dogs do, being half dead,
Unwitting, as I deem: so then
Godmar turn'd grinning to his men,
Who ran, some five or six, and beat
His head to pieces at their feet.

Then Godmar turn'd again and said:
"So, Jehane, the first fitte* is read!   *part of poem or tale
Take note, my lady, that your way
Lies backward to the Chatelet!"
She shook her head and gazed awhile
At her cold hands with a rueful smile,
As though this thing had made her mad.

This was the parting that they had
Beside the haystack in the floods.

THE METRICAL TALE

One further narrative type, the *metrical tale*, should be mentioned. Since a metrical tale is by definition a tale told in meter, all of those considered so far might be considered of this type, and they are. But this leaves many stories in verse that are not ballads, epics, or metrical romances, and they can be grouped together simply as metrical tales. Among these are many of the stories in Chaucer's *Canterbury Tales*, and such poems as William Cowper's delightful *The Diverting History of John Gilpin*,

Burns's *Tam o' Shanter*, John Masefield's *The Everlasting Mercy* and *Dauber*, or Robert Frost's *Brown's Descent*.

Dramatic Poetry

Like the narrative, *dramatic poetry* also tells or implies a story, but with a maximum emphasis on character, and with techniques that relate it closely to the drama as such. As with narrative poetry, also, the characteristics of the dramatic types must be taken as suggestive only, and no single example of the subtypes should be expected to contain all of the characteristics enumerated here. The structural elements hinted at in the narrative or dramatic triangle will vary in application, even as they did in the earlier discussion, and both complete and implied triangles will need to be considered in connection with examples.

POETIC DRAMA

The drama, as usually conceived, is a complete story intended for presentation on a stage, and the speeches are "in character," rather than in the person of the poet. Some dramas, it is true, are written for reading rather than presentation. Even in these, however, the material is arranged in dialogue form, as if to be spoken, but the stage becomes the unlimited stage of the reader's imagination. Normally today the dramas we see in theaters or on television are *prose dramas,* and their lack of emotional demand is such that prose serves adequately for their communication. But occasionally one may feel that what he is hearing "sounds almost like poetry." When this happens it is quite possible that the language is approaching the borderline between prose and poetry; and we may speak of such plays as *prose drama with poetic quality.* J. M. Synge's *Riders to the Sea,* Sean O'Casey's *The Plough and the Stars,* and Marc Connelly's *The Green Pastures* are of this type. It is only when the next step is taken, however, and the play is in fact written in verse, with all of the possibilities opened up by verse techniques, that there results what can be truly called *poetic drama*. The plays of Shakespeare, Marlowe, Dryden and others; and, in our own day, plays by such writers as Maxwell Anderson, Archibald MacLeish, Christopher Fry, and T. S. Eliot illustrate poetic drama intended for stage presentation; while such works as Shelley's *Prometheus Unbound* or Thomas Hardy's *The Dynasts* were written for reading rather than staging and are sometimes referred to as *closet drama*.

The following (Act II, Scene ii) from Shakespeare's *Macbeth* is an admirable example of poetic drama. Macbeth, driven by the prophecy of the witches, as well as by his own and Lady Macbeth's ambition, has gone to murder King Duncan, a guest in Macbeth's castle, after Lady Macbeth has drugged the guards. It is "at dead of night" and Lady Macbeth, alone, awaits her husband's return:

Lady M. That which hath made them drunk hath made me bold;
  What hath quench'd them hath given me fire. Hark! Peace!
  It was the owl that shriek'd, the fatal bellman,
  Which gives the stern'st good-night. He is about it:
  The doors are open, and the surfeited grooms
  Do mock their charge with snores: I have drugg'd their possets,
  That death and nature do contend about them,
  Whether they live or die.
Macb. (*within*).   Who's there? what, ho!
Lady M. Alack, I am afraid they have awaked
  And 'tis not done: the attempt and not the deed
  Confounds us. Hark! I laid their daggers ready;
  He could not miss 'em. Had he not resembled
  My father as he slept, I had done't.

           Enter Macbeth

                My husband!
Macb. I have done the deed. Didst thou not hear a noise?
Lady M. I heard the owl scream and the crickets cry.
  Did you not speak?
Macb.   When?
Lady M.   Now.
Macb.   As I descended?
Lady M. Ay.
Macb. Hark!
  Who lies i' the second chamber?
Lady M.   Donalbain.

Macb. This is a sorry sight. (*Looking at his hands.*)

Lady M. A foolish thought, to say a sorry sight.

Macb. There's one did laugh in's sleep, and one cried "Murder!"
    That they did wake each other: I stood and heard them:
    But they did say their prayers, and address'd them
    Again to sleep.

Lady M.   There are two lodg'd together.

Macb. One cried "God bless us!" and "Amen" the other,
    As they had seen me with these hangman's hands:
    Listening their fear, I could not say "Amen,"
    When they did say "God bless us!"

Lady M. Consider it not so deeply.

Macb. But wherefore could I not pronounce "Amen"?
    I had most need of blessing, and "Amen"
    Stuck in my throat.

Lady M.   These deeds must not be thought
    After these ways; so, it will make us mad.

Macb. Methought I heard a voice cry "Sleep no more!
    Macbeth does murder sleep"—the innocent sleep,
    Sleep that knits up the ravell'd sleave of care,
    The death of each day's life, sore labor's bath,
    Balm of hurt minds, great nature's second course,
    Chief nourisher in life's feast,—

Lady M.   What do you mean?

Macb. Still it cried "Sleep no more!" to all the house:
    "Glamis hath murder'd sleep, and therefore Cawdor
    Shall sleep no more: Macbeth shall sleep no more."

Lady M. Who was it that thus cried? Why, worthy thane,
    You do unbend your noble strength, to think
    So brainsickly of things. Go get some water,
    And wash this filthy witness from your hand.
    Why did you bring these daggers from the place?
    They must lie there: go carry them, and smear
    The sleepy grooms with blood.

Macb.   I'll go no more:
    I am afraid to think what I have done;
    Look on't again I dare not.

Lady M.   Infirm of purpose!
    Give me the daggers: the sleeping and the dead
    Are but as pictures: 'tis the eye of childhood
    That fears a painted devil. If he do bleed,
    I'll gild the faces of the grooms withal,
    For it must seem their guilt.

                          (*Exit. Knocking within.*)

Macb.   Whence is that knocking?
How is't with me, when every noise appals me?
What hands are here? ha! they pluck out mine eyes!
Will all great Neptune's ocean wash this blood
Clean from my hand? No; this my hand will rather
The multitudinous seas incarnadine,
Making the green one red.

Re-enter Lady Macbeth

Lady M. My hands are of your color, but I shame
To wear a heart so white. (*Knocking within.*) I hear a knocking
At the south entry: retire we to our chamber:
A little water clears us of this deed:
How easy is it then! Your constancy
Hath left you unattended. (*Knocking within.*) Hark! more
  knocking:
Get on your nightgown, lest occasion call us
And show us to be watchers: be not lost
So poorly in your thoughts.
Macb. To know my deed, 'twere best not know myself.

(*Knocking within.*)

Wake Duncan with thy knocking! I would thou couldst!

(*Exeunt.*)

Two or more persons talking on a stage will, of course, never
assure a dramatic presentation. To be dramatic there must be,
as in the scene just given, conflict, development of plot, development of character, and action to bring these elements into balance, and to arouse in the reader an empathic response to what
is taking place before him. Someone once said, "They all want
to play Hamlet," but in a very real sense we all *do* play Hamlet
or other characters if the drama we are viewing is well done.
Through empathy we become the different characters, and the
action of the play becomes for the moment the reality of life.
And this is true of dramatic poems as well as of poetic drama.

DRAMATIC POEMS

Dramatic Dialogue

Certain techniques employed by playwrights in the past have
been used by poets for works clearly not intended to be staged.

One such technique is dialogue. We have already met with this, for *Lord Randal* and *Johnny Randall* (pp. 126, 128) are in dialogue throughout. These poems were given as ballads because the preponderance of their characteristics dictated this classification, and because ballads frequently use dialogue, but they are quite dramatic in content. They could thus, with respect to these selected characteristics, also be thought of as *dramatic dialogues* (but with less character development than is usually found in the dramatic poem). On the other hand, A. E. Housman's poem below is obviously not a ballad and *is* a dialogue, and even though it may not appear at first glance to compare in suspense with the deaths and murders of the poems named, there is a growing tension as the poem develops, characters are individualized, and the dramatic elements are adequate for this classification:

> "Is my team ploughing,
>   That I was used to drive
> And hear the harness jingle
>   When I was man alive?"
>
> Ay, the horses trample,
>   The harness jingles now;
> No change though you lie under
>   The land you used to plough.
>
> "Is football playing
>   Along the river shore,
> With lads to chase the leather,
>   Now I stand up no more?"
>
> Ay, the ball is flying,
>   The lads play heart and soul;
> The goal stands up, the keeper
>   Stands up to keep the goal.
>
> "Is my girl happy,
>   That I thought hard to leave,
> And has she tired of weeping
>   As she lies down at eve?"
>
> Ay, she lies down lightly,
>   She lies not down to weep:
> Your girl is well contented.
>   Be still, my lad, and sleep.

"Is my friend hearty,
   Now I am thin and pine,
And has he found to sleep in
   A better bed than mine?"

Yes, lad, I lie easy,
   I lie as lads would choose;
I cheer a dead man's sweetheart,
   Never ask me whose.

The dramatic dialogue, then, is objective, with the poet "in character" as he writes; the story should be developed entirely, or mainly, through dialogue (when the poet steps in, as Frost does briefly in *The Death of the Hired Man*, the effect is similar to the use of "stage directions" in the regular drama); there should be a dramatic situation, suspense, and tension, although melodramatic intensity is not necessary nor desirable; and evidence of character or character development should be present, although it may be relatively slight as compared with a stage play since the dramatic dialogue usually implies rather than tells the full story.

The Aside

The *aside*, while similar in most of the characteristics just given for the dramatic dialogue, differs in one important respect: others are present but do not hear the words of the speaker, who is in effect thinking out loud because the audience needs certain information. The author thus puts in verbal form something similar to that which is going on in our minds as, in the midst of a conversation, we indulge thoughts that we would not wish to share with our companions. So Hamlet, in what is usually called a soliloquy (see below), is in his famous "To be or not to be . . ." technically giving an aside if we assume as we must from the text that Ophelia is actually onstage.

Clearly it is easier for the dramatist to use the aside than it is for the poet, since the others on the stage are in view of the audience and it is evident from the action that they do not hear what is said. The poet, to use this same technique in a poem, must indicate from the lines that someone else is present but does not hear, and that the speaker is addressing only the reader (i. e., thinking aloud). In the following selection from *The Last Ride Together*, Browning has fulfilled these requirements in an effective poem. The speaker has been rejected by the girl he loves, but she grants his request for one final ride with her. It is apparent from the lines that he is not speaking to her, nor to the poet, sculptor or musician referred to. He is "thinking aloud" and we are permitted to listen, as an audience in a theater might during a play:

> I said—Then, dearest, since 'tis so,
> Since now at length my fate I know,
> Since nothing all my love avails,
> Since all my life seemed meant for, fails,
>   Since this was written and needs must be—
> My whole heart rises up to bless
> Your name in pride and thankfulness!
> Take back the hope you gave,—I claim
> Only a memory of 'he same,
> —And this beside, if you will not blame,
>   Your leave for one more last ride with me. . . .
>
> Fail I alone, in words and deeds?
> Why, all men strive, and who succeeds?
> We rode; it seemed my spirit flew,
> Saw other regions, cities new,
>   As the world rushed by on either side.
> I thought,—All labour, yet no less
> Bear up beneath their unsuccess.
> Look at the end of work, contrast
> The petty done, the undone vast,
> This present of theirs with the hopeful past!
>   I hoped she would love me; here we ride.
>
> What hand and brain went ever paired?
> What heart alike conceived and dared?
> What act proved all its thought had been?
> What will but felt the fleshly screen?
>   We ride and I see her bosom heave.
> There's many a crown for who can reach.
> Ten lines, a statesman's life in each!
> The flag stuck on the heap of bones,
> A soldier's doing! what atones?
> They scratch his name on the Abbey-stones.
>   My riding is better, by their leave.

What does it all mean, poet? Well,
Your brains beat into rhythm, you tell
What we felt only; you expressed
You hold things beautiful the best,
    And place them in rhyme so, side by side.
'Tis something, nay 'tis much: but then,
Have you yourself what's best for men?
Are you—poor, sick, old ere your time—
Nearer one whit your own sublime
Than we who never have turned a rhyme?
    Sing, riding's a joy! For me, I ride.

And you, great sculptor—so, you gave
A score of years to Art, her slave,
And that's your Venus, whence we turn
To yonder girl that fords the burn!
    You acquiesce, and shall I repine?
What, man of music, you grown gray
With notes and nothing else to say,
Is this your sole praise from a friend,
"Greatly his opera's strains intend,
But in music we know how fashions end!"
    I gave my youth; but we ride, in fine.

The Soliloquy

When the actor or the speaker in the poem gives his lines
with no one else present to hear him, we have the *soliloquy*
("words alone"). In this, as in the aside, since no one is listening there can be a more open, frank, and honest statement made,
and a more direct revelation of character given, than would be
possible with others present and listening, just as we frequently
express opinions of ourselves or others, to ourselves in private,
much more bluntly than would otherwise be the case. This will
be eminently clear from Browning's *Soliloquy of the Spanish
Cloister*, spoken by a monk who hates his brother monk. He
speaks in no uncertain terms as he watches, unobserved, while
Brother Lawrence moves about the garden (in effect, "off-
stage"). As with all of the dramatic types, tension is present
(within the speaker in this case); there is character revelation,
both of the speaker (his hatred instead of the love he has sworn,
his reaction to the girls washing their hair, his knowledge of the

exact page on which the worst picture is to be found in his
pornographic novel), and of Brother Lawrence (he is admittedly a bore, but the hatred of the speaker is likely to give us
the feeling that Lawrence is just the opposite of the hypocrite
he is described as being); the poem is objective (these are
clearly not Browning's thoughts); and it is an implied narrative,
for we are at the climax, framed in the question: Will the
speaker carry out his threats? and we are given hints (however
biased) of what has taken place before this moment, and of
what may or may not follow:

Gr-r-r—there go, my heart's abhorrence!
    Water your damned flower-pots, do!
If hate killed men, Brother Lawrence,
    God's blood, would not mine kill you!
What? your myrtle-bush wants trimming?
    Oh, that rose has prior claims—
Needs its leaden vase filled brimming?
    Hell dry you up with its flames!

At the meal we sit together:
    *Salve tibi!** I must hear   *Save thee
Wise talk of the kind of weather,
    Sort of season, time of year:
Not a plenteous cork-crop: scarcely
    *Dare we hope oak-galls,** I doubt:*   *for making ink
What's the Latin name for "parsley"?
    What's the Greek name for Swine's Snout?

Whew! We'll have our platter burnished,
    Laid with care on our own shelf!
With a fire-new spoon we're furnished,
    And a goblet for ourself,
Rinsed like something sacrificial
    Ere 'tis fit to touch our chaps—
Marked with L. for our initial!
    (He-he! There his lily snaps!)

Saint, forsooth! While brown Dolores
    Squats outside the Convent bank,
With Sanchicha, telling stories,
    Steeping tresses in the tank,
Blue-black, lustrous, thick like horsehairs,
    —Can't I see his dead eye glow,
Bright as 'twere a Barbary corsair's?
    (That is, if he'd let it show!)

When he finishes refection,
   Knife and fork he never lays
Cross-wise, to my recollection,
   As do I, in Jesu's praise.
I the Trinity illustrate,
   Drinking watered orange-pulp—
In three sips the Arian* frustrate;   *a doctrine that denied
   While he drains his at one gulp!   the Trinity

Oh, those melons! If he's able
   We're to have a feast; so nice!
One goes to the Abbot's table,
   All of us get each a slice.
How go on your flowers? None double?
   Not one fruit-sort can you spy?
Strange!—And I, too, at such trouble,
   Keep them close-nipped on the sly!

There's a great text in Galatians,
   Once you trip on it, entails
Twenty-nine distinct damnations,
   One sure, if another fails:
If I trip him just a-dying,
   Sure of Heaven as sure can be,
Spin him round and send him flying
   Off to Hell, a Manichee.*   *heretic

Or, my scrofulous French novel
   On gray paper with blunt type!
Simply glance at it, you grovel
   Hand and foot in Belial's gripe:
If I double down its pages
   At the woeful sixteenth print,
When he gathers his greengages,*   *plums
   Ope a sieve and slip it in 't?

Or, there's Satan!—one* might venture   *the speaker
   Pledge one's soul to him, yet leave
Such a flaw in the indenture
   As he'd miss till, past retrieve,
Blasted lay that rose-acacia*   *i.e. Brother Lawrence
   We're so proud of! *Hy, Zy, Hine** ...   *vesper bells' sound?
'St, there's Vespers! *Plena gratia*
   *Ave, Virgo!** Gr-r-r—you swine!   *Hail Virgin, full of
                                       grace

The Dramatic Monologue

Browning was very skillful in writing the dramatic poem, his major contribution to the subtypes being the *dramatic monologue*, which he perfected with such mastery that it can be said that in a very real sense he invented the form as we know it today.

Like the other dramatic types, the dramatic monologue is objective; a conflict should be present (either within the speaker's mind or between the speaker and others); and the dramatic triangle will normally be implied as the action centers near the climax of what would be the full story. As in the soliloquy there is but one speaker. The characteristics that distinguish the monologue are to be found in the fact that others are present, that they may speak or act but what they say or do must be indicated only through the words of the single speaker, that since the speaker is talking to others there will be less direct revelation of character than in the soliloquy (but about the same as in the dramatic dialogue), that the characters of the others will be revealed through the prejudices of the speaker (since they have no chance to speak in their own persons while we listen), and that, since confusion with the soliloquy might otherwise result (as it does in Tennyson's *Ulysses*), the reader should be made aware of the others early in the poem. Browning's *My Last Duchess*, where the person addressed is clearly established by the fifth line, illustrates the foregoing characteristics and also shows how fully the poet can reveal character, both of the speaker and the one spoken about (with the latter colored by the bias of the Duke, even as was that of Brother Lawrence by the speaker in the soliloquy above):

> That's my last Duchess painted on the wall,
> Looking as if she were alive. I call
> That piece a wonder, now: Frà Pandolf's hands
> Worked busily a day, and there she stands.
> Will 't please you sit and look at her? I said
> "Frà Pandolf" by design, for never read
> Strangers like you that pictured countenance,
> The depth and passion of its earnest glance,
> But to myself they turned (since none puts by

The curtain I have drawn for you, but I)
And seemed as they would ask me, if they durst,
How such a glance came there; so, not the first
Are you to turn and ask thus. Sir, 'twas not
Her husband's presence only, called that spot
Of joy into the Duchess' cheek: perhaps
Frà Pandolf chanced to say, "Her mantle laps
Over my lady's wrist too much," or "Paint
Must never hope to reproduce the faint
Half-flush that dies along her throat": such stuff
Was courtesy, she thought, and cause enough
For calling up that spot of joy. She had
A heart—how shall I say?—too soon made glad,
Too easily impressed; she liked whate'er
She looked on, and her looks went everywhere.
Sir, 'twas all one! My favor at her breast,
The dropping of the daylight in the West,
The bough of cherries some officious fool
Broke in the orchard for her, the white mule
She rode with round the terrace—all and each
Would draw from her alike the approving speech,
Or blush, at least. She thanked men,—good! but thanked
Somehow—I know not how—as if she ranked
My gift of a nine-hundred-years-old name
With anybody's gift. Who'd stoop to blame
This sort of trifling? Even had you skill
In speech—(which I have not)—to make your will
Quite clear to such an one, and say, "Just this
Or that in you disgusts me; here you miss,
Or there exceed the mark"—and if she let
Herself be lessoned so, nor plainly set
Her wits to yours, forsooth, and made excuse,
—E'en then would be some stooping; and I choose
Never to stoop. Oh, sir, she smiled, no doubt,
Whene'er I passed her; but who passed without
Much the same smile? This grew; I gave commands;
Then all smiles stopped together. There she stands
As if alive. Will 't please you rise? We'll meet
The company below then. I repeat,
The Count your master's known munificence
Is ample warrant that no just pretence
Of mine for dowry will be disallowed;
Though his fair daughter's self, as I avowed
At starting, is my object. Nay, we'll go
Together down, sir. Notice Neptune, though,
Taming a sea-horse, thought a rarity,
Which Claus of Innsbruck cast in bronze for me!

Combined Types

The interrelationship of the dramatic types is interestingly illustrated by Leonard Bacon's *An Afternoon in Artillery Walk*, where the aside is frequently interrupted by dramatic monologue. The poem is based on the relationship between Milton and his daughters who, because of his blindness, served as his copyists. It is Mary's turn, at home in Artillery Walk, and she resents her task as she thinks of her sisters Anne, who was lame, and Deborah, enjoying themselves with their loves (Anne married her carpenter, but Deborah, not Mary, married Abram Clark; Mary died single). Her quite un-Puritan daydreaming is constantly interrupted by the demands of her Puritan father, whose questions and requests are clear from her responses. If the selections from *Paradise Lost* (pp. 66, 136) are recalled, Bacon's skill in his selection of imagery will be apparent. (The quotation being dictated at the end of the poem is the opening of Book II.)

I think it is his blindness makes him so,
He is so angry, and so querulous.
Yes, Father! I will look in Scaliger.
Yes, Cousin Phillips took the notes—I think—
May all the evil angels fly away
With Cousin Phillips to the Serbonian Bog,
Wherever that may be. And here am I
Locked in with him the livelong afternoon.
There's Anne gone limping with that love of hers,
Her master-carpenter, and Deborah
Stolen away. Yes, Father, 'tis an aleph*   *Hebrew *a*
But the Greek glose on't in the Septuagint   *Bible translation
Is something that I cannot quite make out.
The letter's rubbed.

Oh, thus to wear away
My soul and body with this dry-as-dust
This tearer-up of words, this plaguey seeker
After the things that no man understands.
'Tis April. I am seventeen years old,
And Abram Clark will come a-courting me.
Oh what a Hell a midday house can be!
Dusty and bright and dumb and shadowless,

Full of this sunshot dryness, like the soul
Of this old pedant here. I will not bear
Longer this tyranny of death in life
That drains my spirit like a succubus.*   *demon or fiend
I am too full of blood and fire for this—
This dull soul-gnawing discipline he sets
Upon our shoulders, the sad characters.
Chapter on chapter, blank and meaningless.
Now by the May-pole merry-makers run,
And the music throbs and pulses in light limbs,
And the girls' kirtles are lifted to the knee.
Ah would that I were blowsy with the heat,
Being bussed by some tall fellow, and kissing him
On his hot red lips—some bully royalist
With gold in's purse and lace about his throat
And a long rapier for the Puritans.
Or I would wander by some cool yew-hedge,
Dallying with my lover all the afternoon,
And then to cards and supper—cinnamon,
Some delicate pastry, and an amber wine
Burning on these lips that know a year-long lent.
Then to the theatre, and Mistress Nell*   *Nell Gwynn
That the king's fond of. Mayhap gentlemen
About would praise me, and I should hear them buzz,
And feel my cheek grow warm beneath my mask,
And glance most kindly—

I was in a muse.
I have the paper, Father, and the pens.
Now for the damnable dictation. So!
"High—on a throne—of royal state—which far
Outshone—the wealth of 'Ormus' "—S or Z?
How should I know the letter?—"and of Ind.
Or where—the gorgeous East—with richest hand
Showers—on her kings—barbaric—pearl and gold,
Satan exalted sate."

The Character Sketch

Related to the foregoing dramatic types is the *character sketch*, in which the poet is concerned less with matters of story, complete or implied, than he is with arousing our sympathy, antagonism, or merely interest for an individual. These poems are presented, usually, from the point of view of the writer as

observer and commentator, and are not involved in an inner
revelation of character in the words of a speaker or speakers, as
in the truly dramatic types. They do, however, differ from
poems written simply *about* people, of which there are many
(to Shakespeare, to Milton, etc.), by incorporating an element
of suspense, conflict, or tension. Edwin Arlington Robinson
could be most effective in this genre, as his *Miniver Cheevy,*
Cliff Klingenhagen, Richard Cory, Reuben Bright, and others
attest. One of his most touching, surely, is *Mr. Flood's Party,*
which deals with an old man who has outlived his earlier friends
and finds himself alone and lonely, consoling himself with a bit
of drink, and carrying on a game of conversation with himself.
Note especially how sentimentality has been avoided through
the touching humor, and how an element of courage, even grandeur, is suggested by the allusion to Roland. Roland too was
alone, fighting bravely to the end, if the allusion is to the epic
Chanson de Roland; or equally alone and facing his dark tower
as Eben Flood is facing his if we find a more meaningful allusion in Browning's *Childe Roland to the Dark Tower Came:*

> Old Eben Flood, climbing alone one night
> Over the hill between the town below
> And the foresaken upland hermitage
> That held as much as he should ever know
> On earth again of home, paused warily.
> The road was his with not a native near;
> And Eben, having leisure, said aloud,
> For no man else in Tilbury Town to hear:
>
> "Well, Mr. Flood, we have the harvest moon
> Again, and we may not have many more;
> The bird is on the wing, the poet says,
> And you and I have said it here before.
> Drink to the bird." He raised up to the light
> The jug that he had gone so far to fill,
> And answered huskily: "Well, Mr. Flood,
> Since you propose it, I believe I will."
>
> Alone, as if enduring to the end
> A valiant armor of scarred hopes outworn,
> He stood there in the middle of the road
> Like Roland's ghost winding a silent horn.

Below him, in the town among the trees,
Where friends of other days had honored him,
A phantom salutation of the dead
Rang thinly till old Eben's eyes were dim.

Then, as a mother lays her sleeping child
Down tenderly, fearing it may awake,
He set the jug down slowly at his feet
With trembling care, knowing that most things break;
And only when assured that on firm earth
It stood, as the uncertain lives of men
Assuredly did not, he paced away,
And with his hand extended paused again:

"Well, Mr. Flood, we have not met like this
In a long time; and many a change has come
To both of us, I fear, since last it was
We had a drop together. Welcome home!"
Convivially returning with himself,
Again he raised the jug up to the light;
And with an acquiescent quaver said:
"Well, Mr. Flood, if you insist, I might.

"Only a very little, Mr. Flood—
For auld lang syne. No more, sir, that will do."
So, for the time, apparently it did,
And Eben evidently thought so too;
For soon amid the silver loneliness
Of night he lifted up his voice and sang,
Secure, with only two moons listening,
Until the whole harmonious landscape rang—

"For auld lang syne." The weary throat gave out,
The last word wavered; and the song being done,
He raised again the jug regretfully
And shook his head, and was again alone.
There was not much that was ahead of him,
And there was nothing in the town below—
Where strangers would have shut the many doors
That many friends had opened long ago.[8]

[8] A first version of this final stanza, found in the manuscript of the poem in the Lewis M. Isaacs Collection of Robinsoniana in the New York Public Library, was called to my attention by my colleague, Professor Robert Stevick. It shows the remarkable skill with which Robinson made the revision from the obvious weakness of the original to the telling force of the received version (compare the Wordsworth revision of *She Dwelt Among the Untrodden Ways*, discussed above, pp. 32–36, as well as pp. 183f, 212n, and the frontispiece of this book):

The Lyric and Its Modern Voice

Poetic tools are, of course, used in all kinds of poetry, including narrative and dramatic, but their effects are likely to be more evident in the singing voices of the *lyric*.[9] This in itself suggests a paradox, however, that can be resolved only by recognition of the fact that there are many lyric elements in the other types of poetry, even though these elements may appear to be subordinated to the story or dramatic scene as developed by the poet. We have seen, for example, that traditional ballads were usually sung, and surely there could be no question of the lyric quality, with or without music, in this stanza from *Sir Patrick Spens*:

> Late, late yestreen I saw the new moone,
>   Wi the auld moone in her arme,
> And I feir, I feir, my dear master,
>   That we will come to harme.

Browning called a group of his poems, including *My Last Duchess* (pp. 154–55), "Dramatic Lyrics," while Shelley described his *Prometheus Unbound* (pp. 66–67) as a "Lyrical Drama." This is to suggest how loosely, even paradoxically, the term has come to be employed in recent centuries, and correspondingly how difficult it is to define.[10]

'For auld lang syne.'—The weary throat gave out;
The last word perished, and the song was done.
He raised again the jug regretfully,
And without malice would have rambled on;
But hearing in the bushes a new sound
He smote with new profanity the cause,—
And shook an aged unavailing fist
At an inhuman barrage of applause.

[9] The word is derived from the musical instrument, the lyre, and the historical importance of this quality is found in many of the subtypes of the genre: songs, madrigals, airs, hymns, odes, elegies, and sonnets (i.e., "little songs").

[10] A recent attempt by James William Johnson is meaningful: "In its modern meaning, a lyric is a type of poetry which is mechanically representational of a musical architecture and which is thematically representational of the poet's sensibility as evidenced in a fusion of conception and image. In its older and more confined sense, a lyric was simply a poem written to be sung; this meaning is preserved in the modern colloquialism of referring to the words of a song as its 'lyrics.'"

Despite overtones of the lyric quality in other types, however, it is possible to distinguish, if only suggestively, its principal characteristics as we know it today. First, and most important, of these is the impression gained that the lines are spoken by the poet himself, giving expression to his personal feelings, aspirations, or attitudes. In other words, the lyric is, or should give the impression of being, subjective (even though the "I" of the poem may not be literally the poet), as against the other, more objective genres, when the author stands outside as narrator, or "gets into" the character of the dramatic piece.

Thus, in terms of the illustration above, while the rest of the poem is direct and seemingly factual, the stanza from *Sir Patrick Spens,* with its beautiful use of personification, appears rather a sudden revelation of the poet's attitude and emotional response to the phenomenon than a mere indication of a sailor's superstition. Browning, in his turn, seems to use "Dramatic Lyric" to differentiate his group of poems from stage drama: they are dramatic in nature, but if it is assumed that the character (e.g., the Duke) is himself writing the poem, it would then be a lyric, since it would express the Duke's (but not necessarily Browning's) feelings. And *Prometheus Unbound* might well be called a "Lyrical Drama" because it is rich in incidental songs and was never intended for the stage, even though it uses a full range of devices found in the drama. But more importantly, it is "lyric" in the sense that it makes full use of Shelley's ideas and emotions—the characters in many instances are truly Shelley's spokesmen under a thin dramatic disguise. It can, of course, be argued that this is true of any drama or narrative of serious intent: the writer writes because he has something to say. The determining factor is the degree to which objectivity, on the one hand, is maintained (as in *Macbeth*) and subjectivity, on the other, is permitted to color the work (as in *Prometheus Unbound*) or to dominate it.

Secondly, since the lyric is the expression of an emotion, and since emotions cannot be long sustained, the lyric will normally be relatively brief, or will, in a longer poem, develop a wave-like motion of flooding and ebbing feeling. Further, the reader will experience an impression of controlled unity, into which

will be worked the fullest possible play of the imagination and
the most skillful use of the devices for rhythm and sound. But
the latter should not be construed to mean that, in the modern
sense of the word, all lyrics should be susceptible of or suggest
musical settings. If Ben Jonson's "Drink to me only with thine
eyes" is a lyric, so is Walter Savage Landor's *On His Seventy-
Fifth Birthday*:

> I strove with none, for none was worth my strife;
>   Nature I loved, and next to Nature, Art;
> I warmed both hands before the fire of life;
>   It sinks, and I am ready to depart;

and so is that large body of subjective expression in blank verse,
free verse or other forms that permit philosophical contemplation or other expressions of lyrical mood.

Form, subject matter, and mood all play their parts with particular force in the lyric. Indeed, as someone has suggested, the
lyric is "a direct arrow-like flight, a spontaneous flash of emotion which makes its own music." We have learned earlier how
the tools of the poet contribute to this music, and especially
how figures of speech and imagery add their magic to the total
impression.

Since lyric poems usually express deep feeling, it is natural
that the majority of them should deal with love, death, or religious considerations. But the range of subject matter is limited
only by the limits of the poet's responses, and nature, persons,
patriotism, social or political conditions, even lighthearted humor, or any other mood, subject, or combination of subjects may
find their way into this form of expression. If the reader will
review the poems used to illustrate the earlier chapters of this
book he will find ample evidence of this.

A final and highly significant element in the lyric is what
Coleridge called "The shaping spirit of Imagination"—for it is
this spirit that lifts the commonplace into the sphere of poetry
in whatever genre, the spirit that makes the early and anonymous lyric,

> O western wind, when wilt thou blow,
> That the small rain down can rain?
> Christ, if my love were in my arms
> And I in my bed again,

different from

> I put my hat upon my head
> And walked into the Strand;
> And there I met another man
> Whose hat was in his hand.

In the former the *idiom* communicates a depth of feeling and passion entirely lacking in the other, and the anonymous writer of the early sixteenth century draws us to him as a highly distinctive personality.

Idiom is that quality of expression peculiar to a given writer (or age) which sets him apart from others, and which has been related to *individuality* in our discussion of the creative personality (see p. 27). It involves the poet's choice of words and imagery, but also that indefinable "way of saying" that results in the memorable phrase, line, or poem.[11] In the lyric, to a degree found in no other single genre, this quality can be discerned, and the illustrative poems below have been grouped by subject matter—and within the groupings chronologically—to emphasize this. The groupings have further been planned especially to acquaint the reader more directly than has been done in earlier sections of this book with the distinctive qualities of modern (mid-twentieth century) poetry. By offering several poems from different periods on a given theme, with each poem in an idiom reasonably characteristic of the period in which it was written, touchstones will be supplied by which to test the reader's response.

Before turning to the selections, however, a word should be said about the modern poems in these groupings. For readers (and there are, unfortunately, still many) whose school experience of poetry ended with the literature of the late nineteenth century, the modern selections may require certain adjustments in perception. Some of the lines may seem startling rather than striking, some laced with phrases better suited to a laboratory than to a poem, some burdened with commonplace detail that is not what we usually think of as "poetic." But this is to take

---

[11] Compare Lascelle Abercrombie's statement: "A poet does not compose *in order to* make of language delightful and exciting music; he composes a delightful and exciting music in language *in order to* make what he has to say peculiarly efficacious in our minds."

words and phrases out of context, to hear only the single notes in a balanced chord of music. Each poem has been selected for its integrated unity as well as for its contemporary feeling, and should be read and reread until the mind has become oriented and the individuality of the poetry emerges—emerges not *in spite of* but in its own right *because of* the idiom in which it has been shaped.

It is true, of course, that in any period—even the most recent—many excellent poems are written that are reminiscent of earlier idioms, and many readers, because of their training, are more "comfortable" with these than they are with the more experimental verse structures, or the involved, obscure, even dense imagery and allusions (frequently bordering on the stream-of-consciousness) which they look upon as typically "modern" and therefore unintelligible (or, conversely, which they decide must be good because they cannot understand them). If extremes are avoided, however (and extremes are never typical), the modern idiom can be refreshing and rewarding. It should, of course, never replace a sense of appreciation for poetry of the past (there is ample room for both in the creative reader's mind); rather it should be welcomed as a new strand in the tapestry of poetry that has been, and will continue to be, woven over the centuries. A careful reading of the poems below (for which comments have been kept to a minimum) will form an admirable preparation for the extended analyses of the lyrics to be found in the next chapter.

CITIES

Our first group will have to do with the reactions of three poets to cities observed in the early morning hours. On September 3, 1802, Wordsworth left England for a visit to France. As the coach taking him to his ship paused for a moment on the bridge across the Thames leading out of London, the poet looked back on the sleeping city and wrote his *Composed upon Westminster Bridge*, wrote it in the quiet tone, the typical phrasing, and what now seems the archaic use of words like "doth" and "glideth," with which we have already become acquainted (see pp. 19, 67):

> Earth has not anything to show more fair:
> Dull would he be of soul who could pass by
> A sight so touching in its majesty:
> This city now doth like a garment wear
> The beauty of the morning; silent, bare,
> Ships, towers, domes, theatres, and temples lie
> Open unto the fields, and to the sky;
> All bright and glittering in the smokeless air.
> Never did sun more beautifully steep
> In his first splendor, valley, rock, or hill;
> Ne'er saw I, never felt, a calm so deep!
> The river glideth at his own sweet will:
> Dear God! the very houses seem asleep;
> And all that mighty heart is lying still!

If we turn now to a poem first published in 1932 we quickly sense not only the changes that have marked the modern metropolis but also those that have marked the modern idiom. Douglas Malloch's *Waking of a City* offers a stanza (the third) that is quite conventional—a stanza, indeed, that might have been written by a contemporary of Wordsworth (or by Wordsworth himself as he suggested the fusion of the city with nature in the early light)—but it is a stanza that, with its sentimentality, serves to point up the realistic tone of the second stanza, and the complete contrast with Wordsworth's sleeping London in the last stanza:

> We fools who cannot sleep have heard it waken
>   So many times
> We cannot count, a giant roughly shaken,
>   For whom no chimes
> Make glad the housewife, send the man afield:
>   Its matin call
> Is noise, the many-voiced and many-wheeled,
>   Where noise is all—
>
> The growling dawn, and then the sullen roaring
>   From street to street,
> Then human life within the hopper pouring
>   With hurried feet,

The crowded street cars, women hip to hip
　　　With men unclean,
Crushed in a nauseating fellowship
　　　Of day's machine.

Oh, I have seen the dawn above a mountain
　　　That floods a plain,
Where life wells up, like water from a fountain,
　　　All sweet again,
Have seen the world awaken like a child
　　　With eyes of blue,
That stretched its arms, breathed deeply then, and smiled
　　　That night was through.

But cities have no peaks, they have but valleys,
　　　No verdant breast,
From restless sleep crawl out of darkened alleys
　　　To day's unrest.
On streets stone-curbed the first gray shadows break,
　　　And lives stone-curbed,
For at the dawning cities do not wake—
　　　They are disturbed.

Malloch's poem is, in a sense, a stepping-stone to the final
selection in this group. With rimed stanzas dropped, Delmore
Schwartz is better able to concentrate on fresher rhythms, and
on vivid detail whose cumulative effect in the broader context
of the poem is the important thing and goes well beyond the
Malloch selection. The opening allusion to Plato's cave[12] is immediately brought home to today's world by the reflected headlights of line two, but bridges the intervening catalogue of details
(many of them touched with sensitive originality) to culminate
in the philosophical suggestion of the closing lines. The poem
takes its title from its first line:

　　　In the naked bed, in Plato's cave,
　　　Reflected headlights slowly slid the wall,

　　　[12] Plato's analogy of the cave is found in the *Republic*, Book VII, and
has to do with appearance and reality. A fire throws shadows of objects
on a wall of the cave in which prisoners are chained so they have never
seen anything but these shadows, which are thus the only reality to them.
One prisoner frees himself, discovers the source of the shadows, and
beyond the fire the bright light of the true Reality, which dazzles his eyes.

Carpenters hammered under the shaded window,
Wind troubled the window curtains all night long,
A fleet of trucks strained uphill, grinding,
Their freights covered, as usual.
The ceiling lightened again, the slanting diagram
Slid slowly forth.
                Hearing the milkman's chop,
His striving up the stair, the bottle's chink,
I rose from bed, lit a cigarette,
And walked to the window. The stony street
Displayed the stillness in which buildings stand,
The street-lamp's vigil and the horse's patience.
The winter sky's pure capital
Turned me back to bed with exhausted eyes.

Strangeness grew in the motionless air. The loose
Film grayed. Shaking wagons, hooves' waterfalls,
Sounded far off, increasing, louder and nearer.
A car coughed, starting. Morning, softly
Melting the air, lifted the half-covered chair
From underseas, kindled the looking-glass,
Distinguished the dresser and the white wall.
The bird called tentatively, whistled, called,
Bubbled and whistled, so! Perplexed, still wet
With sleep, affectionate, hungry and cold. So, so,
O son of man, the ignorant night, the travail
Of early morning, the mystery of beginning
Again and again,
                while History is unforgiven.

LOVE

The second group deals with the many-faceted subject of
love, and the poems have been selected to illustrate some of the
different ways in which the poet says "I love you" (three words
that in themselves make perhaps the most perfect of love
poems). In the first two the position is taken that despite imper-
fections there is something that sets the loved one above all
others. Shakespeare, in the typical Elizabethan idiom of his
Sonnet 130, exaggerates in the direction of under-evaluation in
order to "show up" those lovers who (especially under the in-

fluence of Platonic love precedents) had gone to the opposite
extreme in their attempt to idealize their mistresses by equally
"false compare":

> My mistress' eyes are nothing like the sun;
> Coral is far more red than her lips' red;
> If snow be white, why then her breasts are dun;
> If hairs be wires, black wires grow on her head.
> I have seen roses damasked, red and white,
> But no such roses see I in her cheeks;
> And in some perfumes is there more delight
> Than in the breath that from my mistress reeks.
> I love to hear her speak, yet well I know
> That music hath a far more pleasing sound.
> I grant I never saw a goddess go:
> My mistress, when she walks, treads on the ground.
>   And yet, by heaven, I think my love as rare
>   As any she belied with false compare.

More than two hundred years later Hartley Coleridge used
much the same approach, but without the vivid details brought
in by Shakespeare, and with what we should now recognize as
nineteenth-century tone and imagery. Again the first line is the
title:

> She is not fair to outward view,
>   As many maidens be;
> Her loveliness I never knew
>   Until she smiled on me.
> O then I saw her eye was bright,
> A well of love, a spring of light.
>
> But now her looks are coy and cold,
>   To mine they ne'er reply,
> And yet I cease not to behold
>   The love-light in her eye:
> Her very frowns are fairer far
> Than smiles of other maidens are.

The following poems, again from the Elizabethan and nineteenth-century periods, raise the question of the basis of love,
but arrive at somewhat different answers. The first is an anonymous poem, *Love Not Me for Comely Grace*, lighter in tone
than the second, and it suggests that one should not seek logical

reasons for love, but know love rather as a woman "knows"—by feminine intuition:

> Love not me for comely grace,
> For my pleasing eye or face,
> Nor for any outward part,
> No, nor for my constant heart,—
> > For these may fail, or turn to ill,
> > So thou and I shall sever:
> Keep therefore a true woman's eye,
> And love me still, but know not why—
> > So hast thou the same reason still
> > To doat upon me ever!

When Elizabeth Barrett Browning, in her *Sonnets from the Portuguese*, raised the same question, she sought a more philosophical answer and found it in the timeless and everlasting quality of love itself, which goes beyond all transitory attractions and never diminishes. The nineteenth-century idiom will be apparent:

> If thou must love me, let it be for naught
> Except for love's sake only. Do not say
> "I love her for her smile—her look—her way
> Of speaking gently—for a trick of thought
> That falls in well with mine, and certes brought
> A sense of pleasant ease on such a day"—
> For these things in themselves, Beloved, may
> Be changed, or change for thee—and love, so wrought,
> May be unwrought so. Neither love me for
> Thine own dear pity's wiping my cheeks dry—
> A creature might forget to weep, who bore
> Thy comfort long, and lose thy love thereby!
> But love me for love's sake, that evermore
> Thou mayst love on, through love's eternity.

To this pair of poems might be added another having to do with the ways of love, but this time with an unusual approach. It is from the twentieth century and is in the pure lyrical voice of Sara Teasdale's *Night Song at Amalfi*.[13] Restraint is the keynote here, both in the theme and in the expression, and a remarkable unity is obtained by the integration of the imagery and the thought. The naturalness and seeming simplicity of the

---

[13] A seaport town on the beautiful Gulf of Salerno in Italy.

words and rhythms should be noted, but also the haunting effect
of the feeling achieved by these qualities:

> I asked the heaven of stars
>   What I should give my love—
> It answered me with silence,
>   Silence above.
>
> I asked the darkened sea
>   Down where the fishers go—
> It answered me with silence,
>   Silence below.
>
> Oh, I could give him weeping,
>   Or I could give him song—
> But how can I give silence,
>   My whole life long?

The final pair of love poems brings us more fully into the distinctive idiom and attitude of the modern poet, and the contrast will again be pointed up by linking an early poem with one
from the twentieth century. The emphasis in both of these
poems, in contrast to those so far considered, is on the sensuous
attractions that lead to love. Poets in other periods have sought
to deny or play down the physical. The modern poet, reflecting
the changed attitudes and standards of our day, and the resulting escape from what was so often a false reticence in the past,
is free to develop a franker, more outspoken acknowledgment
of the physical as an important component in the experience of
love. Although good taste is sometimes violated in such treatments (notably in the modern novel, but at times in poems also)
it need not be, as our example will show. But first we turn to
the seventeenth century and Robert Herrick's *Upon Julia's
Clothes.* The physical motion of Julia is delightfully suggested
in the key word "liquefaction" of the first stanza, and then
strengthened in the "vibration" of stanza two—but it is suggested only, because the poem is ostensibly a description of the
silk Julia is wearing, and she remains a somewhat vague figure
behind the glittering façade:

> Whenas in silks my Julia goes,
> Then, then, methinks, how sweetly flows
> That liquefaction of her clothes.

Next, when I cast mine eyes and see
That brave vibration each way free,
Oh, how that glittering taketh me!

How much more direct and honest, and how much more vivid
and compelling is the expression in Theodore Roethke's *I Knew
a Woman, Lovely in Her Bones*. Here the character is sharply
etched, with deft shadings in the fresh and challenging details
of the imagery. Reticence is overwhelmed by the ebullient outpouring of the poet's feeling, and the range of his figures of
speech leaves no room for the trite or commonplace phrase
(note that there is not one of these in the entire poem). Here,
then, is the modern poetic idiom in forceful use, set in a restrained metrical pattern that offers no distraction to the rich
content, and with a free rime placement that points up the singing spirit of the poet as he contemplates the fact that he is a
"martyr to a motion not my own":

I knew a woman, lovely in her bones,
When small birds sighed, she would sigh back at them;
Ah, when she moved, she moved more ways than one:
The shapes a bright container can contain!
Of her choice virtues only gods should speak,
Or English poets who grew up on Greek
(I'd have them sing in chorus, cheek to cheek.)

How well her wishes went! She stroked my chin,
She taught me Turn, and Counter-turn, and Stand;[14]
She taught me Touch, that undulant white skin:
I nibbled meekly from her proffered hand;
She was the sickle; I, poor I, the rake,
Coming behind her for her pretty sake
(But what prodigious mowing we did make).

Love likes a gander, and adores a goose:
Her full lips pursed, the errant note to seize;
She played it quick, she played it light and loose;
My eyes, they dazzled at her flowing knees;
Her several parts could keep a pure repose,
Or one hip quiver with a mobile nose
(She moved in circles, and those circles moved).

---

[14] These are, appropriately in the light of lines five to seven above,
terms associated with Greek drama and with the divisions of the Pindaric
ode (see p. 79). But their secondary suggestion in this context should not
be overlooked.

Let seed be grass, and grass turn into hay:
I'm martyr to a motion not my own;
What's freedom for? To know eternity.
I swear she cast a shadow white as stone.
But who would count eternity in days?
These old bones live to learn her wanton ways:
(I measure time by how a body sways).

THE HOUSE FLY

As we turn to our third group of poems the subject is the common house fly, and we should keep in mind that when the eighteenth-century poems below were written there was little knowledge of the part played by flies in the transmission of disease. They were looked upon rather for their symbolic properties. They typified the shortness of life in which man, comparatively speaking, also shared, or they represented the unity of all life. The former view is reflected in William Oldys' *On a Fly Drinking Out of His Cup*, the very title of which is probably enough to make a modern reader shudder. But not so this poet, who welcomes the stranger with a fine spirit of comradeship:

Busy, curious, thirsty fly!
Drink with me and drink as I:
Freely welcome to my cup,
Couldst thou sip and sip it up:
Make the most of life you may,
Life is short and wears away.

Both alike are mine and thine
Hastening quick to their decline:
Thine's a summer, mine's no more,
Though repeated to threescore.
Threescore summers, when they're gone,
Will appear as short as one!

At the end of the century William Blake, having put an early end to the short summer of a single fly, saw in what he had done the uncertainty of life for man as well as insect, each susceptible of being destroyed by a thoughtless force. Blake is not bitter, as is Gloucester in *King Lear*, who could cry, "As

flies to wanton boys, are we to the gods; / They kill us for
their sport." But he does find a common ground of existence,
and draws his extreme parallels accordingly, in *The Fly*:

> Little Fly,
> Thy summer's play
> My thoughtless hand
> Has brushed away.
>
> Am not I
> A fly like thee?
> Or art not thou
> A man like me?
>
> For I dance,
> And drink, and sing,
> Till some blind hand
> Shall brush my wing.
>
> If thought is life
> And strength and breath,
> And the want
> Of thought is death;
>
> Then am I
> A happy fly.
> If I live,
> Or if I die.

In our own century Karl Shapiro, like Blake, is aware of his
position as a man facing what is now recognized as a potentially
deadly insect, but he offers no concessions in the name of
brotherhood, and his revulsion is apparent. "My peace is your
disaster" leaves no question as to where the ultimate values lie.
The reader may find certain details of this poem—called, like
Blake's, simply *The Fly*—repulsive, but he might find difficulty
in arguing that they are not suited to the subject, or that as a
result of the vocabulary this is not truly a poem.[15] It is a poem,

---

[15] Shapiro prepared for writing this poem by making scientific notes on
what he called "the habits and life-cycle of the common fly." A comparison of his second of two sets of notes with the poem itself will offer a
rewarding insight into the mind of the artist as craftsman: "Spins like a
top with terrific buzz in f. Hobbles on a wing with broken balancers. A
spot of gauze. Musca agonistes. Washing yr hairy hands and feet with
hands and feet. I swat. Your grease, your brown stuff and your body—
paste. Smeared for an inch. I swat you with my hate. You drank of

and a strong one whose sordid details take their proper place
in an imaginative projection of feeling that is filled with fascinating overtones for the careful reader (even without searching
for symbolic intent). Not all poetry is "pretty," but the test of
quality in any poem lies elsewhere:

> O hideous little bat, the size of snot,
> With polyhedral eye and shabby clothes,
> To populate the stinking cat you walk
> The promontory of the dead man's nose,
> Climb with the fine leg of a Duncan-Phyfe
> The smoking mountains of my food
> And in a comic mood
> In mid-air take to bed a wife.
>
> Riding and riding with your filth of hair
> On gluey foot or wing, forever coy,
> Hot from the compost and green sweet decay,
> Sounding your buzzer like an urchin toy—
> You dot all whiteness with diminutive stool,
> In the tight belly of the dead
> Burrow with hungry head
> And inlay maggots like a jewel.
>
> At your approach the great horse stomps and paws
> Bringing the hurricane of his heavy tail;
> Shod in disease you dare to kiss my hand
> Which sweeps against you like an angry flail;
> Still you return, return, trusting your wing
> To draw you from the hunter's reach
> That learns to kill to teach
> Disorder to the tinier thing.
>
> My peace is your disaster. For your death
> Children like spiders cup their pretty hands
> And wives resort to chemistry of war.
> In fens of sticky paper and quicksands
> You glue yourself to death. Where you are stuck
> You struggle hideously and beg
> You amputate your leg
> Imbedded in the amber muck.

Lovelace cup. Blake's cup. Your broken feet your stomach-brain is slain.
Wing pulled sidewise, head pulled down over your body like a drunkard's
hat. Lying on your back like airplanes. In amber full of blood. With sticky
feet wings down like a wet crow, a drenched rat. I beat you like a rat."
(Richard Lovelace wrote a poem titled *A Fly About a Glass of Burnt
Claret*. For Blake's poem see above.)

But I, a man, must swat you with my hate,
Slap you across the air and crush your flight,
Must mangle with my shoe and smear your blood,
Expose your little guts pasty and white,
Knock your head sidewise like a drunkard's hat,
   Pin your wings under like a crow's,
     Tear off your flimsy clothes
And beat you as one beats a rat.

Then like Gargantua I stride among
The corpses strewn like raisins in the dust,
The broken bodies of the narrow dead
That catch the throat with fingers of disgust
I sweep. One gyrates like a top and falls
   And stunned, stone blind, and deaf
     Buzzes its frightful F
And dies between three cannibals.

MAN AND GOD

Man's speculation with respect to his place in the universe
and, more specifically, with respect to his relationship to his
God (in whatever form he conceives the Deity) has led to a
body of poetry that is as varied as the personalities involved
in the search. In ancient days the pastoral surroundings of life
led to imagery that reflected both the rural setting and a deep
sense of personal closeness to God, and in the Psalms there is
seldom any sense of struggle or uncertainty. In 1611 the King
James Authorized Version of the Psalms was set in a flowing
rhythmical prose that needed only to be spaced, as was later
done, in the form of free verse to emphasize the phrasing, the
parallelism, and the phonic recurrences to make them, in appearance as well as in quality, poems. The best of the rich
idiom of Elizabethan English went into the translation, as the
Twenty-third Psalm which follows will attest:

The Lord is my shepherd; I shall not want.
He maketh me to lie down in green pastures;
He leadeth me beside the still waters.
He restoreth my soul;
He leadeth me in the paths of righteousness for his name's sake.

Yea, though I walk through the valley of the shadow of death,
I will fear no evil: for thou art with me;
Thy rod and thy staff they comfort me.
Thou preparest a table before me in the presence of mine enemies:
Thou anointest my head with oil; my cup runneth over.
Surely goodness and mercy shall follow me all the days of my life,
And I will dwell in the house of the Lord forever.

It was at about this same date that John Donne was writing his *Holy Sonnets,* but the tone and attitude of the following poem from this sequence could scarcely have been farther removed than it is from the psalm just read. The cry for salvation is almost desperate; the poet seems to demand more than to pray. And if modern elements of idiom seem blended with the Elizabethan, this will not be surprising when it is pointed out that the influence of Donne on mid-twentieth-century writers has been extensive:

> Batter my heart, three-personed God, for you
> As yet but knock, breathe, shine, and seek to mend;
> That I may rise and stand, o'erthrow me; and bend
> Your force to break, blow, burn, and make me new.
> I, like an usurped town, to another due,
> Labor to admit you, but Oh, to no end.
> Reason, your viceroy in me, me should defend,
> But is captived, and proves weak or untrue.
> Yet dearly I love you, and would be loved fain,
> But am betrothed unto your enemy:
> Divorce me, untie or break that knot again;
> Take me to you, imprison me, for I
> Except you enthrall me, never shall be free,
> Nor ever chaste, except you ravish me.

With the rise of rationalism and scientific thought following the period of Donne, it was inevitable that attitudes about the nature of the Deity would change, and it was perhaps to reassure those who were swayed too strongly by the evidence of their senses that William Cowper in the late eighteenth century wrote his *Light Shining Out of Darkness,* a hymn that has long been a favorite wherever hymns are sung. The song quality will be immediately apparent, and the idiom, with its quiet assurance, will be recognized as appropriate to the subject and the time:

> God moves in a mysterious way,
>   His wonders to perform;
> He plants his footsteps in the sea,
>   And rides upon the storm.
>
> Deep in unfathomable mines
>   Of never-failing skill,
> He treasures up his bright designs,
>   And works his sovereign will.
>
> Ye fearful saints fresh courage take;
>   The clouds ye so much dread
> Are big with mercy, and shall break
>   In blessings on your head.
>
> Judge not the Lord by feeble sense,
>   But trust him for his grace;
> Behind a frowning providence
>   He hides a smiling face.
>
> His purposes will ripen fast,
>   Unfolding every hour:
> The bud may have a bitter taste,
>   But sweet will be the flower.
>
> Blind unbelief is sure to err,
>   And scan his work in vain;
> God is his own interpreter,
>   And he will make it plain.

But the advance of science, the break from authoritarianism in religion, and the increasing questioning and uncertainty were all leading to a weakening of the fibers of faith. By the mid-nineteenth century Tennyson felt it when he wrote in the *Proem* to *In Memoriam*:

> Let knowledge grow from more to more,
>   But more of reverence in us dwell;
>   That mind and soul, according well,
> May make one music as before . . .

and Matthew Arnold knew it and in his *Stanzas from the Grande Chartreuse* recorded how he felt as he stood before the monas-

tery of the Grande Chartreuse in Switzerland and thought of
the men who had made this withdrawal from life:

> Wandering between two worlds, one dead,
> The other powerless to be born,
> With nowhere yet to rest my head,
> Like these, on earth I wait forlorn.
> Their faith, my tears, the world deride—
> I come to shed them at their side.

But there was another voice in late nineteenth-century England
that chose to speak in a different accent—with the biting sharp-
ness of satire. In *The Latest Decalogue* Arthur Hugh Clough
rewrote the Ten Commandments in the changed terms of his
day, and suggested strongly that this was, indeed, the pattern
of conduct recognized by too many of his compatriots:

> Thou shalt have one God only; who
> Would be at the expense of two?
> No graven images may be
> Worshipped, except the currency.
> Swear not at all; for, for thy curse
> Thine enemy is none the worse.
> At church on Sunday to attend
> Will serve to keep the world thy friend.
> Honor thy parents; that is, all
> From whom advancement may befall.
> Thou shalt not kill; but need'st not strive
> Officiously to keep alive.
> Do not adultery commit;
> Advantage rarely comes of it.
> Thou shalt not steal; an empty feat,
> When it's so lucrative to cheat.
> Bear not false witness; let the lie
> Have time on its own wings to fly.
> Thou shalt not covet, but tradition
> Approves all forms of competition.

In our own period we have, to a degree at least, worked
through the difficulties that came so overwhelmingly to the
nineteenth century. But the struggle for identity continues, and
the third stanza of José Garcia Villa's *The Way My Ideas Think
Me* looks back to something of the spirit of John Donne's sonnet
above (p. 176). Villa has adopted for his opening what may

appear at first reading to be an obscure involvement in paradox, and in a very meaningful sense it is, for it reflects the state of mind from which the remainder of the poem comes. The other stanzas are not involved to the same degree, but they do demand of the reader careful attention to the implications of the described struggle and the imagery by which it is presented. It is a poem that is remarkably contemporary, not only in its idiom and free rhythms, but also in the way it voices the plight of modern man, who finds it so difficult to accept—yet so impossible to reject—some stable force in the universe:

> The way my ideas think me
> Is the way I unthink God.
> As in the name of heaven I make hell
> That is the way the Lord says me.
>
> And all is adventure and danger
> And I roll Him off cliffs and mountains
> But fast as I am to push Him off
> Fast am I to reach Him below.
>
> And it may be then His turn to push me off,
> I wait breathless for that terrible second:
> And if He push me not, I turn around in anger:
> "O art thou the God I would have!"
>
> Then He pushes me and I plunge down, down!
> And when He comes to help me up
> I put my arms around Him, saying, "Brother,
> Brother." . . . This is the way we are.

DEATH

The final group of poems is related to the foregoing, but centers in the moving subject of death; death, however, not in its general sense, but in the frequently more lyrically elegaic expression which involves the poets' reactions to individuals. In few areas of poetry is there liable to be more trite, sentimental writing, largely because, genuine as the emotions are, deep feeling is not matched by a corresponding mastery of craftsmanship. Restraint is, of course, the key to the successful poem of this kind, although it need not be as strictly observed as in the brief, impersonal but highly suggestive couplet epitaph from the early seventeenth century, Sir Henry Wotton's *Upon the Death of Sir Albert Morton's Wife*:

> He first deceased: she for a little tried
> To live without him, liked it not, and died.

Only slightly longer, but more characteristic of the type, is Robert Herrick's tenderly conceived *Upon Prue His Maid*:

> In this little urne is laid
> Prewdence Baldwin (once my maid)
> From whose happy spark here let
> Spring the purple violet.

We have already met with one expression of Wordsworth's restrained tribute to the dead Lucy (p. 32), but here, in *A Slumber Did My Spirit Seal*, although we still feel "the difference to me," there is a sense of the shock and disbelief attending his loss. Then, in the closing lines, he amplifies the theme and moves out from his personal grief into a more cosmic awareness of the return of the girl to the earth (but no longer a girl —now one with the inanimate things of nature). As might be expected, the same idiom, the same purposely limited range of imagery, and the same tone as in the companion piece prevail here. There is only a hint (but a suggestive one) in the closing lines of what a twentieth-century poet, schooled in the advances of science, might have made of the imagery:

> A slumber did my spirit seal;
> I had no human fears:
> She seemed a thing that could not feel
> The touch of earthly years.
>
> No motion has she now, no force;
> She neither hears nor sees;
> Rolled round in earth's diurnal course,
> With rocks, and stones, and trees.

As we move from the early into the late nineteenth century we find a poem that is at first apparently as concerned with the finality of death as is Wordsworth's. But in Christina Rossetti's *Rest* the initial shock is over and the sense of finality is welcomed, only to be tempered by the hopefulness of the closing lines. The changes in idiom and imagery from the earlier poems in this group will be evident, but it will be noted also that they have a nineteenth-century "flavor"—the "hath" and "holdeth," the personification, the conventional references to Paradise and Eternity—even though there is an individual touch in the context in which these things are presented:

> O Earth, lie heavily upon her eyes;
> Seal her sweet eyes weary of watching, Earth;
> Lie close around her; leave no room for mirth
> With its harsh laughter, nor for sound of sighs.
> She hath no questions, she hath no replies,
> Hushed in and curtained with a blessed dearth
> Of all that irked her from the hour of birth;
> With stillness that is almost Paradise.
> Darkness more clear than noonday holdeth her,
> Silence more musical than any song;
> Even her very heart has ceased to stir:
> Until the morning of Eternity
> Her rest shall not begin nor end, but be;
> And when she wakes she will not think it long.

The poems so far included have all spoken *about* rather than *to* the dead one. We should now consider two that offer the latter point of view. From the same period as the Rossetti poem, and correspondingly similar in its idiom, comes Coventry Patmore's *Departure*. Written in the rhythms and irregular riming of the Arnold type of free verse, it is a poem that may, for some readers, border too closely on the sentimental in its imagery. But it has two quite individual features that defend it from that charge and justify its inclusion here. First is the indirect approach made to the real concern of the poem; if it were not included in a grouping such as this the reader, for many lines, might well believe it to be merely the record of a temporary parting that had left the speaker disturbed by its nature. Only as the thought develops do we gradually realize that the one addressed is indeed dead. The second unusual quality, the tone of the poem, stems from the first—the speaker actually chides his loved one for having left him as she did. This might be quite natural if it were in fact but a brief separation, but it is a daring approach in the light of the real theme. And it is suc-

cessful because it is psychologically and imaginatively correct
—perhaps only in this way could the speaker control the real
depths of his feelings:

> It was not like your great and gracious ways!
> Do you, that have naught other to lament,
> Never, my Love, repent
> Of how, that July afternoon,
> You went,
> With sudden, unintelligible phrase,
> And frighten'd eye,
> Upon your journey of so many days,
> Without a single kiss, or a good-bye?
> I knew, indeed, that we were parting soon;
> And so we sate, within the low sun's rays,
> You whispering to me, for your voice was weak,
> Your harrowing praise.
> Well, it was well
> To hear you such things speak,
> And I could tell
> What made your eyes a growing gloom of love,
> As a warm South-wind sombers a March grove.
> And it was like your great and gracious ways
> To turn your talk on daily things, my Dear,
> Lifting the luminous, pathetic lash
> To let the laughter flash,
> Whilst I drew near,
> Because you spoke so low that I could scarcely hear.
> But all at once to leave me at the last,
> More at the wonder than the loss aghast,
> With huddled, unintelligible phrase,
> And frighten'd eye,
> And go your journey of all days
> With not one kiss, or a good-bye,
> And the only loveless look the look with which you pass'd:
> 'Twas all unlike your great and gracious ways.

As we turn to the final poem in this group, David Wagoner's
To My Friend Whose Parachute Did Not Open, we need no
date to tell us how far we have come from the others—and
not in years alone, but in the incisiveness with which the contemporary scene is made a part of the poem, in the laboratory
details of the second stanza that have been lifted out of their
ordinary role by a gifted imagination, in the empathy that

shares each moment of the fall (dramatically intensified in the last line) and finds the voice of poetry in each—and in the craftsmanship that gives the idiom and imagery their maximum effectiveness in a restrained iambic pentameter, yet enhances them with the shifting pattern of exact and approximate rime. It is a fine poem, a worthy touchstone for the distinctive characteristics of the modern voice of poetry, and a fitting close for our study of the lyric. For convenient study and comparison the first drafts and the final version of the poem face one another on the two pages which follow. As with the Keats transcription used as a frontispiece for this book, detailed comparison offers important insight into the working of the creative imagination as the artist in his role as craftsman moves toward final achievement.

David Wagoner's *To My Friend Whose Parachute Did Not Open*

The First Drafts

[Somebody wished you luck, or you did it yourself, or prayed,
Then [fell] stepped through the doorway and went down]

[Backwards first, head over heels in the wind
Propelled [in] like streamers from the wing to tail,
You tumbled]

[Backwards first, head over heels in the wind
Propelled like solid streamers from the wing,
Then down the slope of your trajectory,
As perfect as physics]

Thrown backwards first, head over heels in the wind
Like solid streamers from the wing to tail,
You counted whatever [seconds] [stutters] pulses came to mind—
The black and the bright—and at the third, you pulled—
And pulled again at the ring clenched in your hand.

[And d] Down the smooth slope of your trajectory,
Obeying physics[,] [intertia] like a chunk of hail,
Sixteen feet per second per second[,] hurled
Toward treetops, [houses] cows and clip-held gravity
From the unreasonable center of the world.

You saw the cords trail out from below your breast,
[And] Rise up and stand, tied to a piece of cloth
Whose edges wobbled [and] but would not spring wide
Nor [take] borrow a cup of air to [hold] stay you both.
And [O] that tall shimmer [told you y] whispered you were dead.

You had no thoughts. To hell with thinking then.
[This] That was no time for mucking with the past
Which had, like your whirling, weightless flesh, grown thin.
I [hope] know angelic wisdom leaped from your mouth,
But not in words, for words can be afraid.

You sang an anthem at the speed of sound
And held the unwilling air within your head
[And made] Making it fountain upward like a cowl.
And if you didn't, then you touched the ground.
And if you touched the ground, which of us died?

May 8, 1957

Interlinear insertions have been brought into the lines. Brackets indicate
deletions.

David Wagoner's *To My Friend Whose Parachute Did Not Open*

THE FINAL VERSION

Thrown backwards first, head over heels in the wind
Like solid streamers from the wing to tail,
You counted whatever pulses came to mind—
The black, the bright—and at the third, you pulled,
Pulled savagely at the ring clenched in your hand.

Down the smooth slope of your trajectory,
Obeying physics like a bauble of hail,
Thirty-two feet per second per second hurled
Toward treetops, cows, and crouching gravity
From the unreasonable center of the world.

You saw the cords trail out from behind your back,
Rise up and stand, tied to a piece of cloth
Whose edges wobbled, but would not spread wide
To borrow a cup of air and hold you both.
O that tall shimmer whispered you were dead.

You outraced thought. What good was thinking then?
Poor time—no time for plunging into luck
Which had, like your whirling, weightless flesh, grown thin.
I know angelic wisdom leaped from your mouth,
But not in words, for words can be afraid:

You sang a paean at the speed of sound,
Compressed miraculous air within your head
And made it fountain upward like a cowl.
And if you didn't, then you struck the ground.
And if you struck the ground, both of us died.

It will be clear from the foregoing excursion into the reaches of poetry (and many byways have been neglected in a necessarily limited selection of themes) that the serious reader will find an almost limitless world of subject matter, mood, form, idiom and style on which he can draw to the enrichment of his own creative personality. It is hoped that this and earlier chapters—made meaningful as they have been by the important body of poetry with which they have been enhanced—have played their part.

To this point there has been a necessary step-by-step fragmentation of material. The analysis and selection of details with which we have been involved must at last find their justification in the synthesis on which the total experience of reading poetry ultimately rests. We turn next to a more comprehensive demonstration of what may be involved in that final step.

≺ 8 ≻

The Poet and His Poem: A Reading of Six Sonnets from Five Centuries

WITH the types and tools of poetry discussed at such length as space has permitted, we now reach the point in our study when these details should be brought to bear more inclusively upon poems. Special attention will be given to what might be called the "pattern of imagery" which, supported by the devices for rhythm and sound, enables the poet to create mood, tone, and attitude; to communicate meaning; to achieve the rounded whole which forms the work of art. For this approach our discussion will be limited to lyrics whose comparative brevity makes extended explication feasible.[1]

We have already considered the significance of the sonnet as a lyric form. It offers, in small space, an opportunity for the employment of every device at the poet's command, and at the same time it presents a challenge for him to use these devices with the greatest economy and maximum effectiveness. In longer poems, also, the same poetic tools will be employed, but there they can be used with more leisure since there is ample opportunity for extended development of a theme. It should be noted, of course, that many sonnets will be written quite simply with respect to these devices; the six chosen for discussion here have been selected to acquaint the reader with as many as possible of the approaches with which he might be faced in reading and interpreting any poem. If, in the light

[1] The illustrative poems in the final section of the preceding chapter, as well as many throughout the book, have been chosen to include lyrics susceptible of such scrutiny, but it should be remarked that the reading techniques here demonstrated are not limited to lyrics. It is hoped that, with the aid of these explications, the reader will be guided, in poems of whatever genre, to work out for himself the nature of the effectiveness of figurative language in its poetic setting.

of what has gone before, he can follow these explications with understanding, and gain from them some hints as to how poetry should be read, this book will have served its purpose.

The six sonnets cover a span of five centuries[2] and offer insight as to the changing uses of a form that, despite its rigid limitations, has been susceptible of interesting variety both in subject matter and technique. As a lyric it will reflect the personalities of the different writers, the different themes to which they were attracted, and the changing techniques that mark not only the individuality of the writer but also in many instances the idiom of a period. The single genre permits these characteristics to be pointed up more sharply than would be possible otherwise.

The sonnets chosen are from the Elizabethan period, with Shakespeare as spokesman; the seventeenth century, through the voice of Milton; the early nineteenth century, with Keats as one of its finest artists in the sonnet form; the late nineteenth century, as Gerard Manley Hopkins introduces his sprung rhythm technique to the pattern and anticipates our own day with his influence; and two stages of contemporary development of the form: first in Robert Frost, with an idiom that represents a transition to the later and more pronounced extremes, both in form and content, of the second, in George Barker.

Shakespeare's *Sonnet XXX*

Our first poem for discussion will be an untitled sonnet, number XXX from the sequence of 154 by Shakespeare, a sequence on which we have already drawn for other illustrations (see pp. 79, 111, 168):

> When to the sessions of sweet silent thought
> I summon up remembrance of things past,
> I sigh the lack of many a thing I sought,
> And with old woes new wail my dear time's waste.
> Then can I drown an eye, unus'd to flow,
> For precious friends hid in death's dateless night,

[2] The reader should review the historical sketch, beginning on p. 96, in which the development of sonnet usage is seen in relation to that of other poetic structures. The present chapter will serve to amplify that outline.

And weep afresh love's long since cancell'd woe,
And moan th' expense of many a vanish'd sight.
Then can I grieve at grievances foregone,
And heavily from woe to woe tell o'er
The sad account of fore-bemoaned moan,
Which I new pay as if not paid before.
But if the while I think on thee, dear friend,
All losses are restor'd, and sorrows end.

Since this is a poem without a title, the reader is given no preliminary hint as to his possible approach to the subject. The fact that it is number thirty in a sequence suggests that a careful reading of the other sonnets might give a desirable perspective, even though sonnets (including this one) should be capable of being read as individual poems. In this instance one would learn from the others that this is one of 125 written to a young man, a friend of the poet, on various aspects of their friendship. Since friendship is the theme, it is impossible to tell at times whether a given poem is addressed to a man or woman, as in the present instance where the approach is quite general.

A preliminary reading offers no difficulty as to the main theme: Thinking about his many failures of personal accomplishment, and his many friends who have died, the poet becomes depressed, but is rescued from his dark mood by thoughts of a friend who is not dead but available for continuing friendship. If it is felt that such a statement falls short of the effect of the sonnet, let us consider what the poet has done that this summarizing sentence has not done.

1 When to the sessions of sweet silent thought
2 I summon up remembrance of things past . . .

Certain key words give us the clues with which we must start. "Sessions," for example, can have a number of connotations: the morning session of a school-class, a session of Congress, a court session, etc. With the word "summon" in line two it should be clear that the latter meaning is intended: As an individual is summoned before a court, so Shakespeare summons his memories before the court of his thoughts. But this is to be a gentle ("sweet") court, examining evidence rather than meting out punishment (although the latter follows as the painful memories come before him); it is a court of "sweet silent thought," and "remembrance of things past" is much more specific than simply "memories" would be.[3]

> 3 I sigh the lack of many a thing I sought,
> 4 And with old woes new wail my dear time's waste . . .

The first memory that comes before the poet is an unhappy one, and immediately strikes a negative note (as indeed do all the memories through line twelve, for a reason to be revealed only in the closing couplet). He has failed to attain (he "lacks") many things he sought, and for this he not only sighs but, in a stronger word, "wails." Line four suggests that the things that made up his "lack" were important enough to be considered "woes." This is a word that will carry its overtones into the next quatrain, but for the moment we know only that (1) because he is wailing anew for the woes of the past his precious time is wasted now ("waste" for "wasted" would not be unusual in Elizabethan poetry), or (2) as he remembers the old woes he wails anew for the precious time wasted then in seeking that which he did not attain. Either reading is possible, with a slight preference for the former since one does indeed waste his time regretting events of the past about which nothing can be done. Even before a court, where we go to recover losses, we frequently waste our time if recovery is outside the jurisdiction of the court.

> 5 Then can I drown an eye, unus'd to flow
> 6 For precious friends hid in death's dateless night . . .

From the general "many a thing" which has dominated the first quatrain the poet now specifies the principal cause of his grief: the death of his friends, indeed a cause for woe. The wailing is augmented by the tears which express it, but doubly so in the fact that these eyes, which are normally dry, are now "drowned" (a forceful metaphor) in what must be an uncontrollable flood of weeping.

At this point (line six) the court imagery returns and is

[3] To those who know Marcel Proust's *Remembrance of Things Past* the allusion and the appropriateness of this title for the English version will be evident.

strengthened throughout the remainder of the sonnet. Dates
are important in legal proceedings, for on them rests our hope
of evidence that may help us to recover our losses, but when
friends go into (become "hidden in") the night of death there
are no calendars by which to time actions, no light by which
to find them. So again the poet finds cause for weeping:

> 7 And weep afresh love's long since cancell'd woe,
> 8 And moan th' expense of many a vanish'd sight . . .

He now balances the "new wail" and "old woes" of line four
(and thus integrates this section of the poem) with "weep
afresh" and "long since cancell'd woe," the latter now centered
on the love for his friends which was canceled by death (as
a contract is canceled by a court). The mood is sustained in
the next lines with "moan," "grieve," "heavily . . . tell o'er,"
and again "moan" (lines eight through eleven). But these are
not merely repetitions, for each return is enriched by the context. In line eight, for example, he now moans the "expense"
(again a legal connotation attends this word), a payment for
something that has vanished. (The "many a thing I sought"
of line three is now particularized, since the "many a vanished
sight" will inevitably be associated with the friends who have
dominated lines four to eight).

> 9   Then can I grieve at grievances foregone,
> 10 And heavily from woe to woe tell o'er
> 11 The sad account of fore-bemoaned moan,
> 12 Which I new pay as if not paid before . . .

The progression of thought and imagery has now carried us
through the first two quatrains. The third quatrain now sum-
marizes and generalizes, recapitulating, but always with a difference to avoid mere repetition. Line nine indulges a play on
words (dear to the Elizabethans), "grieve at grievances," to
carry the basic idea forward. The "grievances foregone" are, of
course, the "old woes," but we go to court to have our grievances adjudicated. It is too late. Since no court can restore
the basis of his grievance (the "precious friends hid in death's
dateless night"), it is all past ("foregone") and, waste of time
or not, all he can do is grieve. But his grief now particularizes

its sources: "many a thing," "friends," and "many a vanished sight." Each separate item (or "woe") in the record ("account"; again a legal connotation is present) must be counted ("told") with a "heavy" heart, for it is a "sad account." Each item of it has already been bewailed ("fore-bemoaned moan," another play on words; note that *bemoaned* is pronounced as three syllables) or "paid before," but in spite of this, it must be paid anew. No court, no "session of sweet silent thought," can finally cancel the debt of the memory of lost friends. Only one thing can alleviate such losses: another friendship that is so rich it makes one forget, for the moment at least, what the past has taken. And this is the burden of the closing couplet:

> 13   But if the while I think on thee, dear friend,
> 14   All losses are restor'd, and sorrows end.

We see now that the three quatrains have presented as dark a picture as possible for a carefully planned reason. The highest compliment one can pay a friend is that association with him is so meaningful and vital that he does in fact compensate for the losses experienced when other friends have died. So Shakespeare, out of the depths of grief stirred by painful memories, has balanced twelve lines on the debit side of the ledger with two on the credit side that bring the account into balance and make further sorrow fruitless, for the losses are restored. The poem thus closes in key with the dominant image of courts and the transactions undertaken there, including the official auditing of accounts.

But in our final reckoning we do not read, nor do we analyze, this sonnet to find pleasure in the legal knowledge or terminology Shakespeare possessed. We read it because we find in it a compassion which we can share today—but for which we may not be able to find words—and because we realize as we read that the fabric of human experience is of one piece, each thread of which may throw any other into a fresh perspective. We are our own judges, to a point at least, and must weigh carefully the evidence from the past and the present that each of us summons up to his own "sessions of sweet silent thought."

Although we need Shakespeare as spokesman, we meet him on this common ground.

The richness of the imagery here discussed is, of course, made more effective by the devices for rhythm and sound employed by the poet.[4] With only two enjambement lines (lines one and ten), and only three medial pauses (in lines five, thirteen, and fourteen, all light), the principal rhythmical variety is obtained through the use of variant feet. Each quatrain, for example, opens with a trochee, emphasizing the unit of thought developed therein. Beyond this, a natural reading gives pyrrhics and spondees, with one anapest in line three and one in line eight, that alleviate what might otherwise be a too-regular iambic movement. The spondees are especially important in giving emphasis to key phrases or words (*sweet si*lent, *things past, time's waste, death's date*less, *love's long, new pay, not paid, All loss*es). In general, however, it can be said that the sonnet is written with rhythmical restraint, and the four-line segments of thought progress naturally to the counter-thought of the closing couplet.

Turning next to the poetic devices for sound, the rime, as would be expected, follows the English or Shakespearean pattern *ababcdcdefefgg*. It is used conservatively to unify the segments of thought as they develop through the quatrains and into the couplet. Single rimes are used throughout, and the exact type predominates, although at two points variety is given through the use of approximate sound (*past-waste* and *foregone-moan*). The overall result is that the reader moves forward with confidence and with a minimum of overt attention to the line ends, but with a sense of satisfaction as the phrases and sentences are brought to natural completion at the key rime points.

[4] Details relative to rhythm will depend on the text of a given poem. In the present instance there is no evidence that Shakespeare guided his sonnets through the press when they were published in 1609 (many of them had been written in the early 1590's), and the punctuation, frequently faulty, has been amended in different ways by later editors. But the variants are minor. Any reading will, of course, be valid for the chosen text only.

Equally significant with rime, and even more dependent on the basic rhythm for its effectiveness, is the manner in which alliteration and assonance have been used. We will select for illustration here instances of relative importance, together with representative minor occurrences, which link and emphasize key words and phrases. In this way the reader should gain some idea of how meaningfully the pattern of harmony is sustained, even within the limits of a definition (see p. 58) that was designed to subordinate the mere repetition of letters. A schematic representation of the key sounds may be helpful and is given opposite.

> 1   When to the sessions of sweet silent thought
> 2   I summon up remembrance of things past,
> 3   I sigh the lack of many a thing I sought . . .

If we consider first the major sounds as they relate to content (and, for this first analysis, we will separate alliteration and assonance for clearer distinction) we note that the opening three lines carry a dominant *s*, with "the *s*essions of *s*weet *s*ilent thought" picked up in "*s*ummon" of line two, while line three not only carries the *s* forward but in itself is balanced by the opening "*s*igh" and the closing "*s*ought" (a pattern of opening and closing sound that will be met with frequently). The *s* sounds are additionally intensified by the repetition and phrasing of "I summon," "I sigh," and "I sought" (while "I drown" will parallel the structure in line five). Secondary alliteration is found in the *th* of "*th*ought," "*th*ings," and "*th*ing."

The principal assonance in these lines rests in the short *e* of "Wh*e*n to the s*e*ssions," which carries to "rem*e*mbrance" in line two; and in the long *i* of "s*i*lent" plus the repeated "I" noted above. Minor assonance is found in "s*u*mmon *u*p," and in "p*a*st" and "l*a*ck."

> 4   And with old woes new wail my dear time's waste.
> 5   Then can I drown an eye, unus'd to flow,
> 6   For precious friends hid in death's dateless night,
> 7   And weep afresh love's long since cancell'd woe,
> 8   And moan th' expense of many a vanish'd sight . . .

Line four now moves away from the heavy *s* and introduces a strong *w* in "*w*ith," "*w*oes," "*w*ail" and "*w*aste" (which is

	ALLITERATION	ASSONANCE[*]
When to the sessions of sweet silent thought	s th	ĕ—ĭ—ī
I summon up remembrance of things past,	s — th m	ĕ—ĭ—ĭ—ŭ—ă
I sigh the lack of many a thing I sought,	s — th m	ī—ĭ—ĭ—ĭ—ă
And with old woes new wail my dear time's waste.	w d	
Then can I drown an eye, unus'd to flow,	d — f	ō—ĭ—ī—ā
For precious friends hid in death's dateless night,	d — f r — r	ō—ĭ—ĭ—ā
And weep afresh love's long since cancell'd woe,	w s — f r — r l	ĕ—ī—ĭ—ă
And moan th' expense of many a vanish'd sight—	s m	ĕ—ĕ—ĭ—ă—ā—ī
Then can I grieve at grievances foregone,	gr f — f	ĕ—ē—ĭ—ā—ā
And heavily from woe to woe tell o'er	w f — f t	ĕ—ĕ—ō—ĭ—ā—ā
The sad account of fore-bemoaned moan,	m — f	ĕ—ē—ō—ō
Which I new pay as if not paid before.	n p f wh	ĭ—ī—ā—ĭ—ā—ō
But if the while I think on thee, dear friend,	f wh	ĭ—ī—ĭ—ē—ē—ĭ
All losses are restor'd, and sorrows end.	s r	ĭ—ē—ō

* Minor variations in sound have been ignored here. Thus, in lines thirteen and fourteen, *thee* has a normal long *e* (ē), *dear* a hooked long *e* (ę̄), and *restored* a half-long *e* (ê). In an introductory study they are sufficiently close to be grouped together as long *e*, although their slight distinctions should be recognized.

probably strong enough to be recalled at line seven, balanced as
it is between an opening "*w*eep" and a final "*w*oe" [compare
line three], with the accompanying *l* and *s* resulting in memorable harmony). But even as the *w* of line four dominates, the
d of "*d*ear" is introduced and strengthened in "*d*rown" and
"*d*eath's *d*ateless" which follow; while *f* and *fr* enter at "*f*low/
For," "*fr*iends" and "a*fr*esh." (Note, in passing, the medial rime
effect of "*pre*cious" and "a*fr*esh.") The section then closes with
a nice balance between "*m*oan" and "*m*any."

Assonance is especially effective in this passage, for the long
o of "*o*ld w*o*es," picked up in "fl*o*w," becomes onomatopoetic
(suggestive of a cry of grief) in the repeated "woe" and "moan"
of lines seven, eight, ten and eleven. The long *a* of "w*ai*l" and
"w*a*ste" contributes to this effect, and the rhetorical balance
between "old" and "new" gives increased intensity to "woes"
and "wail." The repeated "I" of lines one to three is now echoed
at "*ti*me's," repeated at "*I*" and brought through "*eye*" down to
"ni*g*ht." Line five has "can" and "an," and line six "h*i*d *i*n," but
the next extended sound is the short *e* of "pr*e*cious fr*i*ends,"
"d*ea*th's," "a*fre*sh," "*e*xpense" and "m*a*ny." A minor, but interesting, echo is found from "*can*cell'd" to "*An*d" to "*van*ished," and
to "*can*" of line nine.

> 9   Then can I grieve at grievances foregone,
> 10 And heavily from woe to woe tell o'er
> 11 The sad account of fore-bemoaned moan,
> 12 Which I new pay as if not paid before . . .

After an effective parallelism ("Then can I," between lines
five and nine—the opening lines of the second and third quatrains) alliteration on *gr* and *g* picks up with "*gr*ieve at *gr*iev-
ances *f*oregone," while the *f* of the latter word introduces a
blend of alliteration, repetition and medial rime that runs from
"*fore*gone" to "*o'er*" to "*fore*-bemoaned" to "be*fore*" and to "re-
*store*d" (line fourteen). "Bemoaned moan" (anticipated by "woe
to woe") adds to this effect, as does "new pay" and "not paid,"
with which the third quatrain closes.

Assonance is found largely in the repetitions just discussed,

but also in the short *e* of "*heavily*" and "*tell*," which again links
the opening and close of the line.

13   But if the while I think on thee, dear friend,
14   All losses are restor'd, and sorrows end.

Line thirteen now picks up the *wh* of "*Which*" and the *f* of
"*before*" (line twelve) in "*while*" and "*friend*," and links "*while
I*" by the long *i*. The poem then closes with a nicely blended
sound in the circumflex *o* (note that *a* of "*All*" has this same
sound), *l, r,* and *s* of "*All losses* are *restored,* and *sorrows* end."

From the foregoing it will be apparent that much of the im-
pelling effect of this sonnet in an oral reading, and much of the
forcefulness with which the strikingly impressive imagery is
communicated stem from the poetic devices for rhythm and
sound. Whether or not we are as conscious of them as might
be suggested by the preceding analysis, they undergird and
illuminate the poem's main reason for being: the communication of meaning and mood. We have taken them out and put
them under the microscope of our analysis. In doing so, it is
hoped that when they are restored to their proper place and
proportion they will become once again but a part (although
a better appreciated part) of the total poetic experience.[5]

[5] For the skeptical reader who is now convinced that such an approach
is nothing but "letter-picking," and that to assume that a poet goes even
approximately to this length in working out his effects is sheer nonsense,
it should be admitted at once that the poet—even the poet who has
mastered the tools of his craft—does not sit down with a slide rule and
plot the details of his alliteration and assonance. But he will normally be
quite aware of their contribution to his work. Many of the repeated
sounds will, of course, come in accidentally (there are, it should be remembered, only twenty-six letters in the alphabet) or unconsciously, but
it is more than coincidence that as many as we have found are present
in positions of stress and proximity that give them their maximum effectiveness. Practice and a sensitive ear that recognizes the value of these
devices in supporting or strengthening the expression of ideas have made
the poet skillful in forming the effective phrase, and it will not be surprising if many of the key words are linked by sound. The secondary
sounds, to which the poet has probably given little attention, will then
be more evident than might otherwise be the case, through a sort of
verbal magnetism. We indulge in "letter-picking" only to focus attention
on a phenomenon that is too frequently neglected in a silent reading, or
not given full value in an oral interpretation. Let such an analysis be
kept in its proper perspective.

Milton's *On His Blindness*

For our second analysis we shall turn to the seventeenth century when, under Milton's pen, sonnet rhythms became more flexible, and their subject matter more varied. The poem is Milton's *On His Blindness*, a sonnet that involves *allusion*. Allusion may be direct, as in the reference to God as "my Maker," or indirect, as in the key image with which Milton works. In many ways the indirect approach is more suggestive: without identifying the thing to which allusion is made the poet can develop stronger overtones for his principal theme. The indirect allusion is also subtler and correspondingly more illuminating, but this assumes that the reader will recognize it; if he does not, the poem may (indeed should) be meaningful, but it will lack the added dimension to which it is susceptible.

> When I consider how my light is spent
> Ere half my days in this dark world and wide,
> And that one Talent which is death to hide
> Lodged with me useless, though my soul more bent
> To serve therewith my Maker, and present
> My true account, lest He returning chide;
> "Doth God exact day-labor, light denied?"
> I fondly ask. But Patience, to prevent
> That murmur, soon replies, "God doth not need
> Either man's work or his own gifts. Who best
> Bear his mild yoke, they serve him best. His state
> Is kingly: thousands at his bidding speed,
> And post o'er land and ocean without rest:
> They also serve who only stand and wait."

The title, *On His Blindness*, orients the reader immediately, although for full understanding of this sonnet it is necessary to know that Milton became blind in 1652 while serving as Latin Secretary to the Puritan Commonwealth. The question in his mind as he writes (about 1655) is how he can serve his cause without sight. (A second question would be how he could write the great works he had projected. *Paradise Lost* was not started until 1658.)

1 When I consider how my light is spent
2 Ere half my days in this dark world and wide . . .

Instead of saying directly that he has gone blind the poet introduces in the first line the image of spending, while the metaphor "light" suggests much more than "eyes" would have, and anticipates "dark" in the next line. This light has been "spent" before half his life is over. (He was forty-four in 1652, with little statistical chance of reaching the suggested eighty-eight, but the poetic exaggeration [hyperbole] points up the great hopes he had for his future, and his need of time to accomplish these hopes.) Being blind, he now feels himself in a "dark world and wide," an image that combines an expected and also a highly suggestive idea: the world is now literally dark for him, of course, but to one who cannot see, distance suddenly takes on a new meaning. Walk across the room with eyes open and it will be a short distance; repeat this with eyes closed and the distance will appear to have doubled or tripled. All of this psychological truth is packed into the one word "wide." Then follows the key allusion:

> 3 And that one Talent which is death to hide
> 4 Lodged with me useless . . .

The reader will probably first accept the word "Talent" in the modern sense: Milton had a talent for writing, but now questions his ability to use the talent because of blindness. The poem can be read with this interpretation, but if the word "spent" is kept in mind, and if the "hiding" of the talent, the "true account," and the fear of being "chided" (line six) are noted carefully, there may come to mind (as it would immediately for Milton's readers in an age that knew its Bible well) the Parable of the Talents in Matthew 25:14–30, in which a lord who was about to travel called his three servants together and gave one of them five talents (or coins), another two, and another one. The first two servants invested the money and had it ready with interest for an accounting on their lord's return; but the third "went and digged in the earth, and hid his lord's money." On the master's return the first two servants were highly commended for increasing their allotments, but the third was chided as a "wicked . . . slothful . . . unprofitable servant," and instructions were given that he be cast "into outer darkness."

The talent, then, is literally a coin, which picks up the spending image of the first line, and the coin becomes a metaphor for Milton's sight, now "hidden" and useless despite his wish to serve and return a "true account"[6] favorable to God:

> 4   though my soul more bent
> 5   To serve therewith my Maker, and present
> 6   My true account, lest He returning chide . . .

Thus he, like the servant in the parable, may be chided (indeed, he has already been cast into darkness) because his account will show no profit if the coin (his sight) cannot be put to use. But this is the statement of the negative side of the case, and Milton pauses to reconsider the situation.

> 7   "Doth God exact day-labor, light denied?"
> 8   I fondly ask . . .

The poet makes an interesting play on the words "day-labor" and "light denied," suggesting that under the circumstances his question would be a foolish ("fond") one. The word "light" introduces a purposeful ambiguity involving daylight and sight: there can be no day without light; how can there be service or labor without sight? But before the question (a defensive rationalization) can be extended, a personified Patience steps in to answer it:

> 8   But Patience, to prevent
> 9   That murmur, soon replies, "God doth not need
> 10 Either man's work or his own gifts . . .

Note that the early lines of the poem have reflected impatience; this impatience is now balanced by the wisdom of patience. Milton is told that God, unlike the lord of the parable, does not need man's work ("serve," "labor," and "work" link this image pattern together) or his own gifts. Although the pronoun is not capitalized here or below, "his" clearly refers to God and the gift of the talent. God is above these things and asks only a willing acceptance of that which He asks men to bear.

> 10   Who best
> 11 Bear his mild yoke, they serve him best . . .

[6] Compare Shakespeare's use of the same word, also in a commercial sense, in the sonnet just analyzed.

Now the burden, which had seemed so overwhelming earlier, is a "mild" yoke: the shift in attitude is evident and important. Milton, who had assumed that his work was indispensable, now realizes that the thousands who are not faced with a "dark world and wide" can carry out the will of God in their way:

11   His state
12   Is kingly: thousands at his bidding speed,
13   And post o'er land and ocean without rest . . .

Nor is their work undervalued. But God can be served also by man's spirit, by his willingness to say "Thy will, not mine, be done." And this leads to the closing line, frequently quoted but too often out of context:

14   They also serve who only stand and wait.

Turning now to the devices for rhythm and sound employed by the poet to enhance his poem, one is immediately aware of the greater variety in phrasing as compared to Shakespeare's sonnet. This is not alone the result of the present poem's being an Italian sonnet, although the octave-sestet structure of the Petrarchan pattern invites an arrangement of material different from the Shakespearean (see above, p. 79). Milton, it will be noted, goes even beyond the normal octave-sestet division and permits his eighth verse to run over into the ninth. He thus gains an overall integration of the fourteen lines. But he carries his freedom beyond this; indeed, the movement is suggestive of that described by him as desirable for blank verse (see p. 101), although here, of course, rime is employed, and one could scarcely seek, in a short poem, a better example of "the sense variously drawn out from one verse into another." There is, first, the long, sweeping development of lines one to six, in which, cutting across the rime scheme in its urgency, the poet suggests the impatience under which he is writing.[7] Then with shorter phrases he goes on to build up the arguments against his opening premise, gradually quieting down to the calmness

[7] As with Shakespeare's sonnet, details relative to rhythm will depend on the chosen text, of which there are several for this poem. The one used here seems best suited to relationship between form and content.

of acceptance and understanding of the last line. But even within the first six lines there is variety in phrasing, the first three with no medial pauses, the next three with light comma pauses to serve as a transition to the already noted strengthening of caesuras in the rest of the poem. These effects are enhanced by the run-on lines, eight out of the fourteen being of this type, and by the economical use of opening trochees (only at *Lodged with, Either,* and *Bear this*), with spondees reserved for a few key positions (*dark world, day labor, not need, man's work, own gifts, mild yoke, they serve,* and *They also*), and pyrrhics kept to a minimum.

Milton's use of rime is more subtle than that of Shakespeare in the poem considered, partly because he is using a more intricate sonnet form (the Petrarchan with its *abbaabbacdecde* scheme), and partly because his use of enjambement tends to subordinate the rime sounds and blend them into the total harmony of the poem. Moreover, all of the rimes are single exact, and thus call a minimum of attention to themselves, since the ear is most accustomed to accepting such combinations. The reader thus touches the rime sounds very lightly, and moves directly across to the following lines as the thought progresses; but he cannot ignore the rimes, for they represent the major note in oral echoes; they are the "solo voices" against the "accompaniment" of alliteration and assonance, and the extra emphasis found in the fact that they fall at line ends (even enjambement line ends) and are thus held in the ear while the eye must return to the beginning of the next line, gives them their distinction and their importance.

The integration established by rhythm and rime is furthered by alliteration and assonance. As with the Shakespeare selection, the schematic diagram on p. 203 identifies the more important instances, together with representative minor occurrences, in which key words and phrases are emphasized by these devices for sound. With our experience of the earlier poem, in which alliteration and assonance were separated for the analysis, it should be possible here to follow the progression of the blended sound.

1   When I consider how my light is spent
2   Ere half my days in this dark world and wide,
3   And that one Talent which is death to hide . . .

There is an interesting if complex pattern of sound in line one. The opening and close give us assonance on short *e* in "Wh*e*n" and "sp*e*nt" (which is made more prominent by the strong echo, suggestive of rime, of "*When*" and "*spent*"). But between these words is a triple alternation of sound in the order *h*, long *i*, *s—h*, long *i*, *s*, with an additional short *i* linking "consider" and "is" (*When I con*s*ider *h*ow *m*y *light *i*s *s*pent*). Intentional or not, or only partially so, this sets the tone for a sonnet rich in melody. There is a repetition of "my" (assonating with "w*i*de") in line two, where the *h* is also picked up with strong emphasis in "*h*alf," and in line three in "w*h*ich *i*s death to *h*ide." Line two also offers *d* and *w* in "My *d*ays in this *d*ark *w*orld and *w*ide," with a carry-over of *w* to "*o*ne" (remember that the *sound* determines the effect) and of *d* to "*d*eath" in the next line. In the meantime the short *i* has given a secondary emphasis at "*i*n th*i*s" and "wh*i*ch *i*s," while a stronger association is set up in the short *a* of "And th*a*t one T*a*lent."

4   Lodged with me useless, though my soul more bent
5   To serve therewith my Maker, and present
6   My true account, lest He returning chide . . .

Retention of the *l* from "*l*ight" in line one to "*L*odged" in line four is doubtful, although the initial placement of "Lodged" gives it an advantage. In any event there is linkage of the important "*L*odged" and "use*l*ess" in this line, as there is through the long *o* of "th*o*ugh my s*ou*l" and the *m* of the cumulative "*m*e" and "*m*y" leading to the significant "*M*aker." At the same time the cumulative effect of the long *i* in the repeated "m*y*" invites the ear to "ch*i*de" (which closes the line as "My" opened it), and to "l*i*ght den*i*ed" and "*I*." Also, the *s* of "my *s*oul more bent / To *s*erve" unifies that phrase, even as a subordinate harmony is added by the *er* of "s*er*ve" and "Mak*er*" (which possibly is retained until the strong *er* of "m*ur*mur," "Eith*er*," "w*or*k," and the repeated "s*er*ve" and "s*er*ve" below recall it). The short *e* of "pr*e*sent" is then picked up at "l*e*st," even as the *r* of the consonantal diphthongs in "*pr*esent" and "t*r*ue" is brought into the open at "*r*eturning," while the *t* of "*t*rue" is also echoed in "re*t*urning."

> 7 "Doth God exact day-labor, light denied?"
> 8 I fondly ask. But Patience, to prevent
> 9 That murmur, soon replies . . .

A *d* then unifies line seven, at "*D*oth," "*d*ay," and "*d*enied," even as long *a* links "*day-la*bor" (and carries to "*Pa*tience" in the next line), *l* bridges from "*l*abor" to "*l*ight," and short *a* carries from "ex*a*ct" to "*a*sk." The short *o* of "G*o*d" also carries to "f*o*ndly" in line eight, and to "G*o*d doth n*o*t" of line nine. The enjambement of line eight is made more significant as *p* carries across in "But *P*atience, to *p*revent / That murmur, soon re*p*lies."

> 9   "God doth not need
> 10 Either man's work or his own gifts. Who best
> 11 Bear his mild yoke, they serve him best . . .

The next phrase is developed between the *g* recurrence in "*G*od . . . *g*ifts," with, in between, the spondee of "*n*ot *n*eed" made even stronger by the repeated *n*, and with a long *e* in "n*ee*d / *E*ither" (dependent on pronunciation of the latter word); after which the *b* of "*b*est / *B*ear" and "*b*est" unifies lines ten and eleven.

> 11   they serve him best. His state
> 12 Is kingly: thousands at his bidding speed,
> 13 And post o'er land and ocean without rest . . .

At this point the *s* and *b* of "*s*erve him *b*est. His *s*tate" initiates a strong echo of the two sounds in "*b*idding *s*peed" of the next line. But "*sp*eed" in turn initiates alliteration with "*p*ost," even as the latter word introduces a long *o* that blends "p*o*st" with "*o*cean" and, in line fourteen, with "als*o*" and "*o*nly." Through lines ten to twelve the repetitions of "*his*" and "*him*" establish a minor *h* and short *i*, with the latter picked up more strongly in "k*i*ngly" and "b*i*dd*i*ng." Finally, in the last two lines "And," "land," "and," "stand," and "and" add their touch, while the striking last verse opens and closes on long *a*, holds the long

ASSONANCE | ALLITERATION

When I consider how my light is spent

Ere half my days in this dark world and wide,

And that one Talent which is death to hide

Lodged with me useless, though my soul more bent

To serve therewith my Maker, and present

My true account, lest He returning chide;

"Doth God exact day-labor, light denied?"

I fondly ask. But Patience, to prevent

That murmur, soon replies, "God doth not need

Either man's work or his own gifts. Who best

Bear his mild yoke, they serve him best. His state

Is kingly: thousands at his bidding speed,

And post o'er land and ocean without rest:

They also serve who only stand and wait."

o and short *a* from above, and balances the first and last half of the line with *s*:

14   They al*s*o *s*erve who only *s*tand and wait.

Keats's *On First Looking into Chapman's Homer*

Our third example takes us from the mid-seventeenth century into the early nineteenth. It will be recalled that, following the Elizabethan period and the first half of the seventeenth century which culminated in Milton, a retreat into formalism over-shadowed much of the earlier spontaneity and accomplishment, and a coldness of restraint limited most of the poetry for a hundred years to the stiffness of the closed heroic couplet. But a period as mechanical in its effects as was the age of Pope could not, of course, narrow the creative channel for long, and as the stream of literature followed the turn into the nineteenth century it once more found the broader sweep that marks the creative as opposed to the critical attitude.

The Romantic period was marked by imaginative spontaneity, by a spirit of enthusiasm, and by an eagerness to broaden out-looks and give free play to a sense of discovery, whether in philosophy, politics, or literature. Keats's *On First Looking into Chapman's Homer*, written in 1819, is illustrative of these qualities:

> Much have I travell'd in the realms of gold,
> And many goodly states and kingdoms seen;
> Round many western islands have I been
> Which bards in fealty to Apollo hold.
> Oft of one wide expanse had I been told
> That deep-brow'd Homer ruled as his demesne;
> Yet did I never breathe its pure serene
> Till I heard Chapman speak out loud and bold:
> Then felt I like some watcher of the skies
> When a new planet swims into his ken;
> Or like stout Cortez when with eagle eyes
> He star'd at the Pacific—and all his men
> Look'd at each other with a wild surmise—
> Silent, upon a peak in Darien.

The title of this poem offers an initial difficulty to the uninitiated reader. Who was Chapman? Most readers will have heard of Homer, and we have learned that the name here is probably a metonymy and stands for the poems written by Homer, hence a book. Chapman then might be a friend of Keats from whom he borrowed the *Iliad* or the *Odyssey*. But the context of the sonnet does not seem to bear this out, since Keats says "Till I heard Chapman speak out loud and bold." We will probably quickly assume that, since original Greek is not an easy language to learn, this Chapman must have been a translator of Homer, whose translation had a marked impact on Keats. A bit of research will lead us to George Chapman of the Elizabethan period, and we will hold the date in our minds until we determine whether or not it is of importance.

Keats opens his poem (see lines one to four above) with an image of travel, but it quickly becomes apparent that this is not to be taken literally, but as a metaphor for something else. Note that Keats never mentions reading, but the title has given us our clue, and since reading can lead to discovery in a very literal sense, the travel figure is appropriate to it. And we then learn something of where the poet has "travelled," for in six lines he gives us six synonyms that offer definite geographical pictures: realms, states, kingdoms, islands, expanse, and demesne. (The opening word of the poem, "Much," in its accented position, has set the tone for the scope of these images.)

But some of these terms are modified by adjectives, or *epithets*, which give us even more information of a poetic kind: they are realms "of gold"; they are "goodly" states and kingdoms; they are "western" islands; and one is a "wide" expanse. "Gold" and "goodly" indicate quality, and since we know that we must think imaginatively and in figurative terms, Keats is clearly suggesting that he has read "much" in literature of the best writers. "Round many western islands" would then indicate that he was handicapped as to range of reading, not being acquainted with the Greek tongue; and "wide" would supplement "goodly" to indicate the epic scope of the particular work under consideration.

Then we are told that these realms, kingdoms, etc., are held by "bards" (poets) in "fealty" (or faithfulness: a term from feudalism indicating relationship to an overlord) to Apollo (the god, or overlord, of poetry). This confirms our earlier supposition that the basic travel image must refer to reading. But the image from feudalism adds another dimension to the thought, and gives the reader a new association through which to enrich the developing pattern.

This poem, like Milton's, is an Italian sonnet (but of the divided octave-sestet type), and the second quatrain of the octave now concentrates on the translation of Homer, but still under the travel image that unifies the first eight lines:

5   Oft of one wide expanse had I been told
6   That deep-brow'd Homer ruled as his demesne;
7   Yet did I never breathe its pure serene
8   Till I heard Chapman speak out loud and bold . . .

In the sense perhaps that he has read inferior translations that have not spoken out "loud and bold" with the firsthand effect of the original, Keats says that he has been "told" of this "wide expanse" (a perfect image for the scope of Homer's epics which still holds to the geographical detail) which in his turn Homer "ruled as his demesne" in fealty to Apollo. Note that he is "deep-brow'd Homer," since the high forehead traditionally suggested the strength of mind and imagination that made the *Iliad* and *Odyssey* possible. Keats had been told of this expanse, but had not previously breathed its pure atmosphere ("serene": a bold word suggesting also calmness and strength).

It is possible, of course, to assume from the lines that Keats had not previously read Homer; that he had in fact merely been told about the poet. But the word "pure" and the next line suggest very strongly that he might have experienced an "impure" version of the epics, translated by someone who did not "speak out loud and bold." Whose translation might this be? The logical answer would be Alexander Pope, for his was the famous translation that Keats would have read at school. We have already met Pope and his closed, formal heroic couplets with their Neoclassic restraint; and his *Homer* has these limiting characteristics. Chapman, on the other hand, was of the Elizabethan period: vigorous, fresh, forceful, concrete. (Pope himself had described the Chapman translation as animated by "a daring fiery spirit.") All of these facts point to Keats's lines as meaning that suddenly he had found a translation that suggested what must have been the real feeling of the original: he had traveled to Homer's demesne and had discovered the true atmosphere of this wide expanse. Let us follow him in the experience.

From Keats's biography we learn that this sonnet was written after his friend Charles Cowden Clarke, who had borrowed a 1616 edition of Chapman's translation, had invited Keats to share the book. Keats was elated as they read, far into the night, what Clarke called "the famousest passages." Keats's reaction to one of these Clarke described as follows:

One scene I could not fail to introduce him to—the shipwreck of Ulysses, in the fifth book of the "Odysses" where Ulysses is cast up on the shores of Phæacia, and I had the reward of one of his delightful stares upon reading the following lines [lines 608–14 in Chapman]:

> Then forth he came, his both knees faltring, both
> His strong hands hanging downe, and all with froth
> His cheeks and nosthrils flowing, voice and breath
> Spent to all use; and downe he sunk to Death.
> *The sea had soakt his heart through*: all his vaines
> His toiles had rackt t' a labouring woman's paines.
> Dead wearie was he. . . .

The italics are Clarke's, as if to indicate the point at which he was rewarded with Keats's "delightful stare."

If these lines are compared with Pope's translation—general where Chapman is concrete, restricted in movement and idiom where Chapman moves with strength and vitality—light will be thrown on the spirit of the sonnet as a whole, and on what Keats meant by saying that he had "heard Chapman speak out loud and bold." Here is Pope's translation of the above passage (lines 580–87 in his version):

> That moment, fainting as he touch'd the shore,
> He dropp'd his sinewy arms: his knees no more
> Perform'd their office, or his weight upheld:
> His swoln heart heav'd; his bloated body swell'd;

From mouth and nose the briny torrent ran;
And lost in lassitude lay all the man,
Depriv'd of voice, of motion, and of breath,
The soul scarce waking in the arms of death.

The octave, then, has established the travel image, the sense
of discovery, and the land toward which these travels have
been leading. The sestet must now be used to clarify the effect
on Keats, and the spondaic *"Then felt* I" which opens it brings
into focus the personal significance of all that has gone before:

> 9   Then felt I like some watcher of the skies
> 10   When a new planet swims into his ken . . .

With a deft shift in his imagery of discovery we are now led
from land travel to astronomy, with the suggestion that this is
too large an experience to be limited to earth. A strong simile
likens the poet to one who discovers a new planet, and makes
striking use and placement of the word "swims"—an onomatopoetic word for which Keats's friend Leigh Hunt could find
only one epithet: "complete." The heavens are then balanced
by a return to earth and Cortez:

> 11   Or like stout Cortez when with eagle eyes
> 12   He star'd at the Pacific—and all his men
> 13   Look'd at each other with a wild surmise—
> 14   Silent, upon a peak in Darien.

Now the personal search of discovery with which the earlier
lines have dealt is projected outward, shared by Keats with
those other great voyagers who have literally "travell'd in the
realms of gold" and stood in awe before their new worlds. This
serves to round out and confirm the opening, and to stress the
common ground on which the alert mind in whatever field
finds its home.

Cortez, of course, is an error for Balboa in this context, but
only the literal-minded would fail to sense the imaginative cor-
rectness of the error. Keats had been reading about Cortez and
the name slipped in. It does not matter: the whole spirit of
breathless discovery is in these last four lines: the "eagle eyes"
of Cortez "staring" at the Pacific; his men looking at each other
with a "wild surmise" (such phrases are the mark of the great

poetic creator); and their silence as they stand looking from the peak in Darien.

If, to this pattern of imagery, we again add consideration of the principal devices for rhythm and sound, it will be apparent that much of the effective communication of the mood rests in these devices. Rhythmically, this might seem to be contradicted by the fact that the first ten verses are made up of two-line units of thought, without benefit of a single medial pause.[8] But one does not feel a couplet development because of the manner in which the phrasing overlaps the rime scheme through enjambement. In each instance (at *been, told,* and *serene*) where a rimed couplet might intrude, there is no punctuation. This gives a nice variety to these lines, one appropriate here even as the many strong caesuras were appropriate to Milton's quite different content. Such uniformity as does result from the two-line progression serves to make even more effective the remarkable quality of the last four lines, with their skillfully placed pauses. The strong caesuras after *Pacific* and *surmise* come upon us suddenly after the even tenor of the preceding verses and invite us to stop and "stare" with these men; and the separated *Silent,* coming as it does on an opening trochaic substitution, encourages us to pause in silence as we share this breathless moment of discovery. Keats himself once wrote:

I think poetry should surprise by a fine excess, and not by singularity; it should strike the reader as a wording of his own highest thoughts, and appear almost a remembrance.

Its touches should never be half-way, thereby making the reader breathless, instead of content. The rise, the progress, the setting of imagery should, like the sun, come natural to him, shine over him, and set soberly, although in magnificence, leaving him in the luxury of twilight.

One could hardly ask for a better description of the qualities of the rhythm and imagery of this sonnet than is given in Keats's words.

[8] The result, perhaps, of having composed the poem in part at least while walking home from Clarke's rooms in the early morning hours (the poem was sent to Clarke in a note later that same morning). When there is no paper and pen handy one tends to block out units of thought in this way.

Nor are the devices for sound insignificant in creating this effect. The rime scheme, like that of Milton's sonnet, is Petrarchan; but whereas Milton used a *cdecde* sestet, Keats follows the pattern *abbaabbacdcdcd*, which is more consistent with the rhythmical development discussed above. Again the rimes are all of the single exact type, as they were in Milton's use, unless we make *been* of line three approximate in sound through United States rather than British pronunciation. Unlike Milton, however, Keats follows the normal octave-sestet division of thought. The first quatrain introduces the general subject of travel, as we have seen, and closes firmly on the word *hold*. Then the second quatrain is linked to the first by *told*, even as the thought is linked in that it is an extension of the opening theme to the particular work under discussion, and the octave closes with the fourth occurrence of the unifying sound in *bold*. Appropriately, the sestet gives Keats's reaction to what has taken place, and this turn of thought is accompanied by the change in rime pattern; but the possible suggestion of a quatrain on *cdcd* is avoided by permitting an enjambement at *men*, which leads the reader directly into the closing *cd* and unifies the sestet, even as the octave had been unified through its *abbaabba*.

1 Much have I travell'd in the realms of gold,
2 And many goodly states and kingdoms seen;
3 Round many western islands have I been
4 Which bards in fealty to Apollo hold . . .

For the alliteration and assonance the diagram on p. 213 will again plot the principal sounds in the poem. In considering this harmony, we note that the *r* of "travell'd" and "realms," and the short *a* of "have" and "travell'd" (with a possible echo at the repeated "and" of line two) unify the first line. But in this line also the *m* of "Much" anticipates "many," and the *g* of "gold" anticipates "goodly," in line two. Line two then finds its own unity in the *s* of "states" and "seen." Line three picks up the *r* of line one in the strong initial position of "Round," and repeats the "many" of line two for parallelism; but this repetition is picked up with assonance in the sound of short *e* between "many" and "western." Then the prominent *b* of "been" leads over to "bards" in the following line and, if given the

British pronunciation to rime exactly with "seen," the long *e* of "*been*" anticipates "fealty." If given the conventional United States pronunciation (thus making it a rime approximate in sound) the short *i* of "*been*" anticipates "Wh*i*ch" and "*i*n." But the long *i* of "*i*slands" and "*I*," the *h* of "*h*ave," "W*h*ich," and "*h*old," the *w* of "*w*estern" and "*w*hich," the broad *a* of "b*a*rds," together with the same sound in the first *o* of "Ap*o*llo," and the *t* of "feal*t*y" and "*t*o" also contribute their bit to the texture; as, most effectively, does the long *o* of "Ap*o*ll*o*" and the vowel of "h*o*ld." So subtle is this blending of alliteration and assonance that it will be well to read the lines aloud with an ear attentive to the effects (but see also p. 195*n*):

> R*o*und m*a*ny *w*estern *i*slands *h*ave *I* *b*ee*n*
> *Wh*ich *b*ards *i*n fealty *t*o Ap*o*llo *h*old . . .

The richness of sound continues as we turn into the second quatrain of the poem, which is linked to the first both by the rime (the long *o* of which carries to "H*o*mer" in line six) and by the *p* of "A*p*ollo" and "ex*p*anse":

> 5 Oft of one wide expanse had I been told
> 6 That deep-brow'd Homer ruled as his demesne;
> 7 Yet did I never breathe its pure serene
> 8 Till I heard Chapman speak out loud and bold . . .

Line five has a strong alliterating spondee in "*o*ne *w*ide" (again, the sound and not the letter determines alliteration), with assonance contributing the long *i* of "w*i*de" and "*I*" and the short *a* of "exp*a*nse" and "h*a*d" (the latter picked up with "Th*a*t" of line six). Then the earlier *b* (lines three and four) is reintroduced in the repetition of "*b*een," and carries with impressive force through "*b*row'd," "*b*reathe," and "*b*old" to the conclusion of the octave. In some of these words, however, the *b* is part of a consonantal diphthong *br*, the *r* of which is echoed in "*r*uled" and "se*r*ene." Add to these sounds the supporting *d* of "*d*eep," "*d*emesne" and "*d*id," the *h* of "*H*omer," "*h*is" and "*h*eard," the short *i* of "h*i*s," "d*i*d," "*i*ts," and "T*i*ll," the short *e* of "Y*e*t" and "n*e*ver," the *p* of "*p*ure" and "s*p*eak," the short *a* of "Ch*a*pman" and "*a*nd," the expanding length of the long *e* which binds lines six, seven, and eight together, plus the

major note of *ou* in "*ou*t *lou*d"—and again only an oral reading
with careful attention can fully reveal the quality of Keats's use
of these devices.[9]

> 9   Then felt I like some watcher of the skies
> 10 When a new planet swims into his ken;
> 11 Or like stout Cortez when with eagle eyes
> 12 He star'd at the Pacific—and all his men
> 13 Look'd at each other with a wild surmise—
> 14 Silent, upon a peak in Darien.

The sestet continues with equally effective music. The opening *e* of "Th*e*n f*e*lt" is picked up (and "Then" is strongly echoed,
even to the point of medial rime) in "Wh*e*n," "k*e*n," "wh*e*n"
and "m*e*n." "Then f*e*lt" is immediately followed by the assonance of "*I* l*i*ke," and this in turn gives way to a most interesting blend of *s* and *w*, either independent or brought together
in the consonantal diphthong of the key word "*sw*ims." These
sounds, plus the related consonantal diphthong *st*, integrate the
entire sestet. They have been anticipated by "*s*erene" and "*s*peak"
of lines seven and eight, and appear now in the following
order: "*s*ome," "*w*atcher," "*s*kies," "*w*hen," "*sw*ims," "*st*out,"
"*w*hen," "*w*ith," "*st*ar'd," "Pacific," "*w*ith," "*w*ild," "*s*urmise,"
and "*S*ilent." Accompanying these sounds are others that add
their voices: "*l*ike" of line nine (anticipated by "*l*oud" of line
eight) comes through the diphthong of "p*l*anet" in line ten and
is repeated in line eleven, with a strong possibility that it will
carry to the firm initial position of "*L*ook'd" (with its associated
k) in line thirteen; lines eleven and twelve have the *h* of

[9] In the first draft of the sonnet, Keats wrote for line seven: "Yet could
I never judge what men could mean." He changed it, Clarke said, because the poet felt it was "bald and too simply wondering." By this he
probably meant that it was flat and non-suggestive, as it certainly was in
comparison to the splendid figure at which he finally arrived. The many
monosyllabic words, the unrewarding repetition of "could," the repetition
rather than effective rime of d*e*m*e*sne-m*e*an, and the weakness of the
short *e* assonance in n*e*v*e*r-t*e*ll-m*e*n as compared with the expansive reso-
nance (so in keeping with the imagery) of the long vowels in br*ea*the-
p*u*re-ser*e*ne—all point to the superiority of the revision as the mark of a
young poet destined for growth and greatness. The promise is confirmed
by Keats's change of the original *low-brow'd* to *deep-brow'd* and
wond'ring eyes to *eagle eyes*. (Compare Wordsworth's revision above,
pp. 32–36, as well as pp. 159*n*, 183*f*, and the frontispiece of this
book.)

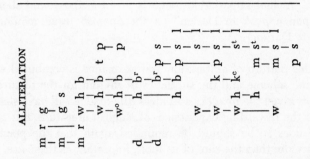

ALLITERATION   ASSONANCE

Much have I travell'd in the realms of gold,

And many goodly states and kingdoms seen;

Round many western islands have I been

Which bards in fealty to Apollo hold.

Oft of one wide expanse had I been told

That deep-brow'd Homer ruled as his demesne;

Yet did I never breathe its pure serene

Till I heard Chapman speak out loud and bold:

Then felt I like some watcher of the skies

When a new planet swims into his ken;

Or like stout Cortez when with eagle eyes

He star'd at the Pacific—and all his men

Look'd at each other with a wild surmise—

Silent, upon a peak in Darien.

"when," "he" and "his"; lines twelve and thirteen introduce the *m* of "men" and "surmise"; the *i* of "swims" in line ten is given a remarkable effect by the trochaic substitution of "into" (followed also by the *i* of "his"), which seems almost onomatopoetic in its force ("swims into"); the *k* of "ken" is picked up in the hard *c* of "Cortez," the long *e* of "eagle" in "He," "each," and "peak," a long *i* in three consecutive words, "wild surmise— / Silent." A final remarkable touch is given in the *p* and short *o* of "upon a peak in Darien" (if the Spanish pronunciation is given to Darien).

If this pattern of alliteration and assonance is combined with the rime scheme and the subtleties of rhythm for the texture of support given the imagery and ideas, the reader will have shared one of the rewarding experiences of English literature. But even as he does so he should be reminded again that the poem is finally more than the sum of its tools, important as these are.

Hopkins' *The Windhover*

In turning now to the late nineteenth century we will be concerned with a sonnet that will appear strangely different from those discussed above. The general shape will be familiar; and the rime scheme, despite a first-line oddity, follows the Petrarchan pattern to which we have become accustomed. But on beginning the reading we will ask what has become of the iambic pentameter that is supposed to represent the sonnet norm, and we will find ourselves threatened with an overwhelming wave of sound through which it may be difficult to distinguish the meaning that lies beneath.

The poem is Gerard Manley Hopkins' *The Windhover*, which carries a dedication, "To Christ Our Lord." The appropriateness of the latter is evident when we recall that the poet was a Jesuit priest. Mention of Hopkins' name should remind us also of the discussion of sprung rhythm above (p. 88), a form he introduced in the late nineteenth century, and one that was to exert an important influence in later decades. For, although Hopkins died in 1889 (*The Windhover* was written in 1877), his poems

were not published until 1918 when his friend and editor, the
Poet Laureate Robert Bridges, transcribed a number of the
manuscripts and saw the work through the press. A correspond-
ence between Bridges and Hopkins has preserved for us many of
Hopkins' ideas on his art, as well as his own interpretation of
what he intended sprung rhythm to accomplish. A brief glance
at these will prove helpful in reading the poem.

In the first place, Hopkins confirms an idea that has been
stressed several times in this book. When Bridges returned some
of Hopkins' poetry, noting that friends who read it had found
it most difficult, the poet guessed at once that the reading had
been a silent one, and he urged that all should "take breath
and read it with the ears, as I always wish to be read, and my
verse becomes all right." If it is reasonable to assert, as we have
done, that poetry is truly poetry only when it is read aloud,
then it is especially true of Hopkins in his sprung rhythm
verses; for, as we shall see, the devices for sound and rhythm
form a major part of their impact.

As to sprung rhythm itself, Hopkins pointed out that ordinary
rhythm (what he called "Running Rhythm") has a tendency to
become "same and tame" unless variety is worked in. Poetic
technique, as we have seen, is able to accomplish this admirably,
but—foot-patterns being what they are—only within restricted
limits. So Hopkins developed sprung rhythm (whose debt to
Old English rhythms he recognized), and described it as con-
sisting "in scanning by accents alone or stresses alone, so that
a foot may be one strong syllable or it may be many light and
one strong." Clearly, this is a long step in the direction of freedom from metrical regularity, but it is a disciplined freedom
in which "the feet are assumed to be equally long or strong and
their seeming inequality is made up by pause or stressing." So
in *The Windhover* or other of Hopkins' sonnets an oral reading
will *suggest* five accents to the line, even though the reader may
be tempted to stress more or fewer syllables than five. It is
clearly Hopkins' intent that some of the seemingly excessive
stresses be subordinated, that the seemingly diminished lines be
spaced out with pauses, but that none of them be forced into
a mechanical tempo.

Properly read, this apparent license gives a vitality and force to the poet's ideas and imagery that were to Hopkins "the nearest rhythm to the native and natural rhythm of speech." It is, however, the rhythm that appears when speech is marked by the urgency of excitement and emotional intensity. Sprung rhythm permits the poet's ideas to be conveyed in a rush of words when that is desirable in the light of the context, with one adjective treading on another's heel, so fast they follow, and with alliteration, assonance, and medial rime bursting like rockets from the lines—but, again like rockets, offering light as well as sound. At times this is accompanied by an omission of the niceties of grammatical construction that leaves us groping for meaning, or opens the way for divergent interpretations of the lines. It makes for exciting poetry and, although few writers have used the technique to the degree that Hopkins has in the following sonnet (Dylan Thomas frequently approaches it), his precedent has encouraged others since the nineteen twenties to use greater freedom in their rhythms, and to grant him the flattery of imitation of many of the devices he employed.

But let us now observe this theory as it is practiced in a poem that Hopkins himself called "the best thing I ever wrote"— *The Windhover*:

> I caught this morning morning's minion, king-
> dom of daylight's dauphin, dapple-dawn-drawn Falcon, in his
> riding
> Of the rolling level underneath him steady air, and striding
> High there, how he rung upon the rein of a wimpling wing
> In his ecstasy! then off, off forth on swing,
> As a skate's heel sweeps smooth on a bow-bend: the hurl and
> gliding
> Rebuffed the big wind. My heart in hiding
> Stirred for a bird,—the achieve of, the mastery of the thing!
>
> Brute beauty and valour and act, oh, air, pride, plume, here
> Buckle! AND the fire that breaks from thee then, a billion
> Times told lovelier, more dangerous, O my chevalier!
>
> No wonder of it: shéer plód makes plough down sillion
> Shine, and blue-bleak embers, ah my dear,
> Fall, gall themselves, and gash gold-vermilion.

In this instance the reader may or may not receive help from the title, since the word is largely limited to British usage. But it is suggestive of something that hovers on the wind, and this appears to be confirmed by the allusion to the falcon in line two. Reference to the dictionary (which may prove to be a frequent necessity in reading this poem) shows the windhover to be a small European kestrel, a bird about a foot long which frequently hovers for some time in the air, against the wind.

> 1 I caught this morning morning's minion . . .

The poem then—or at least its opening—is to be about a bird; but one is struck immediately by the characterization given this falcon, which Hopkins tells us he "caught." (It soon becomes clear that this is a figurative use of the word, as when we say "I caught him in a mistake," or "I caught his act at the theater.") Very simply, then, he saw a bird. But "caught" is stronger than "saw," and suggests that he seized it with his eyes and held it with the force of his feeling. And he did not "seize" merely a bird: the falcon becomes so meaningful to him that he conceives of it as a personality—it is the favorite ("minion") of the morning. "Minion" is associated with court relationships, and this idea is carried into the next line where the bird is further characterized as the prince ("dauphin") of the "kingdom of daylight" (i.e. of the morning):

> 1   king-
> 2 dom of daylight's dauphin, dapple-dawn-drawn Falcon . . .

Further description shows the morning to be a "dapple-dawn," and here the poet's excitement begins to come through in the speeded-up rhythm as he shortens the normal "dappled-dawn" and intensifies our natural tendency to elide the final *d* by eliminating it—as if, in his rush to get the moment into words before it passes, he has no time for formal grammar. "Dappled," of course, means parti-colored, and refers here probably to the scattered clouds catching the first light; and this dawn has either (1) attracted ("drawn") the falcon and brought it out of its resting place, or (2) the falcon seems pulled along ("drawn") by the movement of the clouds, or (3) as it hovers the bird seems to be sketched ("drawn") against the dappled sky as background. This is one of the ambiguities that occur so frequently in Hopkins' work, enriching the content with multiple suggestion, but also challenging the reader in his interpretation. Other words of this kind, to be noted below, and the resulting differences of opinion as to their true meaning in this context, have led Elizabeth Drew to declare that the present sonnet "must be one of the most argued-about poems in the English language."

2   in his riding
3   Of the rolling level underneath him steady air, and striding
4   High there, how he rung upon the rein of a wimpling wing
5   In his ecstasy! . . .

The description of the bird, with its suggestion of nobility, now gives way to a delineation of the falcon's movement, and again the lines are charged with Hopkins' excitement as he responds to what is taking place before him. At first, as the bird hovers, it is quite literally "riding" the wind (note the appropriateness of "riding" with "dauphin"), but with such mastery that it is not thrown about by the "rolling" motion (we learn below that it is a "big" wind); rather, in the brilliant paradox of "rolling level underneath him" the bird makes the air seem flat and steady beneath it. And then it flies! Small as it is against the broad sky, it seems to "stride" upward as it spirals ("rung" means "spiraled in flight") in a circle controlled by wings that guide its "ecstatic" flight. "Wimpling wing" is a bold phrase, but we should not be surprised by verbal boldness in a writer who exhibits originality so fully in every other phase of his craft. A wimple is a head covering, worn by women in the middle ages (and still used by some nuns), fashioned by winding a cloth over the head and around the neck and chin, turning it as they did so and permitting it to ripple as the folds fell into place. A "wimpling wing" then is a wing that ripples and turns or folds in flight.

5   then off, off forth on swing,
6   As a skate's heel sweeps smooth on a bow-bend . . .

But now the controlled spiral gives way to a freer movement as the falcon "swings" into the wind in a "sweep" that Hopkins likens to the action of an ice skater as he "smoothly" accomplishes his turn, controlled by the "heel" of his skate, and makes his "bow-bend" (probably the familiar "figure eight" which looks like a tied bow).

6   the hurl and gliding
7   Rebuffed the big wind . . .

The two motions of the bird are then keyed by two words: "hurl" and "gliding." Whether by "hurling" itself (compare "striding" of line three and "off forth on swing" of line five) into the wind, or by moving gracefully as it "glides" with the wind (compare "riding" of line two and "rung upon the rein" of line four) the falcon is the master: the attempt of the "big wind" to overcome it has been checked or turned aside ("rebuffed"). "Rebuffed" is again a bold word, one sense of which, although rare, is to "blow back." If Hopkins was aware of this meaning it is particularly effective in its relationship to the wind; but even the more usual connotation of "rebuff" as "snub" would carry interesting overtones for the principal meaning.

7   My heart in hiding
8   Stirred for a bird,—the achieve of, the mastery of the thing! . . .

The poet then tells us that, as he watched, his heart was in hiding, but was moved deeply ("stirred") by the achievement and mastery that had been demonstrated before him. Again (see line two), the shortening of "achievement" to "achieve" gives us the feeling of excitement as Hopkins gropes for words to describe the experience—as much as to say: "The achieve . . . no, no—more than the achievement—the *mastery* of the thing —that's what I'm trying to say."

As to the "heart in hiding," note that there would be no reason for him to hide physically—he is too far from the falcon to make that necessary. It is rather that, either (1) in comparison with the free flight and unfettered scope of the bird his heart is in effect hidden from such activity (perhaps he is thinking of his position as a priest), but is moved by it; or (2) —and this seems more meaningful in the light of the sestet— his deepest feelings, emotions, and insights ("heart") are hidden beneath the surface of his sense responses, which, in their turn,

had been excitedly responding only to the surface beauty of
the falcon and the scene in which it played its part. With the
stirring of his heart, however, all that follows in the sestet
becomes possible; without it there would be no material for
the sestet except more details of the same order as those in the
octave.

    9   Brute beauty and valour and act, oh, air, pride, plume, here
   10   Buckle! . . .

As the sestet opens there is an important shift to the present
tense which suggests that, because of the stirring of his heart,
what took place before suddenly comes home to him with fresh
awareness of its true significance. We again get a rush of words
as the poet tries to capture the qualities that made the details
of the octave possible. Hopkins has, in fact, been seeking what
he called "inscape"—the discernment of the inner quality of
the subject of his observation (as a painter in a *landscape*
might seek the outer quality). But in the excitement of the
action he had scarcely been aware of the search. Now he draws
closer to its real meaning. The first manifestation of this inner
quality was natural or material beauty ("Brute beauty"); then
valor (a word appropriate to the princely "dauphin" above and
the "chevalier" below); then action, so brilliantly particularized
in the octave; then (introduced by the spontaneous exclamation
"oh") "air," "pride," and "plume." "Air" offers another ambiguity. It can be taken as the atmosphere through which the
bird has been flying, but its neighboring word "pride" offers a
more attractive alternative, suggesting that the "air" of the bird
in its proud mastery of the dawn wind is rather its manner or
appearance (as we say, "He has a proud air about him"). This
would fit better with "plume" also, since the latter not only de-
notes the plumage of the bird, but also connotes the headdress
of both dauphin and chevalier; and it is reminiscent of the
spirit of knighthood and chivalry that has colored other passages
of the poem. Whichever reading is taken for "air," all of these
qualities, representative as they are of the details of the first
eight lines, "here / Buckle!" And we are suddenly faced with
the two most controversial words in the poem.

The difficulty lies in the possibility of reading "here" in two related ways, and in reading "buckle" in two opposite ways. "Here" may refer either to place or time. If the former, the logical reference would be to the poet's heart which has "stirred for a bird." If the latter, the meaning would be "now," at this point in his experience.[10] "Buckle," in its turn, can mean either "join together," "grapple," "struggle," or, conversely, "collapse" or "fall apart" (as when a bridge "buckles" under too much weight).

> 10   Buckle! AND the fire that breaks from thee then, a billion
> 11   Times told lovelier, more dangerous, O my chevalier! . . .

These possibilities lead, with the remainder of the first tercet, to two principal alternative readings, the first as follows: The appearance, action, spirit, and environment of the falcon suddenly come together ("buckle" as "join") for the poet in a heart that has been out of touch with ("hidden" from) such things; AND (the capitals are important for emphasis) as the combined

[10] The phrase "here / Buckle!" has also been taken as an imperative: "Let these things buckle in this place or at this time." There seems no good reason for assuming the imperative mood, but as paraphrased in the preceding sentence it would not affect the essentials of either of the readings offered below. However, a more serious circumstance arises if, as has in effect been done, the imperative is paraphrased: "Let these things buckle in my heart and the fire that will break from *it* (my heart) will be a billion times told lovelier than the flashing beauty of the falcon, because mine will be a spiritual rather than a physical manifestation."

The objection to this interpretation of the imperative lies in the fact that with it the final tercet becomes an anticlimax. The plough and the embers are of the physical order of the bird, not of the spiritual order of the heart. There is no great "wonder" that these comparable things should reveal an inner consistency despite their surface differences. But if the progression from bird to plough to embers is suddenly interrupted by a tangential introduction of a climactic spiritual experience in which the heart becomes the subject, rather than the respondent to the subject, the unity of the poem is threatened if not destroyed.

If, on the other hand, the falcon is made the subject of the first eleven lines of the poem, with consideration moving from its outward beauty to its inner revelation as seized by the heart rather than the senses of the poet, the contrast of the closing tercet finds its maximum impact: the "moral," that one should not be deceived by outward show in a world that is compact of a beauty much deeper than the physical, is given its major statement.

All of which is not to deny any reader his right to read the poem as an *analogy* to a human experience, which is quite different from ascribing to the poet that with which the poem is invested by the reader.

elements that he has observed strike him suddenly and fully when the union has been effected ("then"), it is as though the whole becomes greater than the sum of its parts, and the flashing of the bird in the sunlit dawn is intensified to the point of "breaking" forth (compare "gash" below) into flaming beauty ("fire": compare "embers" below), many times (note the hyperbole of "a billion") "lovelier" than he at first realized, and correspondingly "more dangerous" to a heart that might wish to remain hidden and untempted by such physical beauty. Consistent with the "dauphin" and the "plume" images above, the bird then becomes a knight addressed by the poet in the exclamatory "O my chevalier!"

The second, and preferable, possibility takes "buckle" in the sense of "collapse": The physical beauty the poet has been observing suddenly collapses at the moment when he has seized it most fully with his senses. The collapse, let it be noted, follows immediately on the "stirring" of a heart that, as has been suggested above, was "hidden" beneath the surface response of his senses. This stirring has had a seismic effect: it has shaken open or cut through (compare "gash" below) the mass of physical beauty, AND (the capitals imply that *this* is the important thing) as the mass "then" buckles, the fire of the spiritual beauty within "breaks from" it ("from thee": the falcon as the epitome of physical beauty in form and action), just as a fire within a building breaks out when the walls buckle under the force of the inner flame. But this is no physical fire: it is a light, an insight revealing the significance of an overwhelming spiritual beauty that can be fully seen only when the physical has split open to reveal it. And this revelation is incomparably ("a billion /Times") more "lovely" than is the merely exciting beauty of the physical scene before him. It is an inner, refined beauty revealed *through* the gross, material outer beauty (the "Brute beauty"), and it involves a correspondingly "more dangerous" experience since a greater risk must be assumed in penetrating to the mystery of the universe as reflected in its external manifestations: the spiritual realization always involves greater hazards for the individual soul than does the physical. Hopkins then closes the tercet with his final gesture to the falcon that has made the realization possible, his "chevalier."[11]

12 No wonder of it: sheer plod makes plough down sillion
13 Shine, and blue-bleak embers, ah my dear,
14 Fall, gall themselves, and gash gold-vermilion.

The final lines of the poem then extend the thought and give it an unexpected turn. Actually, he says, the wonderful thing he has been describing is not so surprising or wonderful, since even the most uninspired or unrelieved plodding[12] (about as far as it is possible to get from the sweeping flight of the bird) down the length of a furrow[13] makes the plough shine and flash its fire as it is polished by the earth[14]; and superficially unattractive embers, blue in color and bleak in appearance (with a suggestion of drabness in "blue-bleak") may fall, rub against something ("gall themselves") and in breaking open ("gash") expose the red-gold fire at their heart. Or, to put it simply, not only the exciting, awe-inspiring manifestation of nature, but also the meanest, least promising thing is potentially a shining revelation. The suggestion is not unlike that of Shelley in lines from *Epipsychidion*:

> The spirit of the worm beneath the sod
> In love and worship blends itself with God.

The sonnet thus balances the description of a superficially ecstatic experience with the inner response to its deeper significance, and confirms the reality of the latter by drawing par-

[11] With this tercet compare Shelley's *Hymn to Intellectual Beauty* (p. 20) for a similar emotional response when, through the spring beauty of physical nature, "Sudden, thy shadow fell on me; / I shrieked, and clasped my hands in ecstasy!"
[12] "sheer plod": note again the abbreviated word, as in "achieve" (line eight).
[13] English has no "sillion." Compare French "sillon" (a furrow) or the earlier English "selion" (a strip of land dividing an open field).
[14] Grammar would appear to dictate this reading here, but the intent may be, as Elisabeth Schneider suggested, that the furrow itself is made to shine by the motion of the plough, since Hopkins has a journal entry: "the near hill glistening with very bright newly turned sods." Perhaps "shine" applies to both plough and furrow, the latter being gashed as is the ember below.

allels with activities that are seemingly anything but ecstatic or significant.

But have we gone far enough in thus interpreting the poem? Have we overlooked the dedication, "To Christ Our Lord," and its possible bearing on some of the lines? Have we taken adequate account of Hopkins' role as a Jesuit priest? Let us admit at once that the above reading has been kept as conservative as possible in these matters simply because others have gone to unreasonable and unnecessarily subtle lengths to find meanings that are as "hidden" (but in a more literal sense) as was the heart of the poet, if they are present at all.[15]

Certainly it is legitimate, in the light of Hopkins' other work, to suggest that the beauty of the falcon, like the beauty of all nature, praises God, even as does the shining plough as it meets the earth, or the flashing beauty of an apparently bleak ember when its inner quality is revealed. But to suggest, as has been done, that "O my chevalier" and "ah my dear" refer to Christ, and that "gash gold-vermilion" is an allusion to the crucifixion, is, to be charitable, at least questionable, and such interpretations have surely gone beyond the evidence of the poem. They have rested too heavily on the dedication "To Christ Our Lord" *of a poem to the windhover.* The dedication is potentially misleading, it is true, but it should be remembered that Hopkins considered this sonnet "the finest thing I ever wrote"—an eminently sufficient reason for an inscription such as this from a Jesuit priest. And, as another Jesuit priest, W. A. M. Peters, S.J., has pointed out: "Hopkins did not dedicate this poem to Christ until some six years after he had written it!"

A great deal has already been said in these pages about the rhythmical effects of Hopkins' sonnet. It remains here only to point out some of the details of the application of sprung rhythm as the poem develops. The first line, for example, is actually metrical in its iambic pentameter regularity, although the reader will be struck by the devices for sound and by the

[15] See some of the items in the suggested readings at the end of this book.

unexpected division of "kingdom" at the line end. This metrical regularity sets the five-stress pattern expected of a sonnet, and the mind attempts to bring each following verse into agreement with it; although in line two, toward which we are moved quickly by the division of "king/dom," we find, not the expected ten syllables, but sixteen. By sprung rhythm, however, the five-stress agreement can be maintained. Hopkins indicated markings for the poem (although they have largely been ignored when the poem has been printed) and in the present discussion these markings, as identified by W. H. Gardner from a collation of the manuscripts, have been used.[16] Line two is as follows:

dom of daylight's dauphin, dapple-dawn-drawn Falcon, in his riding

The line is thus hurried, it is true, and the feeling of speed is increased by the alliteration; but most of the octave is "hurried" in this sense, because the subject calls for it, and this line anticipates the mood of excitement that results. The third line, also of sixteen syllables, offers something of the same effect, while line four returns to a more regular, but still rapid, movement with three conventional anapests:

Of the rolling level underneath him steady air, and striding
High there, how he rung upon the rein of a wimpling wing . . .

This basically metrical fourth line leads directly into line five, which returns to a dominantly iambic pentameter movement, offering a desirable contrast to the preceding lines and to the fifteen syllables of line six:

In his ecstasy! then off, off forth on swing . . .

With the sprung rhythm principle as guide, the entire sonnet then falls into the accented pattern indicated on the accompanying schematized presentation for rhythm and sound (see below, p. 231). But line nine should be noted in passing, since it presents a unique problem with its six nouns. The indicated marking brings it into the five-stress pattern:

Brute beauty and valour and act, oh, air, pride, plume, here . . .

[16] W. H. Gardner. *Gerard Manley Hopkins*, I, 99.

The poet has started his listing without haste ("and" . . . "and"), but suddenly, after the exclamatory "oh," he drops the connectives and rushes toward the phrase "here/Buckle!" with what is, in effect, *air-pride-plume* as a triplet resting in a single accent. Admittedly, although the reading gives adherence to a five-accent line, individual readers (in the light of the dominant irregularity of so many lines, combined with a pattern of alliteration and assonance that divides the reader's attention between rhythm and sound) might find a more natural emphasis in a reading that gave six stresses to the six nouns, or even a seventh to *here*. The defense of Hopkins' scansion is to be found in the application of another of the poet's rhythmical principles to which we should turn.

It will be noted that six lines in the octave, and three of those in the sestet, are enjambement lines. The effect normally gained by the run-on, however, is magnified greatly in sprung rhythm, and was consciously exploited by Hopkins (compare Marianne Moore's *Poetry*, p. 7, for similar enjambement freedom). He pointed out that it was natural for sprung rhythm lines to be "*rove over,* that is for the scanning of each line immediately to take up that of the one before, . . . and in fact the scanning runs on without break from the beginning, say, of a stanza to the end and all the stanza is one long strain, though written in lines asunder." If for "stanza" we substitute "octave" and "tercets" (of the sestet) the poem under discussion, with the added inducement to run-on given by the many feminine endings, is a perfect example of this principle. It accounts for the division of *king / dom*; for an onomatopoetic effect in the feminine rhythm of "in his riding / Of the rolling level underneath him"; and for what, in an oral reading, becomes an essentially falling rhythm sought by the poet.[17] With it,

---

[17] Perhaps Hopkins' admonition should be repeated here: "Take breath and read it with the ears, as I always wish to be read, and my verse becomes all right." As to the falling rhythm, the poet noted that in sprung rhythm feet the stress "falls on the only syllable, if there is only one, or, if there are more, . . . on the first, and so gives rise to four sorts of feet, a monosyllable and the so called accentual Trochee, Dactyl, and the First Paeon." The first paeon is / x x x. For Hopkins' full statement on sprung rhythm see the reading list given at the end of this book.

also, the necessity for pedantic stress-counting can be subordinated to an awareness of the vigor, freshness, and stimulation to be found in verse of this scope.

Looking at the larger rhythmical effects, we see that the long, sweeping first statement, varied only by light comma pauses, carries down to *ecstasy!* in line five, where it hesitates only long enough to change direction and carry the bird to its final rebuff of the wind in line seven. Then comes a short personal note as the new sentence divides the line and carries into the next verse, but it is a momentary digression only, and the bird once more dominates as it returns in full mastery to close the octave.

The sestet then divides into two tercets, the rhythms of the first reflecting the excitement of the new discovery the poet has made. But one discovery leads to another, and while a quieter statement might be expected for the contrast of the second tercet, the rhythm is actually only slightly less forceful than that of the first; for it must hold the mood of what has gone before and support the true, if less exciting, miracle: the realization that humble things share fully the wonder of being.

To unify this sweeping expression of the poet's experience there is a rime scheme that offers some interesting differences from those we have met earlier. There is no surprise in the conventional *abbaabbacdcdcd* pattern, and the integrated octave (without division into two quatrains) is reminiscent of Milton's *On His Blindness*, discussed above, although Hopkins, unlike Milton, does not carry the octave into the sestet by enjambement. But in the present sonnet the rime sounds of the octave all involve an *ing*, alternating between the single exact rime of *king-wing-swing-thing* and the double exact rime of *riding-striding-gliding-hiding*. It should be noted that these are *different* rime sounds, but the overlapping repetition of *ing* serves to stabilize the octave as it bears the pressure of both sprung rhythm and an intensified alliteration and assonance. Assisting in this, also, is the format in which the poem is presented. The indention of lines with corresponding rime sounds guides the ear as well as the eye, and leads the reader forward through the units of thought.[18]

The sestet, too, offers an interesting difference from many sonnets that employ the *cdcdcd* pattern and that develop the thought in two-line segments corresponding to the progression of the sounds; for Hopkins, by playing off two separated tercets against this scheme, gives an excellent example of variety within uniformity. The first tercet, *cdc*, offers a complete thought, as does the second, *dcd*. But there is a close relationship, as we have seen, between the ideas of the two parts, and this likeness-with-a-difference in idea is balanced by the likeness-with-a-difference in the rime sounds, with something of a contrapuntal effect in the interplay. Moreover, an interesting parallel to the octave is found in the fact that the sestet uses the same rimer' types employed above: single exact in *here-chevalier-dear*, and double exact in *billion-sillion-vermilion*.

The end rimes are also given support throughout the sonnet in Hopkins' use of repetition and medial rime. The *ing* endings which we have seen in such an important role in the octave are anticipated by the repetition of "morn*ing* morn*ing*'s" in line one, followed almost immediately by "k*ing*-," and extended (combined with alliteration) in "rid*ing* / Of the roll*ing*." Then comes the expected rime, "strid*ing*," but the *ing* is intensified in line four by "wimpl*ing* w*ing*," again strengthened by alliteration. These medial repetitions of *ing* increase the general impact of the poem's sound, but they are supplemented by normal medial rimes at *dawn-drawn* in line two; *air-there* between lines three and four; *Stirred-bird* in line eight; *sheer* (as an intermediate rime) between the normal pair of end-rimes, *chevalier-dear* in lines eleven and thirteen; and *Fall-gall* in the last line.

One might expect that this concentration of rime sound would

[18] Sonnets are sometimes printed flush in solid blocks of fourteen lines (or with the closing couplet of the Shakespearean pattern indented) as in other examples in this book. Or they may be spaced by quatrains and closing couplet for the English pattern, by octave and sestet for the Italian. Sometimes indentions are given as guides to the rime scheme, sometimes not. Frequently these variations in printing are determined by editorial judgment, but when, as in the present instance, the clearest evidence of relationship between form and content is important, it is well to make the indicated divisions and indentions.

serve the poet's purpose, with, possibly, minimal alliteration
and assonance for harmony. But such is not the case. Indeed,
so richly textured is the poem in the use of these devices that
one must conclude that they have been carried about as far as
is possible in a serious poem. The risk in a use as extensive as
this is great, since the reader may be tempted merely to let
the sound play across his consciousness like music, with little
concern for the ideas that may be present. And the risk is
doubly great when the verbal ambiguities we have encountered
add their weight to the normal difficulties of interpretation.
But once the reader has accustomed himself to this music he
will realize that here is no idle toying with sound, but a carefully controlled support for the facets of emotion that break
through the words and the lines. This will be clear if some of
these effects are explored.

The alliteration is so prominent that no good purpose can
be served by tracing it as closely as has been done in the other
poems of this chapter. (The diagram on p. 231, like the
others, will enable the reader to locate the principal occurrences,
as well as many of those of lesser importance.) Even the dullest
ear will be impressed by the combined repetition and alliteration of "morning morning's minion" in line one, the concentration of *d* in line two, and the obvious examples of a similar kind
throughout the poem. But there are a few particularly interesting applications of alliteration that should be noted, as well
as examples of assonance that are liable to be overlooked in the
fortissimo of the consonants.

1 I caught this morning morning's minion, king-
2 dom of daylight's dauphin, dapple-dawn-drawn Falcon, in his
     riding
3 Of the rolling level underneath him steady air, and striding . . .

Line one, in addition to the obvious *m*, recalls a pattern of
sound that we have met several times in these explications, in
which the opening and close of the verse are linked—here by
the hard *c* of "caught" and the *k* of "king-." Less prominent,
but increasingly marked as line two develops, is the assonance
of "caught," "morning," "morning's," "dauphin," "dawn," "drawn,"

and, for those who use the preferred British pronunciation, "Falcon" (*faw*con). This is followed by a progression that is, in effect, a series of stepping-stones of sound. First there is the *r* of "in his *r*iding of the *r*olling"; then the *r* of "*r*olling" gives way to *l*, and we have "*r*o*ll*ing *l*eve*l*"; then, a few syllables later, "*st*eady" and "*st*riding" close line three.

```
3                                              striding
4   High there, how he rung upon the rein of a wimpling wing
5   In his ecstasy! then off, off forth on swing,
6   As a skate's heel sweeps smooth on a bow-bend . . .
```

Line four offers a tripartite alliterative structure on *h*, *r* (which also echoes the *r* and st*r* above), and *w* ("*H*igh," "*h*ow *h*e *r*ung," "*r*ein," "*w*impling *w*ing"), with "*w*imp*l*ing *w*in*g*" linked, by the assonance of short *i*, to "*I*n h*i*s" of the next line. The long *i* of "str*i*ding / H*i*gh there" seems almost to reach upward onomatopoetically, and the phrase "*o*ff, *o*ff *f*orth" with its strong accentuation and its blended *o* and *f* sounds, is, in turn, suggestive of the action it describes, even as the *sw* and *s* of "on *sw*ing / As a *s*kate'*s* heel *sw*eeps *s*mooth" asks only a sensitive ear to catch the hiss of steel on ice.

```
6                              bow-bend: the hurl and gliding
7   Rebuffed the big wind. My heart in hiding
8   Stirred for a bird,—the achieve of, the mastery of the thing! . . .
```

Shorter word combinations are emphasized by oral links: "*b*ow-*b*end," "*r*ebuffed the *b*ig wind," and "*M*y *h*eart in *h*iding." The strong *b* introduced in line six then unites the octave and the sestet through "*b*ird" of line eight, "*B*rute *b*eauty" of line nine, and "*B*uckle," "*b*reaks," and "*b*illion" of line ten.

```
9    Brute beauty and valour and act, oh, air, pride, plume, here
10   Buckle! AND the fire that breaks from thee then, a billion . . .
```

Note that the sestet opens with an enclosing pattern of sound (on *b*), similar to that in line one, although here it is not completed until the first word of line ten. Within the *b* extremes there is a two-step progression on *a* and *p*, with "*a*nd v*a*lour *a*nd *a*ct" and "*p*ride, *p*lume" (with a subordinate *r* that may come through in "*B*rute" and "*p*ride"; and with a strong feeling

I caught this morning mórning's mínion, king-

dom of dáylight's dauphin, dapple-dawn-drawn Fálcon, in his ríding

Of the rólling level underneath him steady áir, and stríding

Hígh there, how he rung upon the rein of a wímpling wíng

In his ecstasy! then off, off forth on swíng,

As a skáte's heel sweeps smooth on a bow-bend: the húrl and glíding

Rebúffed the bíg wind. My heart in híding

Stírred for a bird,—the achieve of, the mastery of the thíng!

Brute beauty and valour and áct, oh, áir, príde, plúme, hére

Búckle! AND the fíre that breaks from thee then, a bíllion

Times told lóvelier, more dángerous, O my chevalíer!

No wonder of it: sheer plód makes plough down síllion

Shine, and blue-bléak embers, ah my déar,

Fáll, gall themsélves, and gash góld-vermílion.

of medial rime approximate in sound between "air" and "here").
However, "Buckle!" does not conclude the thought or the action,
and a strikingly effective and important balance across the ful-
crum of the capitalized AND is secured through the alliteration
of the key verbs "*B*uckle!" and "*b*reaks." It would be difficult
to imagine a more forceful indication that the breaking fire is
a consequence of the buckling.

> 10   a billion
> 11   Times told lovelier, more dangerous, O my chevalier!
> 12   No wonder of it: sheer plod makes plough down sillion . . .

The word-pair, "*T*imes *t*old," linked by alliteration, then introduces a long *o* that picks up in "*O* my chevalier" and bridges
to the second tercet in the initial "*N*o." This is followed shortly
by another example of enclosing alliteration, with *sh* at the extremes, and again an internal two-step progression, this time
on *pl* and *ou*, with "*sh*eer *pl*od makes *pl*ough d*ou*n sillion /
*Sh*ine."

> 13   Shine, and blue-bleak embers, ah my dear . . .

There follows then the pairing of "*bl*ue *bl*eak" and, in the last
line, a strong gathering (or should we, after the foregoing, now
say "buckling"?) of sound, which starts with the initial rime
"Fall, gall," but gives way to the strengthened *g* of "*g*all,"
"*g*ash," and "*g*old":

> 14   Fall, gall themselves, and gash gold-vermilion.

Inevitably, with a texture of sound as rich as we have here,
the subordinate alliteration and assonance will be diminished
accordingly in their effectiveness. But they are nonetheless
present, supporting the soloists in the spotlight with a meaningful harmony. A few minutes spent in study of the diagram
which shows the sonnet's alliteration and assonance will reveal
the details of this accompaniment. It seems wise to rest here
in the outline just concluded, in the hope that, by judicious
selection, the feeling of some readers that Hopkins must have
been hypnotized by the *Nephelidia* (see p. 59) of his compatriot Swinburne has been dispelled, and that beneath the cas-

cade of sound there will now be sensed the channels that direct it into a disciplined pattern in which the ideas and images are enhanced, not hidden.

Frost's *A Soldier*

In turning now from Hopkins to Robert Frost, the reader will find a much less complex prosody than in the Hopkins poem. Frost's *A Soldier* was written by a writer whose individuality of style was fully matured before Hopkins' poems were belatedly published, and thus who, unlike George Barker (to be considered below), was uninfluenced by Hopkins' experiments. The modernity of Frost's poem is to be found in his adaptation of the sonnet's rime scheme and subdivisions to his needs; in the theme which stems from, but universalizes, his reaction to the First World War (the poem was published in 1928); and especially in the idiom with which he treats, and the force and suggestion with which he develops, the striking figure of speech through which the poem emerges in the full richness of its thought.

> He is that fallen lance that lies as hurled,
> That lies unlifted now, come dew, come rust,
> But still lies pointed as it plowed the dust.
> If we who sight along it round the world,
> See nothing worthy to have been its mark,
> It is because like men we look too near,
> Forgetting that as fitted to the sphere,
> Our missiles always make too short an arc.
> They fall, they rip the grass, they intersect
> The curve of earth, and striking, break their own;
> They make us cringe for metal-point on stone.
> But this we know, the obstacle that checked
> And tripped the body, shot the spirit on
> Further than target ever showed or shone.

In this instance, although the title of the sonnet, *A Soldier*, offers no difficulty, it does offer an interesting choice of article. Another sonnet on this subject, the famous one by Rupert Brooke, called *The Soldier*, may be fruitfully compared. It will be recalled that this poem was personal; Brooke was *the* soldier of whom he was writing as he saw the possibility of his death (which occurred, as if in fulfillment of his prophecy, a short time later). Brooke saw himself as becoming one with the dust of a foreign land in which he would be fighting, and he imagined his body as retaining, and imbuing the place of his burial with, some of the qualities that England had given him. But in Frost's title we have *a* soldier as the subject, and the article implies that he is any soldier who has gone out to die in battle. The difference is important in that there is a more complete objectivity and universality of feeling in Frost as against Brooke; just as there is a fresher, more challenging opportunity offered in the figure of the lance in this context, as against the more conventional nature of Brooke's "dust to dust" theme.

1   He is that fallen lance that lies as hurled,
2   That lies unlifted now, come dew, come rust,
3   But still lies pointed as it plowed the dust . . .

The octave opens in the present tense, emphasizing the universality of the subject, and immediately introduces the metaphor that is to dominate the sonnet. It would be difficult to conceive of a figure more in keeping with the subject than is the lance, for it carries a full freight of association with battle, while at the same time it suggests battle in a day more reminiscent of the tournaments of chivalry than of our modern wars with their mechanized destruction. The significance of this implied attitude will appear as the poem develops. And if there is any question of how seriously the word "fallen" in line one is to be taken, our answer comes in the second line: This is a lance that will not be lifted for further use—a soldier who is dead, and who, like the lance, did not fall of his own choice. He was "hurled" into the war. The lance *should* be lifted to preserve it from the dew that will bring on rust and disintegration, that it may be hurled again; but it is not lifted, for it represents a soldier whose body has no further use in war—the "dew" and "rust" of the grave will play their role as, in Shelley's *Adonais*, "darkness, and the law / Of change, shall o'er his sleep the mortal curtain draw."

But in these first lines Frost emphasizes another aspect of the situation. The word "lies" is repeated three times, always with the same implication that this lance has not yet been touched: it lies "as hurled," "unlifted" and "still pointed" in the direction of its flight, which was ended when it hit no meaningful target but merely "plowed the dust." Here, then, is an action that has come to nothing, that *can* come to nothing except the final disintegration of the instrument that was put into motion without choice. It is a dark picture that the first three lines offer, as dark as the futility of war itself.

> 4   If we who sight along it round the world,
> 5   See nothing worthy to have been its mark,
> 6   It is because like men we look too near . . .

But we are human and subject to human limitations in our evaluations of such things. We think only in terms of the immediate and the near. We sight along the shaft of the lance as we hurl it, or we direct the soldier toward a goal, and when both merely "plow the dust" by falling short of the globe-encircling vision we have had, we assume that nothing worthwhile is to be gained from the mark that was actually hit. Being human we look only at the point in the dust, a point that is too near to be the true touchstone of the experience. We forget that everything we hurl must fall short when measured by the dream or vision we project around the world—the lance literally as it flies toward but not to the target; the soldier figuratively as the war he represents and his part in that war fail to attain the goals for which it is fought.

> 7   Forgetting that as fitted to the sphere,
> 8   Our missiles always make too short an arc.
> 9   They fall, they rip the grass, they intersect
> 10 The curve of earth, and striking, break their own . . .

In a telling image, Frost takes his position in the reaches of space. From this far distance the geometrical relationships between the full curve of the earth and the shorter arc of an airborne missile (which is fitted to the sphere of the earth by the laws of gravity) become clear. The latter must inevitably fall short in comparison with the full arc of the earth itself, or the goals it symbolizes in this context. And since this is so, our missiles, whether lance or soldier, must fall, rip the grass (compare "plowed the dust" above) and, in this far view, intersect the stable curve of the earth in breaking their own curves *against* the earth as they strike.

11   They make us cringe for metal-point on stone . . .

When this shattering moment comes, as the point of the lance finds the stone of its destruction in the dust it plows, we cringe empathically; as the arc of the soldier's fall to earth cuts across the curve of the earth itself, we cringe for the broken body, and our empathy is more poignant in the degree that human flesh is more nearly of us than metal-point can ever be.

12   But this we know, the obstacle that checked
13   And tripped the body, shot the spirit on
14   Further than target ever showed or shone.

If as men we are thus shortsighted, however, and must cringe in the shock of a destruction we cannot understand, it can also be said that as men we have the potential to rise above our shortsightedness and look beyond our loss. The last three lines of the poem reverse the emphasis of what has gone before. In the opening lines the lance figure predominated. Now the figure is dropped (except for "target" in the last line) and the body is named for what it is. As men we know that death is but an incident in the life of the spirit, and when the body has been "checked" (stopped) and "tripped" (compare the image of falling, in line nine), whatever it was that obstructed its normal movement toward its goal, and so became its obstacle, could bring it down like a fallen lance but could not touch the spirit which man has and the lance has not. Indeed, only through checking of the body can the spirit be freed, and when its confines are suddenly taken away completely by death, its sudden release causes it (still in terms of the war imagery) to "shoot" on, beyond the obstacles of wars and bullets, beyond even the brightest goals that man with his limitations has seen in sighting along the arc on which he has projected it. It "shoots on," a missile of spirit rather than of body.

It should be noted immediately that this poem is not a defense of war. It rises above war as such, seeing in it but one of many obstacles against which man's body and spirit must be tested (compare Hopkins' sonnet above). It does, however, imply that the dreams for which men fight their wars, like the ideals for which the knights of old hurled their lances in tournament or battle, must be reckoned with in terms of the spirit that makes men willing to die for a vision. And if the immediate target is too close, and the flight of the body comes short even of that, man's spirit, to the degree that it can be freed, is not limited by these shortcomings.

The rhythm of this sonnet must be considered in relationship to the rime scheme, which is *abbacddceffeff*, with all rimes except one of the single exact type. With only this evidence before us we would immediately anticipate three brace-rime quatrains and a closing couplet, giving something of a cross between a Petrarchan and a Shakespearean form, but with a closely unified sestet centering around the four *f* rimes. In practice, however, we find an opening three-line unit of thought which sets the initial tone of the poem. This is followed by a five-line movement, without medial pauses, to complete the octave. These five lines are all, except for the last, comma end-stopped; but the thought development invites wide variation in the *degree* of pause at the different line ends. After *world* one might reduce this almost to the point of enjambement; after *mark* a stronger stop is called for by the rhetorical structure, and after *near* only slightly less so; while after *sphere* lightness again is suggested. These variations prevent monotony.

Moreover, by holding the greater part of the octave to the natural and direct progression of these five lines (the whole poem, it should be noted, rests on a conservatively consistent iambic movement) the richly varied phrasing of the sestet strikes with greater impact than would otherwise be the case. The five short phrases of lines nine and ten,

> They fall, they rip the grass, they intersect
> The curve of earth, and striking, break their own,

impart a sense of immediacy, and are quite suggestive of the action they delineate; after which "They make us cringe for metal-point on stone" is effectively direct in its uninterrupted statement. (These lines, it will be observed, continue the thought of the octave rather than, as is usual, offering a sestet shift in approach to the theme.) The last three lines of the sestet are then made up of three nicely varied phrases that bring the poem to its close:

> But this we know, the obstacle that checked
> And tripped the body, shot the spirit on
> Further than target ever showed or shone.

But in thus outlining the sestet phrasing we note that the expected division of *effe ff* has not appeared, for there are two separate tercets—separate, at least, in grammatical structure—with the resulting rime division *eff eff*, a division that parallels the *abb* of the opening three lines of the poem. The two tercets are thus closely unified (with an interesting variant in the rime approximate in sound at *on*), and their rime schemes balance the two closely related units of thought framed in them.

To this point, then, Frost has used the sonnet with the freedom available to him. He has chosen to write with a metrical regularity that is about as far as one can get from the sprung rhythm of Hopkins, but he has prevented this regularity from becoming monotonous by the striking imagery of the content, the dignity of the idiom which enhances the iambic movement, and the ingenuity with which the content is related rhythmically to the rime scheme. In the latter instance he has achieved freshness and individuality, but without violating the spirit of the organization on which the sonnet form is predicated.

There is also a fourth element that helps notably to make this sonnet memorable. Woven into its texture is a pattern of alliteration and assonance that strengthens and supports the other factors of which we have spoken, and does so with remarkable effectiveness. Let us consider the principal contributions, with attention, called, as before, to the diagram on p. 240.

> 1 He is that fallen lance that lies as hurled,
> 2 That lies unlifted now, come dew, come rust,
> 3 But still lies pointed as it plowed the dust . . .

Our now familiar pattern of enclosing sound opens the octave, with the *h* of "*He*" and "*h*urled" forming the extremes and the *l* of "*l*ance" and "*l*ies" the means, while a minor note is sounded in the short *a* of "th*a*t," "l*a*nce," "th*a*t," and "*a*s." But the *l* is to be a major note in the first four lines, both through repetition of "*l*ies" and independent occurrences in "un*l*ifted," "p*l*owed," and "a*l*ong." Line two also has its minor assonance in the *u* of "*u*nlifted," "r*u*st" and the corresponding sound in the repeated "*c*ome," a sound that is picked up in the expected rime ("d*u*st") below. The line also introduces an effective balance from "dew" here to "dust" of the next line, with both words in key positions. Line three closes the poem's opening statement by a nicely balanced blend of *l* and *p*: "*l*ies *p*ointed as it *pl*owed."

> 4   If we who sight along it round the world,
> 5   See nothing worthy to have been its mark,
> 6   It is because like men we look too near . . .

The *s* introduced at "*s*till" in line three is now picked up at "*s*ight" and carried to "*S*ee." From line three also, "plo*w*ed" anticipates "round" in line four, even as "a*l*ong" continues the preceding *l* sounds. Line four also introduces in its turn an opening and closing *w* at "*W*e" and "*w*orld," again with a projection to "*w*orthy" in line five; while "w*o*rld" and "w*o*rthy" carry the same tilde *e* sound. And line five, in turn, supplements the repeated sounds with *b* of "*b*een" and *m* of "*m*ark," which carry respectively to "*b*ecause" and "*m*en" of line six, with a possible retention of *n* from "*n*othing" to "*n*ear" in the same lines. The *l* now returns in line six in "*l*ike" (probably with a recall also of the long *i* of the repeated "lies" above). Note, too, the strong relationship between "*l*ike" and "*l*ook," which form, in effect, a medial consonantal rime.

By now we should begin to sense a prevailing characteristic of the alliteration and assonance in this sonnet—a wave-like progression that carries one or more sounds from a given line into the next, at which point one or more additional sounds are introduced and carried forward, only to have new sounds initiated there and the cycle repeated. The result is that the ideas and the images are carried on these waves, and the reader is

ALLITERATION   ASSONANCE

He is that fallen lance that lies as hurled,

That lies unlifted now, come dew, come rust,

But still lies pointed as it plowed the dust.

If we who sight along it round the world,

See nothing worthy to have been its mark,

It is because like men we look too near,

Forgetting that as fitted to the sphere,

Our missiles always make too short an arc.

They fall, they rip the grass, they intersect

The curve of earth, and striking, break their own;

They make us cringe for metal-point on stone.

But this we know, the obstacle that checked

And tripped the body, shot the spirit on

Further than target ever showed or shone.

drawn along with the confidence and the pleasure that comes from even a subconscious awareness of this regularity of recurrence accompanied by variety within uniformity.

7   Forgetting that as fitted to the sphere,
8   Our missiles always make too short an arc . . .

Line seven now picks up the short *e* of "m*e*n" (line six) in "Forg*e*tting," which itself introduces an *f* that carries to "*f*itted" and "*sf*here," and is probably strong enough to be recalled in "*f*all" of line nine, thus contributing to the linkage of octave and sestet. The octave then closes on the *m* of "*m*issiles" and "*m*ake," and the circumflex *o* sound of "*al*ways" and "sh*o*rt."

9   They fall, they rip the grass, they intersect
10   The curve of earth, and striking, break their own;
11   They make us cringe for metal-point on stone . . .

The circumflex *o* of line eight now links with the sestet at "f*a*ll," as does the long *a* of "m*a*ke" (line eight) which likewise carries across to the repeated "th*ey*" of the ninth line, "br*ea*k" of line ten, and "Th*ey* m*a*ke" of line eleven. Other sounds, such as in the repeated "t*oo*" and "t*o*," and the extended short *i* of "*I*f," "*i*t," "*i*ts," "*I*t *i*s"—and a stronger "*fi*tted" and "m*i*ssiles"— color the last four lines of the octave.

The sestet then continues the forward movement of the sound established above. Line nine, as we have seen, repeats *f*, long *a* and circumflex *o*, but in its turn initiates a three-line echo of *r* in "*r*ip," "g*r*ass," "st*r*iking," "b*r*eak," and "c*r*inge," as well as a five-line progression of *s* or *st* in "inter*s*ect," "*st*riking," "*s*tone," "ob*s*tacle," and "*s*pirit." Line ten then adds tilde *e* of "c*u*rve" and "*ea*rth" to the sounds carried over, but as it does so the hard *c* of "*c*urve" anticipates the same sound in "*c*ringe" in the next line, while the short *i* of "cr*i*nge" carries to "th*i*s" and "tr*i*pped" below. In line eleven also the *m* of "*m*ake" and "*m*etal" balance the line nicely.

12   But this we know, the obstacle that checked
13   And tripped the body, shot the spirit on
14   Further than target ever showed or shone.

The long *o* of "*sto*ne" (line eleven) now carries across to "kn*ow*" of line twelve, where, also, the short *o* of the important word "*o*bstacle" (which echoes the lightly touched *o* of "*on*" in line eleven) looks forward to "b*o*dy," "sh*o*t," and the same sound in the *a* of "t*a*rget," in the closing lines. And, finally, the last two lines have their own sound repetitions, with the *t* between "*t*ripped" and "*t*arget," the *sh* of "*sh*ot," "*sh*owed," and "*sh*one," and the long *o* of "sh*o*wed or sh*o*ne." An undertone of a minor *th* runs through the sestet, but the major sounds reduce its significance.[19]

There are three statements by Robert Frost that are pertinent as we close this section. He once said that a poem "begins as a lump in the throat, a sense of wrong, a homesickness, a love-sickness. It is never a thought to begin with. . . . It finds the thought and the thought finds words." Again: "Imagery and after-imagery, that's all there is to poetry." And again: "If I must be classified as a poet, I might be called a Synecdochist; for I prefer the synecdoche in poetry—that figure of speech in which we use a part for the whole." Each of these quotations is a commentary on the present poem. In slightly over a hundred words the poet has framed a statement whose metaphor rests like a seed in the reader's mind, breaking into after-imagery as its implications become increasingly clearer. *A Soldier* is not a poem that is easy to forget once it has been read with care, for it represents a nearly perfect fusion of the ideas expressed above: It is a poem in which a feeling (the "lump in the throat") has found its thought and the thought has found its words; and in which the poet is indeed the synecdochist he wished to be, suggesting an expanding whole from the narrow confines of the part, and offering the reader the opportunity to share in the creation by fleshing out in his own imagination the

[19] It is suggested that the reader now return to Frost's sonnet and, in an oral reading, give careful attention to the full play of the effects here discussed. This should not be done, however, in the spirit of "letter-picking" (see p. 195*n*), but rather with an appreciation of the delicate balance that is maintained between the ideas, the imagery, and the alliteration and assonance related to them. Frost's poem is an admirable illustration of the success with which this balance can be established and maintained.

implications for him of what the poet has said. It is in large part because of these qualities that Robert Frost holds the distinguished position he does in American letters, and, more important perhaps, the affection and admiration of an increasingly wide range of readers who have found in his poems what Keats called "the wording of our own highest thoughts."

Barker's *Sonnet to My Mother*

As we bring this chronological study of sonnets to a conclusion, we turn to a poem that was written in 1940. *Sonnet to My Mother*, by the British poet George Barker, reflects the growing freedom in idiom and form whose development we have been observing in our study of previous writers. Actually, this sonnet is much less extreme than are many of the earlier poems by this author, poems whose verbal complexity and sheer love of sound frequently reflect these traits in Hopkins, and range beside the same characteristics in Barker's compatriot, Dylan Thomas. But there is enough of the contemporary idiom and of the experimental freedom of form in the present example to be typical of a current phenomenon that is becoming increasingly widespread; nor is it limited to the sonnet, as reference to Marianne Moore's *Poetry* (p. 7) and Stephen Spender's *The Express* (p. 106) will attest.

Certain problems are faced by the reader of a poem as recently written as is this one. For our earlier examples we were able to turn to critical studies or biographies for information that supplied us with answers to some of the questions that inevitably must puzzle the uninitiated reader. But we noted even in those instances that such information must always be thought of as a bonus. The poem should, despite shadowy areas in minor instances, communicate its basic ideas and especially its mood and feeling without the reader's possession of this detailed knowledge. And there can be little question of the capacity of Barker's sonnet to do this.

Nevertheless we are, or should be, curious beings, concerned with *what? when? where?* and *why?* As to *what?* the title, *To*

My Mother, offers no problem, and raises only the question of whether the poet will avoid the weak sentimentality so frequently associated with his subject. The reader of this chapter would hardly expect to find the poem here if Barker had not done so, but let us consider the evidence. Here is the sonnet:

> Most near, most dear, most loved and most far,
> Under whose window where I often found her
> Sitting as huge as Asia, seismic with laughter,
> Gin and chicken helpless in her Irish hand,
> Irresistible as Rabelais but most tender for
> The lame dogs and hurt birds that surround her,—
> She is a procession no one can follow after
> But be like a little dog following a brass band.
> She will not glance up at the bomber or condescend
> To drop her gin and scuttle to a cellar,
> But lean on the mahogany table like a mountain
> Whom only faith can move, and so I send
> O all my faith and all my love to tell her
> That she will move from mourning into morning.

The deep affection Barker held for his mother is fully reflected in his lines. But it *is* affection and love for her, sentiment rather than sentimentality, and the mother emerges from these vigorous, tenderly-rough images and figures of speech as a person to be reckoned with; and in this respect the poem is more than merely a personal expression of feeling: it emerges as a character sketch that can stand without apology beside Robinson's *Mr. Flood's Party* (p. 158) or any other that might be called in evidence.

The *what?* of our inquiry is thus defined. The paradox of the first line ("most near . . . and most far") invites the question *when?* or *where?* From the poem itself we cannot know whether the mother is "far" because of separation by distance or through death, but the latter seems to be suggested in the last line where "she will move from mourning [the poet's mourning?] into morning [the morning beyond death?]." At first one is encouraged in this interpretation because of the past tense employed in line two; but before the opening sentence is completed the tense has shifted (with a grammatical freedom typical of this writer and this period) to the present tense. Clearly, though we cannot be sure on this point, the poem is nevertheless eminently enjoyable and, in its broader meaning, understandable without this knowledge.

Actually, the foregoing is an erroneous speculation. It has been permitted to develop because such groping for meaning is one aspect of the initial reading of any poem that is not so simply written as to offer no challenge in its organization, structure, or expression. To be a significant poem it must prove to be worth the effort of learning as much as can be learned about it. The present sonnet promises to be of this kind, so the curious reader will test his hypotheses by gathering such materials as are available in biographical notes, critical comments, or wherever the trail may lead. In the present instance he will be rewarded if he will go, not to the anthology or other book that prints this sonnet as an undated item (remember that we are seeking the *when?*), but to the collection in which it first appeared. This was *Selected Poems* (1941), where the poem appears in a group headed "Pacific Sonnets," with the last seven (of which this is one) subheaded "Personal Sonnets." Following this subgroup there is also the notation, "Japan: March–April 1940." (We might have suspected a war period from "bomber" in line nine.) The meager biographical material available in reference books shows that Barker was teaching English literature in Japan at that time. Thus the poem's composition is dated quite exactly for us, and with these clues in mind we persist and find the poet's *Collected Poems* (1957) inscribed "To the memory of Marion Frances Taaffe, 1881–1955"—his mother. She was therefore alive, but in England, when the poem was written. With these scraps of evidence we have answered our *when?* and *where?* and need only the poem itself to supply us with the *why?* We are now better prepared for the careful reading that has been encouraged throughout this chapter.

1   Most near, most dear, most loved and most far . . .

The four parallel phrases in line one offer a direct, straightforward statement of the poet's attitude. Indeed, the first three phrases are quite conventional, suggesting the cliché "near and dear," but are saved from being disappointingly so by the para-

dox to which reference has already been made. The reader's
mind is immediately attracted by the two words "near" and
"far," and a moment's thought in the light of our biographical
information makes it clear that the mother is indeed literally
far away—half a world away in fact—but that separation from
those we love makes them more near to our hearts, more dear
and better loved than when we are with them. The tone of the
poet's tribute is set, however, not by *more* but by *most*, a superlative that promises a superlative personality for its object, and
in this we are not disappointed.

But "far" has only a light comma pause. The mother, it is
true, is far away, but the poet imagines just what she is doing,
and as he visualizes her under the window she is suddenly not
far away, the opening words "most near" take on fresh overtones to make the phrase effectively literal, and the past tense
of "found" must of necessity give way to the present tense that
follows (line seven). The paradox and its bearing on the meaning are imaginatively right.

Even a superficial reading of the octave shows that the near-
clichés of the opening line make the striking imagery that follows even more dramatic than it might otherwise be. This is
no silver-threads-among-the-gold mother, quietly knitting in her
rocker while the birds carol sweetly outside in the spring
garden. This is a strong, vigorous, earthy mother, still seen by
her twenty-seven-year-old son through the eyes of the boy he
once was; a mother who towered above him and filled the room
with her Irish presence, who carried her stature outside and
filled the streets as she filled the room—but who, for all that,
had about her the compassion of a heart that invited all who
needed help to come to her.

If this is a fair summary of the octave, let us see how the
poet has accomplished this three-dimensional portrait, for it is
that in its effect. Rather than being merely the record of an
appearance, it is what Hopkins called an "inscape." We see her,
yes, but more, we share with her son the magnificent spirit that
is hers, the driving force that sets her apart from other women.

2 Under the window where I often found her
3 Sitting as huge as Asia, seismic with laughter . . .

The first step is direct enough. He has often come upon her as she sat "under" the window, a detail that enables us to visualize the room effectively, just as "found her" suggests that he has, perhaps, interrupted her moment of rest in which she was most relaxed and most herself. The past tense of "found" also serves to carry us back in time and confirm our feeling that this is, indeed, the memory of a boy who ascribes to her now the qualities he remembers from an earlier day.

He sees her "sitting as huge as Asia," a name for which there can be two associations. In mythology Asia was the wife of Iapetus and ancestor of the human race—and there is something primordial about this woman also. But the following metaphor makes it more likely that Barker is thinking of her in terms of the solidity of a continent, something firm and dependable. And as a continent is subject to the shaking force of an earthquake ("seismic"), so her unrestricted laughter shakes the continent of her body. It is a brilliant figure of speech, but one that must not be permitted to overshadow the woman herself.

4   Gin and chicken helpless in her Irish hand,
5   Irresistible as Rabelais . . .

So there she is, exerting the titanic force of her Irish personality on the "helpless" gin and chicken. *Helpless* is a skillfully chosen word, for it extends the continental mass of her personality into her simplest actions. If we get the feeling that she is capable of tearing the chicken apart with those Irish hands in her ebullient high spirits, the next simile encourages us in the reaction. Rabelais, too, was earthy, boisterous, and robust, as this woman clearly is, and one cannot escape the power and attraction of his writing any more than one can escape the compelling personality of this product of Ireland's rich, individual, elemental culture. Both are "irresistible."

5   but most tender for
6   The lame dogs and hurt birds that surround her . . .

Lest we begin to see her as coarse or callous or unapproachable in these qualities, however, the poet quickly disabuses us of the idea and, again through effective contrast, suddenly makes her all tenderness. (Note how "most tender" echoes the parallel phrases of the opening line.) Her unsophisticated naturalness and that element in the human being that has come to be a touchstone of warmth and understanding friendliness—namely, the degree to which the animal world instinctively trusts the human—are here demonstrated as these creatures of the wild "surround" her (another fine choice of word) and she responds with what is in effect a motherly concern for their misfortunes.

> 7 She is a procession no one can follow after
> 8 But be like a little dog following a brass band . . .

Having made this concession to the gentler side of her character, the poet again makes her the commanding figure of line three. She is more than a woman, she is a "procession," and her presence is as unmistakable and as attractive as that of a brass band—an admirable metaphor for bringing the woman of lines three to five into the confines of a village street. So far is she beyond the rest that the proportion can be stated only in terms of the "little" (note the diminutive) dog following the musicians, which little dogs (or little boys) normally do with great delight and with great love.

> 9   She will not glance up at the bomber or condescend
> 10 To drop her gin and scuttle to a cellar,
> 11 But lean on the mahogany table like a mountain . . .

As the sestet opens, the time of the poem becomes important. War had been declared by England on Germany in September, 1939, and Barker knows that the bombing of his country is inevitable. He cannot know when it will start, but he has described a mother who, he knows (and by now we know), will not be cowed into submission. Bombers are at best but mosquito-like irritants to a Rabelaisian Asia whose seismic laughter can match their heaviest roaring—although this is, as we shall see, no time for laughter. Indeed, as he pictures her in this situation, he knows that she will not give them the satisfaction of an upward glance. Certainly she will not lower herself from her basic dignity ("condescend") and her accustomed way of life (for which "gin" has now become a symbol) to "scuttle" as would a rat to a cellar. No, with imperturbable assurance, or with willingness to accept whatever fate may bring, she leans on the mahogany table at which we have pictured her sitting in line three, and in keeping with the preceding figure of speech she is here compared to a mountain.

But there is an important difference, a change in tone and mood, in the last four lines of the poem. The son is clearly concerned for his mother, and he knows that a woman of her compassion, one who is "most tender for / The lame dogs and hurt birds," will in turn be worried and concerned for herself, her family, her friends and her country. All of this is suggested by the word "lean" as it looks forward to the word "mourning" of the last line. One sees her no longer sitting happily amid the comparative comforts of a kind of life now mortally threatened, but rather, humped like a mountain, she leans on the table and awaits, without fear but with a sense of loss and mourning, the worst the bombers can bring.

11   like a mountain
12 Whom only faith can move, and so I send
13 O all my faith and all my love to tell her
14 That she will move from mourning into morning.

There follow lines that in a remarkable way bring into perspective all that has gone before. The poem, as we have seen, has avoided sentimentality by turning, after the first line, to a strong, vital characterization that would be quite objective were it not for the tone—a tone set by the obvious admiration as well as love of the poet for his mother as a strikingly forceful Irish woman. The lines have, except for one interlude in line six, drawn on the brasses of the orchestra of his imagery for their effect, just as he called on a literal brass band for their climactic figure of speech. But now, as the poem draws to its close, there must come the transition back to the subjective response of line one. Barker makes this transition with great skill, for as he likens his mother to a mountain the expected *Which* of line twelve becomes "Whom," and there comes into his mind a bold pun, housed in the allusion to the well known words of Matthew 17:20: "If ye have faith as a grain of mustard seed, ye shall say unto this mountain, Remove hence to yonder place;

and it shall remove; and nothing shall be impossible unto you."
The poet's love *for* her is transmuted into faith *in* her, a faith
so strong (joined to a love so deep) that "nothing shall be impossible unto" it; and faith and love are sent across half a
world to tell her that she will be supported by them. If the
bombers cannot move this mountain of a woman to scuttle into
the darkness of a cellar, she will be moved by this faith and
this love through her night of distress and mourning into the
brightness of a dawn that will come when the threatening
horrors of the war have passed.

In the foregoing discussion we focused our attention on the
development of imagery and the interpretation of ideas. But
as we did so the reader cannot have been unaware of the
contemporary idiom with which Barker has written, and the
occasional evidences of the influence of Hopkins on the lines.
There is, for example, a freshness of expression that is characteristic of modern usage in such phrases as "Sitting as huge as
Asia," "seismic with laughter," "Irresistible as Rabelais," and
"But lean on the mahogany table like a mountain." And there
is a homeliness of imagery that enhances rather than detracts
from the subject. It would be difficult to imagine any of the
poets we have studied, from Shakespeare to Hopkins, writing
in a poem of this kind (although Shakespeare might well have
done so in his plays), "Gin and chicken helpless in her Irish
hand," or "She is a procession no one can follow after / But be
like a little dog following a brass band," or "condescend / To
drop her gin and scuttle to a cellar." As to Hopkins, the first
line is reminiscent of his repetition and medial rime, the "O"
of line thirteen is exactly in the spirit of the exclamations we
have met in *The Windhover*, and the punning of "from mourning into morning" would have delighted him.

The rhythm, too, to which we now turn, is marked by a
contemporary relaxation, although it does not approach the
freedom of sprung rhythm, with which we have dealt above.
It is in fact not sprung rhythm, but it is in the tradition of those
writers who have responded directly or indirectly to the impli-

cations of Hopkins' experiments; and the naturalness of the
speech rhythms in an oral reading, in contrast to the metrical
regularity of earlier sonnets, will make this clear. The long,
compelling phrasing of the octave is reminiscent of the first
eight lines of *The Windhover*, but is, in the present instance,
balanced by a comparable phrasing that spans the sestet as well.

The rhetorical parallelism of line one, on which comment
has already been made, offers likewise a rhythmical parallelism
which emphasizes the ideas. But this parallelism immediately
gives way to the long, sweeping movement to which reference
has just been made, that gathers the details of the description
together in its advance, and carries us (with only one strong
end pause and only one light medial pause) to the completion
of the first phase of the description and to the end of the octave.
Especially interesting in this passage is the very light ending of
line five, where the preposition "for" is touched with minimal
emphasis before it is linked to the following phrase:

> . . . but most tender for
> The lame birds and hurt dogs that surround her,—

Use of the long dash after "her" in line six, which would normally be considered a strong pause, here points directly to what
follows, balancing lines seven and eight against the similar
imagery of the earlier lines and making the interlude of tenderness stand out the more forcefully by its contrast.

The sestet which follows localizes the character of the mother
in a specific situation, and is even more open in its phrasing;
for where the octave had three of eight lines of the run-on
type, the sestet has four of its six, and there is only one medial
comma pause in the entire passage. Since this comma comes
after "move," where more conventional punctuation would unquestionably lead to a stronger pause, it must be concluded that
the poet has consciously written for the effect he has gained,
an effect that is quite apparent. Read aloud and in its entirety,
the sonnet opens with a feeling of the inexhaustible hoard of
qualities possessed by this woman, from which these chosen few
are poured forth quickly, almost recklessly; after which the sestet
continues the catalogue, but leads almost without pause into

the passionate outpouring of the poet's concern for and assurance to his mother. It should be noted, however, that in both
instances where the medial comma pauses occur, they come at
exactly the points needed to prevent a sense of breathlessness
in the reading or monotony in the line phrasing.

If the phrasing is considered for a moment it will be apparent
that great skill has been used in securing the variety within
uniformity. The first line, as we have seen, is the direct statement that is to be developed below, and the rhythm is appropriate to it. There follows an enjambement line that carries to
"Asia" (with its feminine comma pause) which is picked up at
once with the short phrase "seismic with laughter," also ending
in a feminine comma pause. We then must go through nine
lines before we come to another medial pause; but the variety
is maintained through these lines, first by letting line four stand
as a unified statement; then, in the three two-line units of
thought that follow, by permitting the phrasing to cut across
the rime scheme (as it did in Keats's sonnet) and so prevent
the feeling of a couplet development; and finally by having
the full stop at the end of the octave coincide with the second
of the three two-line units. This gives the reader a chance to
pause and approach the first lines of the sestet with a fresh
start. But there will be a carry-over of feeling for this rhythmical two-line pattern, and before it can build into an intrusively
repetitive recurrence it is modified by the comma end-pause
of line ten (whereas the other two units had the long dash
and period stops). This carries the reader quickly into line
eleven, through which he passes directly to the medial comma
pause at "move," and, although he is denied the expected stronger
rest, finds no dissatisfaction in this because the emotional force
of the remainder of the poem sustains the two-and-one-half
unstopped lines.

Supporting this rhythm, as has been suggested, is a rime
scheme that is in its own way typical of the experimental efforts
of our later writers. The eye notes the division into octave and
sestet and is likely to anticipate a Petrarchan sonnet. But the
rime scheme is *abcdabcdefgefh*, which leaves the last line sur-

prisingly unrimed, and integrates the sestet so there is no suggestion of a two-tercet division. If this appears to be a novel
scheme, however, there is more novelty to be found in the relationships of the rime words themselves as they pick up and
echo each other in the closeness of their sounds. The effect is
not unlike that observed in the repetition of the *ing* throughout
the octave of *The Windhover*, where, as here, the repetition
cuts across different rime words. In the present instance, *far*
and *her* might be taken as rime approximate in sound (*far* and
for actually are), as, indeed, might the *ter* of *laughter*, with the
latter approximate in accent also. But the ear cautions us that
her does not stand alone—the rime is actually double exact
composite: *found her-surround her*; and *laughter* is also part
of a double exact pair: *laughter-after*. Only the single exact
rime *hand-band*, widely separated for minimum intrusion, counters this echo. But the same effect occurs, in lesser degree,
between octave and sestet, where *band* of line eight and *condescend* of line nine suggest again rime approximate in sound,
while the latter word is picked up by what is actually repetition: *condescend-send*. There is more variety in these six lines,
however, than was found in the octave, for *cellar-tell her* is a
clear-cut double exact composite rime (the *h* of *her* is subordinated in a normal reading so that it does not intrude).

But what shall be said of a sonnet that ends with an unrimed
line? The answer is to recall once more Hopkins' request: "Take
breath and read it with the ears." If this is done for Barker's
poem, after the experience of the blended and interwoven
sounds of the octave, the average reader who is not concentrat-
ing pedantically on rimes will probably be quite unaware of
the abandonment of the scheme at the end, and for an interesting reason. Starting with *mountain*, which is the word that
would normally be paired in line fourteen, the alliteration and
assonance become especially rich, as we shall see. Here let us
extract only the words involved in alliteration and repetitions:
mountain-move-my-my-move-mourning-morning. The echoing
of *m* and the repetitions of *move* and *my* (together with the
run-on lines that reduce emphasis on rime sounds to a minimum) lull the ear into a sense of satisfaction, and by the time

the listener is actually given a medial rich rime, *mourning-morning*, to close the sestet (as a medial exact rime, *near-dear*, had opened the octave) he is more than willing to accept it as satisfying the contract—he will, indeed, more than likely, be quite unaware of the fact that *mountain* is waiting four lines above for a resolution of its sound.[20]

We turn now to a consideration of the poet's use of alliteration and assonance, where, again, the reader is referred to the diagram on p. 256. There are no extremes in this aspect of the poem. Indeed, the alliteration in the octave is somewhat more widely spaced than has been true of our earlier examples, but the ear of the reader should now be alerted to a point where he will be aware of the harmony present, and of the more significant assonance.

1   Most near, most dear, most loved and most far,
2   Under the window where I often found her
3   Sitting as huge as Asia, seismic with laughter,
4   Gin and chicken helpless in her Irish hand,
5   Irresistible as Rabelais but most tender for
6   The lame dogs and hurt birds that surround her . . .

The repetition of "*most*" and the hooked *e* of the medial rime "*near*" and "*dear*," of course, give a strong blend of these devices. So emphasized is the repeated long *o*, indeed, that the ear will almost certainly hear the echo in "*window*," and this, accompanied by the *f* of "*far*" and "*found*," links the opening two lines—even as the *l* of "*loved*" in line one may well be retained until the same sound in "*laughter*" of line three, and extended to "*helpless*," "*Rabelais*," and "*lame*" in the following lines for similar integration. The *s* of "*Sitting*" and "*seismic*" is especially effective in balancing the two phrases of the third line, a line that also introduces an *h* in "*huge*," an important word that looks forward to two other strong words, "*hand*" and "*hurt*" in lines four and six.

At the same time, long and short *i* sounds blend for a harmonious undertone from lines two to five, the long *i* between "*seismic*" and "*Irish*," and the short *i* from "*window*" to "*Sitting*,"

[20] Compare the parallel situation in Swinburne's *Cor Cordium*, p. 57.

"with," "Gin," "chicken," "in," and "Irresistible." The assonance is especially important through here, and the short *a* of "laughter," "hand" and "Rabelais" (combined with three occurrences of "*as*"), together with the long *a* of "Rabelais" and "lame," and the tilde *e* of "tender," "hurt birds," and "her" all make their contribution.

> 7 She is a procession no one can follow after
> 8 But be like a little dog following a brass band . . .

The tilde *e* then encourages a general but subordinate *r* sound in non-initial positions through lines five to eight, highlighted by the initial prominence of "Rabelais," "procession" and "brass." After a return to *s* in "surround" and "procession," and long *o* in "procession" and "no," the octave closes with what has now become familiar to us as a most effective alliterative pattern, with the extremes (here *b*) enclosing a second sound (here *l*), especially effective in this closing position after the comparative lack of concentrated alliteration above:

> But be like a little dog following a brass band.

The alliteration is enhanced in this line, by the echo of the preceding "follow," and by the assonance of "*a*fter," "br*a*ss" and "b*a*nd."

> 9 She will not glance up at the bomber or condescend
> 10 To drop her gin and scuttle to a cellar . . .

The sestet now picks up the *b*, short *a* and short *o* of line eight of the octave as we are offered "bomber," "glance up at," and "bomber," "drop," and (line twelve) "on the mahogany." There is also a reminiscence of earlier sounds in the tilde *e* of "bomber" and "her," and in the *s* of "condescend," "scuttle" and "cellar."

> 11 But lean on the mahogany table like a mountain
> 12 Whom only faith can move, and so I send
> 13 O all my faith and all my love to tell her
> 14 That she will move from mourning into morning.

At this point the alliteration begins to cluster more noticeably, with line eleven alternating between *l* and *m* in "lean," "mahogany," "like" and "mountain." This *m* then carries to "move,"

Most near, most dear, most loved and most far,
Under the window where I often found her
Sitting as huge as Asia, seismic with laughter,
Gin and chicken helpless in her Irish hand,
Irresistible as Rabelais but most tender for
The lame dogs and hurt birds that surround her,—
She is a procession no one can follow after
But be like a little dog following a brass band.
She will not glance up at the bomber or condescend
To drop her gin and scuttle to a cellar,
But lean on the mahogany table like a mountain
Whom only faith can move, and so I send
O all my faith and all my love to tell her
That she will move from mourning into morning.

ALLITERATION

ASSONANCE

"*m*y," "*m*y," and "*m*ove from *m*ourning into *m*orning" of the following lines. Lines twelve to fourteen give *f* in "*f*aith," "*f*aith" and "*f*rom"; line twelve *s* in "*s*o I *s*end"; and line thirteen *t* in "*t*o *t*ell." The assonance, too (in part associated with repetition), is strongly interwoven through these lines, with the long *a* of "t*a*ble," "f*ai*th" and "f*ai*th," the long *o* of "*o*nly," "s*o*" and "*O*," the long double *o* of "Wh*o*m," "m*o*ve," "t*o*" and "m*o*ve," and the circumflex *o* of "*a*ll," "*a*ll," "m*o*urning," and "m*o*rning." An attentive reading of the last four lines with these sounds in mind will make the reader aware of the oral texture that results from these combinations.

From the foregoing analysis of *Sonnet to My Mother* it will be quite evident that the poet who wishes to do so can and will take such liberties with convention as seem to him best suited to his content. Not all will be as successful as George Barker has been in achieving a blend of rhythm and rime that should make this, for all but the most puristic, not only a moving poem but a moving and skillfully wrought sonnet. Granted that if the liberties taken become so extreme as to sacrifice the integrity of the form (Hopkins' sprung rhythm and Barker's unrimed last line lead in this direction) then freedom becomes license and the bounds of artistic discipline are breached. The result may then be a fourteen-line poem of such interest as the poet can make it, but it will have to be discussed in terms other than those applicable to the sonnet. The above poem has been selected because it has the fascination and the freshness of contemporary treatment in the freedom it reflects, without losing the essential qualities that make it a significant representative of the genre.

Selected Titles for Additional Reading

THE FOLLOWING list of titles makes no pretense at completeness. It has been purposely limited to books to which the student of poetry as an art and craft might well turn for further study, and the bibliographies found in these books will suggest additional titles that might attract him. The titles are arranged in chronological order.

1. THE FAMILY OF THE ARTS

Lessing, Gotthold. *Laokoon,* tr. Sir Robert Phillimore. 1874.

Artistotle. *Theory of Poetry and Fine Art,* ed. S. H. Butcher. 1902.

Babbitt, Irving. *The New Laocoon.* 1910.

Rhys, Ernest. *The Prelude to Poetry.* 1927.

Housman, A. E. *The Name and Nature of Poetry.* 1933.

Greene, Theodore M. *The Arts and the Art of Criticism.* 1940.

Stauffer, Donald A. *The Nature of Poetry.* 1946.

Hagstrum, Jean H. *The Sister Arts.* 1958.

McGinn, Donald J., and George Howerton. *Literature as a Fine Art.* 1959.

2. THE POET AS ARTIST

Prescott, Frederick C. *The Poetic Mind.* 1922.

Lowes, John Livingston. *The Road to Xanadu.* 1927.

Centeno, Augusto. *The Intent of the Artist.* 1941.

Richards, I. A. *Principles of Literary Criticism.* 1948.

Black, Haskell M. *The Creative Vision.* 1960.

   See also readings for Chapter 3.

3. THE CREATIVE PROCESS

Ridley, M. R. *Keats's Craftsmanship.* 1933.

Bate, Walter Jackson. *The Stylistic Development of Keats.* 1945.

Auden, W. H. and others. *Poets at Work.* 1948.

Bartlett, Phyllis. *Poems in Process.* 1951.

Ghiselen, Brewster. *The Creative Process.* 1952.

Scott, A. F. *The Poet's Craft.* 1957.

Roethke, Theodore. *On the Poet and His Craft,* ed. Ralph J. Mills, Jr. 1965.

See also readings for Chapter 2.

4. POETIC TOOLS: DEVICES FOR RHYTHM AND SOUND

Patterson, William. *The Rhythm of Prose.* 1916.

Bridges, Robert. *The Necessity of Poetry.* 1918.

————. *Milton's Prosody.* 1921.

Saintsbury, George. *A History of English Prosody.* 1924.

Andrews, C. E. *The Reading and Writing of Verse.* 1925.

Hamer, Enid. *The Meters of English Poetry.* 1930.

Snyder, Edward. *Hypnotic Poetry.* 1930.

Lanz, Henry. *The Physical Basis of Rime.* 1931.

Allen, George W. *American Prosody.* 1935.

Wood, Clement. *The Complete Rhyming Dictionary.* 1936.

Stauffer, Donald. *The Nature of Poetry.* 1946.

Hemphill, George. *Discussions of Poetry: Rhythm and Sound.* 1961.

5. POETIC TOOLS: STANZA FORMS, POEM FORMS, FREE VERSE
AND SPRUNG RHYTHM

Havens, R. D. *The Influence of Milton on English Poetry.* 1922.

Saintsbury, George. *A History of English Prosody.* 1924.

Hamer, Enid. *The Meters of English Poetry.* 1930.

Allen, George. *American Prosody.* 1935.

————. *A Walt Whitman Handbook.* 1946.

See also readings for Chapter 8.

6. POETIC TOOLS: IMAGERY AND FIGURES OF SPEECH

Empson, William. *Seven Types of Ambiguity.* 1930.

Wood, Clement. *Poets' Handbook.* 1940.

Stauffer, Donald. *The Nature of Poetry.* 1946.

Fogle, Richard Harter. *The Imagery of Keats and Shelley.* 1949.

Kreuzer, James R. *Elements of Poetry.* 1955.
O'Malley, Glenn. *Shelley and Synesthesia.* 1964.

7. THE RANGE OF POETRY: NARRATIVE, DRAMATIC, LYRIC

Narrative

Child, Francis J. *English and Scottish Popular Ballads.* 1882–1898.
Ker, W. P. *Epic and Romance.* 1897.
Rabb, Mrs. Kate. *National Epics.* 1898.
Gummere, Francis B. *The Popular Ballad.* 1907.
Abercrombie, Lascelles. *The Epic.* 1914.
Pound, Louise. *Poetic Origins of the Ballad.* 1921.
——— ed. *American Ballads and Songs.* 1922.
Lawrence, William W. *Medieval Story.* 1926.
Gerould, Gordon. *The Ballad of Tradition.* 1932.
Wells, Evelyn. *The Ballad Tree.* 1950.
Leach, MacEdward. *The Ballad Book.* 1955.
Kroeber, Karl. *Romantic Narrative Art.* 1960.

Dramatic

Kreymborg, Alfred, ed. *Poetic Drama: An Anthology of Plays in Verse.* 1941.
Brooks, Cleanth, and Robert Heilman. *Understanding Drama.* 1948.
Langbaum, Robert. *The Poetry of Experience: The Dramatic Monologue in Modern Literary Tradition.* 1957.
Honan, Park. *Browning's Characters: A Study in Technique.* 1961

Lyric

Erskine, John. *The Elizabethan Lyric.* 1905.
Reed, Edward B. *English Lyric Poetry from Its Origins to the Present Time.* 1912.
Rhys, Ernest. *Lyric Poetry.* 1913.
Schelling, Felix E. *The English Lyric.* 1913.
Drinkwater, John. *The Lyric.* 1916.
Cohen, Helen Louise. *Lyric Forms from France.* 1930.
Shuster, G. N. *The English Ode from Milton to Keats.* 1940.
Yasuda, Kenneth. *The Japanese Haiku.* 1957.

8. THE POET AND HIS POEM: A READING OF SIX SONNETS
FROM FIVE CENTURIES

Crossland, T. W. H. *The English Sonnet*. 1917.

Sterner, L. G. *The Sonnet in American Literature*. 1930.

Hamer, Enid. *The English Sonnet*. 1936.

Zillman, Lawrence J. *John Keats and the Sonnet Tradition*. 1939.

Pottle, Frederick A. *The Idiom of Poetry*. 1947.

Shapiro, Karl. *English Prosody and Modern Poetry*. 1947.

Hubler, Edward. *The Sense of Shakespeare's Sonnets*. 1952.

Shapiro, Karl. *Prose Keys to Modern Poetry*. 1962.

Varied Readings of Hopkins' *The Windhover*

Hopkins, Gerard Manley. "Author's Preface" to *Poems*, ed. Robert
Bridges. Second Edition. 1930.

Gardner, W. H. "The Religious Problem in G. M. Hopkins." *Scrutiny*, June, 1937. Reprinted in Stallman, R. W. *Critiques and
Essays in Criticism*. 1949.

Peters, W. A. M., S.J. *Gerard Manley Hopkins: A Critical Essay
Towards the Understanding of His Poetry*. 1948.

Schneider, Elisabeth. "Hopkins' 'The Windhover.'" *The Explicator*,
January, 1960.

Explications of Other Poems

Brooks, Cleanth. *The Well Wrought Urn*. 1947.

Engle, Paul, and Warren Carrier. *Reading Modern Poetry*. 1955.

Lyon, Harvey. *Keats' Well-Read Urn*. 1958.

Wasserman, Earl. *The Subtler Language*. 1959.

Drew, Elizabeth, and George Connor. *Discovering Modern Poetry*.
1961.

Ostroff, Anthony. *The Contemporary Poet as Artist and Critic: Eight
Symposia*. 1964.

GENERAL

Preminger, Alex, Frank J. Warnke and O. B. Hardison, Jr. *Encyclo-
pedia of Poetry and Poetics*. 1965.

Shapiro, Karl, and Robert Beum. *A Prosody Handbook*. 1965.

Index of Topics

ALEXANDRINE, 65, 68n
Allegory, 133n, 135n
Alliteration, 58
Allusion, 13, 117, 185–257 *passim*
Ambiguity, 131n
Amphibrach, 41n
Amphimacer, 41n
Anacrusis, 45n
Anapest, 39; *see also* Meter
Antibachius, 41n
Antistrophe, 79
Antithesis, 115–16
Apostrophe, 114–15; ex. 42, 45, 51, 54, 61, 74, 75, 94n, 114
Approximate rime, 54–55, 107n
Archaism, 103n
Architecture and poetry, 12, 15
Art and craft, 6–8, 31–36, and *passim*
Arts: relationship to poetry, 5–15; likenesses and differences, 8–9; their underlying principle, 39
Aside, 149; combined with monologue, 156–57
Assonance, 58

BACCHIUS, 41n
Ballad: traditional, 129; ex. 125–28; literary, 129; ex. 130–32
Ballade, 90, 90n, 124n; ex. 90
Ballad stanza, 71; *see also* Common meter
Blank verse, 65–67; ex. 18–20, 66–67, 97–98, 102–3, 105–6, 136, 145–47 (dramatic), 156–57, 166–67; and stanza forms, 65; historical sketch, 96–106; Milton's defense of, 101
Brace rime, 72
Burlesque (mock) epic, 136

CAESURA, 50
Catalexis, 45
Chant royal, 90n

Character sketch, 157–58
Chaucerian heptastich, 74
Cinquain, 94n
Cliché, *see* Triteness
Closet drama, 145; ex. 66–67
Common meter, 71; ex. 32, 34, 57, 62, 71, 72, 125–26, 131–32, 160, 162, 163, 177, 180
Composite rime, 55
Conceit, 113
Connotation, 62
Consonance, 54n
Consonantal rime, 54–55
Couplet: heroic, closed: 68; ex. 14, 53, 68, 100, 116, 137, 180; open: 68; ex. 4, 18, 49, 50, 55, 69, 96, 104–5, 154–55; historical sketch, 96–104; tetrameter, octosyllabic: 69; ex. 47, 55, 69, 82, 139–43, 172, 178; in triple meter: ex. 42, 45, 126–27, 128–29
Craft, *see* Art
Creative personality, 16, 26–27, 33; loss of, 21–23
Creative process, 31–36

DACTYL, 39
Dance and poetry, 13–15
Dimeter, 46; ex. 46–47, 92–93, 173; combined: 60, 61–62, 82, 85–86, 92, 93, 130, 165–66, 170, 182
Double rime, 53
Dramatic dialogue, 147–49; related to ballads, 148
Dramatic irony, 127n
Dramatic monologue, 154–55; ex. 45, 49–50, 154–55; combined with aside, 156
Dramatic poetry, 144–59; *see also* Aside, Character sketch, Dramatic dialogue, Dramatic monologue, Poetic drama, Soliloquy

Dramatic triangle, 124
Duple meter, 39n

ELEGIAC stanza, 73
Empathy, 26–27
Endings (verse), 49–52; masculine, 50; feminine, 50
End rime, 55
English (Shakespearean) sonnet, 79; *see also* Sonnet
Enjambement, 50
Epic, 133–37; traditional: 133–34; literary: 135; ex. 14, 136; mock (burlesque), 136
Epithet, 205
Epode, 80
Exact rime, 52–53

FALLING meter, 39
Fancy and imagination, 18–19, 21
Feminine ending, 40, 45n; and caesura, 50
Figures of speech, 109–18; *see also* Imagery
Foot (prosodic), 39–45
Form-content relationship, 39–45, 68n, 185–257, and *passim*
Free verse, 84–87; Arnold type: 85; ex. 85, 118, 182; Whitman type: 86; ex. 86, 118n, 175; modern type: 87; ex. 7, 88, 179; related to ode, 85n; to sprung rhythm, 88; phrase patterns in, 86–87; not truly free, 86
French forms, 89–93; ballade, 90, 90n; chant royal, 90n; rondeau, 90n, 91; roundel, 90n; sestina, 90n; triolet, 92; villanelle, 93

HAIKU, 94–95
Half rime, 54n
Heptameter, 48; combined, 60
Heroic couplet, 68; *see also* Couplet
Heroic quatrain, 73; *see also* Quatrain
Heroic verse, 65
Hexameter, 48; ex. 44; combined, ex. 22–23, 60, 80–82, 182; *see also* Spenserian stanza
Historical approach to poetry, 96–108, 185–257
Homostrophic ode, 82; *see also* Ode
Horatian ode, 83
Hyperbole, 115

IAMB, 39, 41; *see also* Meter
Identical rime, 55

Idiom, 163; *see also* Poetry, modern
Imagery, 109–18; defined, 109; figures of speech in, 110–18; explications of, 185–250 *passim*
Imagination: defined, 19, 21, 22n; and fancy, 18–19, 21; and synthesis, 32
Implied narrative, 123–24, 127
Incremental refrain, 56
In Memoriam stanza, 72; ex. 61, 72, 177
Inspiration, 17, 20
Italian (Petrarchan) sonnet, 77; *see also* Sonnet
Irony, 127n
Irregular Pindaric ode, 81; *see also* Ode

JAPANESE forms, 94; tanka, 94–95; haiku, 94–95

KINESTHESIA, 62

LIGHT verse, 55, 89–93
Limerick, 93
Line, *see* Verse
Literary ballad, 129; *see also* Ballad
Literary epic, 135; *see also* Epic
Long meter, 71; ex. 42, 45, 64, 71, 113 (doubled), 115, 126, 128, 152 (doubled), 180
Lyric, 160–257; characterized, 160; related to other genres, 160–61

MEDIAL pauses, 49–52
Medial rime, 56, 228
Metaphor, 112; related to allegory, 135n
Meter: uses and advantages, 39–45, 68n, 185–257 *passim*; rising: iambic, 39, 41; ex. *passim*; anapestic, 39, 42; ex. 42, 42n, 92, 93, 126, 128; combined, 42, 46, 81; falling: trochaic, 39, 43–44; ex. 44, 92, 152, 172, 180; combined, 61; dactylic, 39, 44–45; ex. 44; combined, 59; difficulty in reading, 44; duple, 39n; triple, 39n; variant feet: spondaic, 40; pyrrhic, 40; rare feet, 41n; variety in, 39–40, 191, 199–200, 209, 215–16, 224–27, 250–51; metrical silence, 43; Old English, 134; *see also* Free verse, Rhythm, Sprung rhythm
Metonymy, 116–17

Metrical romance, 137–39; ex. 70, 139
Metrical silence, 43
Metrical tale, 143–44
Mock (burlesque) epic, 136
Molossus, 41n
Monometer, 46; combined, 182
Mosaic rime, 55
Music and poetry, 10–15

NARRATIVE poetry, 123–43; *see also* Ballad, Epic, Metrical romance, Metrical tale
Narrative triangle, 124
Near rime, 54n
Nonameter, 48
Normal refrain, 56

OBLIQUE rime, 54n
Octameter, 48; ex. 56, 58, 59; combined, 60
Octave, 77
Octosyllabic couplet, 69; *see also* Couplet
Ode, 79–84; Regular Pindaric: 79–80; related to Greek drama, 79; Irregular Pindaric: 81; ex. 22, 61, 81; related to free verse, 85n, 118n; stanzaic (homostrophic): 82; ex. 20, 76, 82; Horatian: 83
Old English verse form, 134
Onomatopoeia, 60
Ottava rima, 74

PAINTING and poetry, 9–15
Parallelism, 57
Para-rime, 54n
Pathetic fallacy, 113
Pauses, 49–51
Pentameter, 48; ex. 14, 48, 65–68, 70, 74, 89, 105–6, 155, 166–67; 216, and *passim*; combined, ex. 20, 22, 61–62, 80–83. 85, 118, 156, 165, 182; *see also* Spenserian stanza
Personification, 113
Petrarchan (Italian) sonnet, 77; *see also* Sonnet
Phrasing: patterns in, 86–87; variety in, 191, 199, 209, 224–27, 237–38, 250–52; importance of, 49–51, 84
Pindaric ode, 79–81; *see also* Ode, Rhythm
Poem forms, *see* Ballade, Chant royal, Cinquain, Free verse, Haiku, Limerick, Ode, Rondeau, Rondel,

Roundel, Sestina, Sonnet, Tanka, Triolet, Villanelle
Poet, 6–7, 7n, 16–27, and *passim; see also* Creative personality
Poetic drama, 144–45; ex. 66, 97, 118n, 145
Poetry: definitions, 3–6; and other arts, 5–15, 37, 52; and verse, 6–7; and prose, 9, 36, 87, 187; and science, 24; dedication to, 19–21; revision of, 32–36, 159n, 183, 212n, frontispiece; its tools, 37–118; as an oral art, 38–39, 40, 51n, 52–63, 215, 242n; modern idiom in, 107n, 160–84, 176, 243, 250; ex. 7, 106, 166–67, 171, 174, 179, 183f, 233, 244; approach to content, 243–45; *see also* Dramatic poetry, Lyric poetry, Narrative poetry
Prose drama with poetic quality, 144
Prosody, 37
Pyrrhic, 40; *see also* Meter

QUATRAIN, 71–73; heroic: 73; ex. 73, 89, 158 (doubled), 162; with rime skip, 72; brace rime: 72; ex. 72, 177

REFRAIN, 56
Regular Pindaric ode, 79–80; *see also* Ode
Recurrence, *see* Rhythm
Revision of poems, 32–36, 159n, 183, 212n, frontispiece
Rhythm: defined, 37; importance, 49–51, 84; monotonous, 49; basis in recurrence, 52, 84–85; *see also* Meter, Phrasing, Sprung rhythm, Variety within uniformity
Rich rime, 55
Rime: defined, 53; single, double, triple, 53; exact, 53; approximate (half, near, oblique, para-, slant; consonance), 54–55, 107n; composite (mosaic), 55; consonantal, 54–55; end, 55; medial, 56, 228; rich, 55; *scheutel* ("shaking"), 55; brace, 72; concessions to, 56; rime scheme, 64; Keats on difficulties, 107; subtlety and variety in use of, 200, 210, 227–28, 237, 252–53
Rime royal stanza, 74
Rising meter, 39; *see also* Meter
Rondeau, 90n, 91–92
Rondel, 91
Roundel, 90n

Rubáiyát stanza, 72
Run-on (enjambement), 50

SATIRE, 74, 137n
Scheutel ("shaking") rime, 55
Science and poetry, 24
Sculpture and poetry, 12–15
Sestet, 77
Sestina, 90n
Shakespearean (English) sonnet, 79;
see also Sonnet
Short meter, 71; ex. 41 (doubled),
42, 47, 59, 71, 116, 148
Simile, 110–11
Single rime, 53
Slant rime, 54n
Soliloquy, 151–52
Sonnet, 77–79, 185–257; Italian (Pe-
trarchan): 77–78; ex. 51, 57, 77,
99, 107, 108, 114, 165, 169, 176,
181, 196, 204, 216, 233; Spen-
serian: 78; related to Spense-
rian stanza, 78n; English (Shake-
spearean): 79; ex. 79, 111, 154,
182; irregular: ex. 107, 216, 233,
244; historical sketch, 96–108
Sound patterns, 191–95, 200–2, 209–
14, 227–32, 238–42, 252–57
Spenserian sonnet, 78
Spenserian stanza, 75; ex. 9, 62, 75;
historical sketch, 103n
Spondee, 40
Sprung rhythm, 88–89, 214–16, 224–
27; ex. 89, 210; related to free
verse and Old English verse, 88
Stanza, 45, 64
Stanza forms: miscellaneous, 17, 46,
48, 56, 59, 60, 76, 110, 114, 130,
150, 158, 165, 168–74, 183; *see*
Ballad stanza, Couplet, Heroic
quatrain (elegiac stanza), *In Memoriam* stanza, Long Meter, Ottava rima, Rime royal, Rubáiyát
stanza, Spenserian stanza, Stave
of six, Tercet, Terza rima; *see
also* Poem forms
Stanzaic (homostrophic) ode, 82–83;
see also Ode

Stave of six, 73; ex. 73, 178
Strophe, 79
Substitutions (metrical), 39–40
Suggestion in poetry, 94
Syllable: defined and characterized,
38
Symbol, 131n; *see also* Imagery
Synecdoche, 116

TANKA, 94–95
Tercet, 112
Terza rima, 70; ex. 54, 70, 114
Tetrameter, 47; ex. 112-13, 134 (Old
English form), 150, 170–71, 178
(*see also* French forms, *In Memo-
riam* stanza, Long meter, Tetram-
eter couplet); combined: 60, 61–
62, 80, 81–82, 85, 92, 110, 114,
118, 168, 169, 174, 182; *see also*
Common meter, Short meter
(3343)
Tetrameter couplet, 69
Traditional ballad, 129; *see also*
Ballad
Traditional epic, 133
Tragic irony, 127n
Tribrach, 41n
Trimeter, 47; ex. 47, 59, 116, 148;
combined, ex. 17, 22, 41, 42, 44,
61–62, 72, 80–83, 85, 110, 114,
118, 130, 168–70, 174, 182; *see
also* Common meter
Triolet, 92
Triple meter, 39n
Triple rime, 53
Triplet, *see* Tercet
Triteness, 7, 110, 245–46
Trochee, 39; *see also* Meter
Truncation, 45n

VARIETY within uniformity, 39, 49–
51, 191
Vers de société, 83–93
Verse, 45–48; defined, 45; end-
stopped, 49; enjambement (run-
on), 50–51
Verse and poetry, 6–7
Villanelle, 93

Index of Names, Titles, and First Lines

Authors quoted at length are in capitals. Titles of poems, including those formed from first lines, are in bold face. Other first lines, including those of non-initial fragments which hold independent rather than merely illustrative interest, are light face. Asterisks indicate poems that are analyzed. Bold face page numbers indicate where poems or prose passages are quoted.

ABERCROMBIE, LASCELLES, 5, 7, 13, 163n
A billion light years . . . if an ant could see, 108
Abt Vogler, 109
A casement high and triple-arch'd there was, 9, frontispiece
A child said What is the grass . . ., 112
ADEN, CARLIN
    Early Fishermen, 73
Adonais, 15, 103n, 234
Aeneid, 14, 49, 97, 135
Afternoon in Artillery Walk, An, 156
After the first powerful plain manifesto, 106
Ah, leave the smoke, the wealth, the roar, 90
Akenside, Mark, 102
Alastor, 105
A little learning is a dang'rous thing, 116
Amoretti, 98
Anderson, Maxwell, 144
Andrea del Sarto, 105
And slowly answer'd Arthur from the barge, 105
And still she slept an azure-lidded sleep, 62
ANONYMOUS
    From Beowulf, 134
    Bessie Bell and Mary Gray, 57
    Hospital Impressions, 88
    Johnny Randall, 128
    Lord Randal, 126
    Love not me for comely grace, 169
    O Western Wind, 162
    *Sir Patrick Spens, 125
    There was a faith healer of Deal, 93
    Time, stop, 94n
Antigone, 117, 118n
Antony and Cleopatra, 97
ARNOLD, MATTHEW, 85, 117, 177
    Dover Beach, 118
    Philomela, 85
    From Stanzas from the Grande Chartreuse, 178
A slumber did my spirit seal, 180
A sweet disorder in the dress, 69
As You Like It (Incidental Music), 15n
A thing of beauty is a joy forever, 104
Auden, W. H., 105

BACON, LEONARD
    An Afternoon in Artillery Walk, 156
BAKER, CATHERINE
    Five lines, 94n
BARKER, GEORGE, 107n, 186, 233, 243–57
    *Sonnet to My Mother, 244, 256

Batter my heart, three-personed God, 176
Beattie, James, 103n
Bells, The, 60
Be not the first by whom the new are tried, 116
Beowulf, 88, 133, 134
Bessie Bell and Mary Gray, 57
Bible, 175, 197, 249
Biographia Literaria, 4, 22n, 32
Bishop Orders His Tomb, The, 105
Blair, Robert, 102
BLAKE, WILLIAM
    The Fly, 172
Blessed Damozel, The, 15n
Bob Southey! you're a poet—Poet laureate, 74
Boileau, Nicolas, 100
Boy of Winander, The, 27, 67
*Break, Break, Break, *42, 116
Bridges, Robert, 215
Brooke, Rupert, 233–34
BROWNING, ELIZABETH BARRETT, 106
    If thou must love me, let it be for naught, 169
BROWNING, ROBERT, 39, 49–50, 51, 104, 109, 110, 138, 154, 158, 160, 161
    From The Last Ride Together, 150
    My Last Duchess, 154
    Soliloquy of the Spanish Cloister, 152
Brown's Descent, 144
BURNS, ROBERT, 19, 21, 103n, 144
    From Epistle to J. Lapraik, 17
    Ye banks and braes o' bonnie Doon, 71
    Ye flowery banks o' bonnie Doon, 71
Busy, curious, thirsty fly, 172
Butler, Samuel, 56
BYRON, GEORGE GORDON, LORD, 4, 15n, 70, 103n, 104
    From Childe Harold's Pilgrimage, 75
    From The Destruction of Sennacherib, 42
    From Don Juan, 74
    Song of Saul Before His Last Battle, 45
By the rude bridge that arched the flood, 115
By what right did I pick these flowers, 95

Cacoethes Scribendi, 18
Canterbury Tales, The, 96, 143
CARLYLE, THOMAS
    To-Day, 46
Castle of Indolence, The, 103n
Cenci, The, 105
Chanson de Roland, 134, 158
CHAPMAN, GEORGE, 117, 204–5
    From Odyssey, 207
CHAUCER, GEOFFREY, 74, 104, 138, 143
    From Canterbury Tales, The, 96
Childe Harold's Pilgrimage, 75, 103n
Childe Roland to the Dark Tower Came, 138, 158
Christabel, 22, 138
Clarke, Charles Cowden, 207, 209n, 212n
Cliff Klingenhagen, 158
CLOUGH, ARTHUR HUGH
    The Latest Decalogue, 178
COLERIDGE, HARTLEY
    She is not fair to outward view, 168
COLERIDGE, SAMUEL TAYLOR, 27, 74, 124, 132, 138, 162
    From Biographia Literaria, 4, 22n, 32
    *From Dejection: An Ode, 22
    From The Rime of the Ancient Mariner, 62
Collected Poems (Barker), 245
COLLINS, WILLIAM
    Ode to Evening, 83
    Ode Written in the Beginning of the Year 1746, 82
Composed Upon Westminster Bridge, 164, 165
Concord Hymn, 115
Connelly, Marc, 144
Cor Cordium, 57, 254n
Cotter's Saturday Night, The, 103n
Cowley, Abraham, 81
COWPER, WILLIAM, 102, 104, 143
    Light Shining Out of Darkness, 177
Crabbe, George, 104
Cyriack, this three years' day these eyes, though clear, 99

Dante, 15n, 70, 135
Dauber, 144
Death, 64

Death, be not proud, though some have called thee, 114
Death of the Hired Man, The, 105, 149
Death stands above me, whispering low, 64
Debussy, Claude, 15n
Defence of Guinevere, The, 70
Defence of Poetry, A, 4, 16n
*Dejection: An Ode, 22
Delight in Disorder, 69
Departure, 87n, 181, 182
Deserted Village, The, 103
Destruction of Sennacherib, The, 42
Dickinson, Emily, 3, 54
Diverting History of John Gilpin, The, 143
Divine Comedy, 70, 135
DOBSON, AUSTIN, 89
   A Kiss, 92
   You Bid Me Try, 92
   Vitas Hinnuleo, 91
   When I saw you last, Rose, 93
Don Juan, 74
DONNE, JOHN, 98
   Batter my heart, three-personed God, 176
   Death, be not proud, though some have called thee, 114
   From The Ecstasy, 113
Dover Beach, 117, 118
Dramatic Lyrics, 160
Dreamer of dreams, born out of my due time, 74
DRYDEN, JOHN, 14, 80, 81, 100, 101, 104, 145
   From Aeneid, 14
   From A Song for St. Cecilia's Day, 61
Dynasts, The, 145

Early Fishermen, 73
Earth has not anything to show more fair, 165
Earthly Paradise, The, 74, 104
Easy is the triolet, 92
Ecstasy, The, 113
Ere we retired, / The cock had crowed, 19
Eliot, T. S., 111, 145
EMERSON, RALPH WALDO, 4
   Cacoethes Scribendi, 18
   Concord Hymn, 115
   From The Poet, 7n, 25

Endymion, 50, 104
English Bards and Scotch Reviewers, 104
Epipsychidion, 223
Epistle to J. Lapraik, 17
Essay of Dramatic Poesy, 101
Essay on Criticism, An, 53, 65n, 68, 116
Eve of St. Agnes, The, 9, 62, 75, 103n, 138, 212n, frontispiece
Everlasting Mercy, The, 144
Every day the sailing rougher, 55
Express, The, 105, 106, 107n, 243

Faerie Queene, The, 75, 135, 135n, 138
Fair seed time had my soul, and I grew up, 102
Far from the sun and summer gale, 80
Far in a western brookland, 59
Feeling that you were waiting for me, 95
FINCH, HELEN
   Good Night, 46
FITZGERALD, EDWARD
   From Rubáiyát of Omar Khayyám, 72
Five lines, 94n
Five piles standing in the river, 95
Fly About a Glass of Burnt Claret, A, 174n
Fly, The (Blake), 173
Fly, The (Shapiro), 174
Fra Lippo Lippi, 105
Francesca Da Rimini (Symphonic Fantasy), 15n
From the depth of the dreamy decline of the dawn . . ., 59
FROST, ROBERT, 17, 105, 109, 144, 149, 186, 233–43
   *A Soldier, 233, 240
Fry, Christopher, 145

Gardner, W. H., 225, 225n
God moves in a mysterious way, 177
Goldsmith, Oliver, 103
Good nature and good sense must ever join, 116
Good Night, 46
Gorboduc, 97
Gosse, Edmund, 89
Grave, The, 102

GRAY, THOMAS, 131
From The Progress of Poesy, 80
Great roads the Romans built, that men might meet, 73
Green Pastures, The, 144
°Griesly Wife, The, 131
Gr-r-r—there go, my heart's abhorrence, 152
Gummere, Frances B., 134

Had she come all the way for this, 139
Hall, David, 12n
Hardy, Thomas, 145
Hark! Ah, the Nightingale, 85
HARTWICH, ETHELYN MILLER
What Shall Endure, 73
Havens, R. D., 103
°Haystack in the Floods, The, 70n, 138, °139
Hear the sledges with the bells, 60
He first deceased: she for a little tried, 180
He is that fallen lance that lies as hurled, 233, 240
Here Lies a Lady, 35n
HERRICK, ROBERT, 10n
A Meditation for His Mistress, 112
Delight in Disorder, 69
How Roses Came Red, 47
Upon Prue His Maid, 180
Upon Julia's Clothes, 170
Highwayman, The, 138
Hillyer, Robert, 104
HOLMES, OLIVER WENDELL
Cacoethes Scribendi, 18
Holy Sonnets, 98, 114, 176
HOMER, 133n, 204–7
From Odyssey, 207
HOPKINS, GERARD MANLEY, 87n, 88, 186, 214–32, 237, 250, 253, 257
°The Windhover, 216, 231
Horace, 91
Hospital Impressions, 87, 88
House of Life, The, 106
HOUSMAN, A. E., 3, 4
Far in a western brookland, 59
Is my team ploughing, 148
Loveliest of trees, the cherry now, 47
Oh, when I was in love with you, 72
How thou art changed! I dare not look on thee, 66
Howe, Irving, 16n

How like a winter hath my absence been, 111
How long they have been there I cannot tell, 73
How Roses Came Red, 47
How sleep the brave who sink to rest, 82
How soon hath time, the subtle thief of youth, 77
Hughes, Glenn, 95
Hunt, Leigh, 104, 106, 208
Hymn to Intellectual Beauty, 20, 223n
Hyperion, 105

I asked the heaven of stars, 170
I am nae poet, in a sense, 17
I caught this morning morning's minion, king–, 216, 231
Idylls of the King, 138
If all the trees in all the woods were men, 18
If aught of oaten stop, or pastoral song, 83
If by dull rhymes our English must be chain'd, 107
If I could break the hearts of a hundred men, 95
If thou must love me, let it be for naught, 169
I hold it true, whate'er befall, 72
I Knew a Woman, 171
I knew a woman, lovely in her bones, 171
Iliad, 133, 205, 206
Inferno, 15n
In Memoriam, 61, 72, 177
In the mid days of autumn, on their eves, 74
In the Naked Bed, In Plato's Cave, 107n, 166
In this little urne is laid, 180
I put my hat upon my head, 163
Isabella, or the Pot of Basil, 74
I said—Then, dearest, since 'tis so, 150
Is my team ploughing, 148
I strove with none, for none was worth my strife, 162
I think it is his blindness makes him so, 156
I, too, dislike it . . ., 7
It was not like your great and gracious ways, 182

Jarrell, Randall, 35n
Johnny Randall, 128, 148
Johnson, James William, 160n
JOHNSON, SAMUEL, 4
  I put my hat upon my head, 163
Jonson, Ben, 162

KEATS, JOHN, 26, 83n, 103n, 104,
    106, 117, 138, 186, 204–14, 252
  From The Eve of St. Agnes, 9, 62,
    frontispiece
  From Endymion, 50, 104
  From Isabella, or the Pot of Basil,
    74
  From the letters, 27, 32, 209, 243
  °On First Looking Into Chap-
    man's Homer, 117, °204, 213
  On the Sonnet, 107
  From Sleep and Poetry, 4, 69
  To Autumn, 76
KHAYYÁM, OMAR
  From The Rubáiyát, 72
King Lear, 172–73
Kiss, A, 92
Knight's Tale, The, 138
Kubla Khan, 22

Lady of Shalott, The, 110
Lamia, 104
LANDOR, WALTER SAVAGE
  Death, 64
  On His Seventy-Fifth Birthday,
    162
  Proud word you never spoke, but
    you will speak, 48
LANG, ANDREW
  Easy is the triolet, 92
  To Theocritus in Winter, 90
°Laocoön (sculpture), 11–15
Laocoön, Neptune's priest by lot
  that year, 14
L'Après-Midi d'un Faune, 15n
L'Art Poétique, 100
Last Ride Together, The, 150
Late, late yestreen I saw the new
  moone, 160
Latest Decalogue, The, 178
Let knowledge grow from more to
  more, 177
Letter to Robert Frost, A, 104
Lie still, my newly married wife,
  131
Light Shining Out of Darkness, 176,
  177
Lines Composed a Few Miles Above
  Tintern Abbey, 22n, 102

Little Fly, 173
°London, 1802, 51
Longfellow, Henry Wadsworth, 44
°Lord Randal, 56n, °126, 129, 148
Lotus-Eaters, The, 103n
Lovelace, Richard, 174n
Loveliest of trees, the cherry now,
  47
Love not me for comely grace, 168,
  169
Lyrical Ballads (Preface), 4, 5, 19,
  24, 26, 109

Macbeth, 48, 97, 145, 161
MacLeish, Archibald, 145
Mallarmé, Stéphan, 15n
MALLOCH, DOUGLAS
  Waking of a City, 165
Manfred, 15n
Manfred Symphony, 15n
MANIFOLD, JOHN
  °The Griesly Wife, 131
Marlowe, Christopher, 97, 145
Masefield, John, 144
Matthew, Book of, 197, 249
Meditation for His Mistress, A, 112
Mending Wall, 105
Michael, 105
Midsummer Night's Dream, A, 18
Millay, Edna St. Vincent, 106
MILTON JOHN, 56, 80, 98, 101, 103,
    112, 135, 156, 158, 186, 196–
    204, 206, 210, 227
  °On His Blindness, 196, 203
  On His Having Arrived to the
    Age of Twenty-Three, 77
  From Paradise Lost, 66, 111, 136;
    on the verse of, 101
  To Cyriack Skinner, 99
Milton, thou shouldst be living at
  this hour, 51
Miniver Cheevy, 158
Minstrel, The, 103n
MOORE, MARIANNE, 87n, 226, 243
  Poetry, 7
More strange than true. I never may
  believe, 18
MORRIS, WILLIAM, 104, 138
  From The Defence of Guinevere,
    70
  From The Earthly Paradise, 74
  °The Haystack in the Floods, 139
Morte d'Arthur, 105
Most near, most dear, most loved
  and most far, 244, 256
Mr. Flood's Party, 158, 244

Much have I travelled in the realms of gold, 204, 213
My genial spirits fail, 22
My heart has melted into the sea, 95
*My hope was one, from cities far, 34
My Last Duchess, 49, 104, 154, 160
My mistress' eyes are nothing like the sun, 168
Myself when young did eagerly frequent, 72

Nephelidia, 59, 232
Nevertheless, you, O Sir Gauwaine, lie, 70
Nibelungenlied, 134
Nine times the space that measures day and night, 66
Night Song at Amalfi, 169, 170
Night Thoughts, 102
No more, but e'en a woman, and commanded, 97
Norton, Thomas, 97
Not with more glories, in the ethereal plain, 100
Noyes, Alfred, 138

O Bessie Bell and Mary Gray, 57
O'Casey, Sean, 144
Ode: Intimations of Immortality, 81
Ode to Evening, 83
Ode to the West Wind, 54, 70, 114
Ode Written in the Beginning of the Year 1746, 82
Odyssey, 133, 205-6, 207
O Earth, lie heavily upon her eyes, 181
Of Man's first disobedience, and the fruit, 136
O Heart of hearts, the chalice of love's fire, 57
O hideous little bat, the size of snot, 174
Oh, when I was in love with you, 72
Old Eben Flood, climbing alone one night, 158
OLDYS, WILLIAM
On a Fly Drinking Out of His Cup, 172
On a Fly Drinking Out of His Cup, 172
One day I wrote her name upon the strand, 78
*On First Looking Into Chapman's Homer, 117, *204, 213

On His Being Arrived to the Age of Twenty-Three, 77
*On His Blindness, *196, 203, 227
On His Seventy-Fifth Birthday, 162
On the Sonnet, 107
Out of the Cradle Endlessly Rocking, 86
Owen, Wilfred, 35n
O western wind, when wilt thou blow, 162
O where hae ye been, Lord Randal, my son, 126

Pacific Sonnets, 245
Palomar, 108
Paradise Lost, 66, 99, 111, 135, 156; on the verse of, 101
PATMORE, COVENTRY, 87n
Departure, 182
Perry, John Oliver, 16n
Peters, W. A. M., 224
Petrarch, Francesco, 77, 98
Philomela, 85
Pindar, 79
Plato, 166
Pleasures of the Imagination, The, 102
Plough and the Stars, The, 144
POE, EDGAR ALLAN, 5
From The Bells, 60
From The Raven, 56, 58
Poems (Waller), 100
Poet, The, 7n, 25
Poetry, 7, 87n, 226, 243
POPE, ALEXANDER, 101, 102, 104, 137n, 204, 206-7
From An Essay on Criticism, 53, 65n, 68, 116
From Odyssey, 207
From The Rape of the Lock, 100, 137
Prelude, The, 19, 102, 105
Progress of Poesy, The, 80
Prometheus Unbound, 66, 105, 145, 160-61
Prophecy of Dante, The, 70
*Proud Maisie, 127n, *130
Proud word you never spoke, but you will speak, 48
Proust, Marcel, 188n
Psalms, Book of, 175

Rabelais, 247
Ransom, John Crowe, 35n
Rape of the Lock, The, 100, 136-37, 137n

Raven, The, 56, 58
Remembrance of Things Past, 188n
Republic, The, 166n
Rest, 180, 181
Reuben Bright, 158
Richard Cory, 158
Riders to the Sea, 144
Rime of the Ancient Mariner, The, 22, 62, 132
Ring out wild bells, to the wild sky, 61
ROBINSON, EDWIN ARLINGTON, 105, 106, 158, 159n, 244
   Mr. Flood's Party, 158, 159n
ROETHKE, THEODORE
   *I Knew a Woman, 171
Roll on, thou deep and dark blue Ocean—roll, 75
Romeo and Juliet (Overture Fantasy), 15n
Rose kissed me today, 92
Rose Leaves, 92
Roses at first were white, 47
ROSSETTI, CHRISTINA, 42n, 44
   Rest, 181
   Song (When I am dead, my dearest), 41
Rossetti, Dante Gabriel, 15n, 106
Rubáiyát of Omar Khayyám, The, 72
Ruskin, John, 113

Sackville, Thomas, 97
Salt spray, swinging to fling, flash, 89
Sassoon, Siegfried, 35n
SCHNABEL, ARTUR
   Every day the sailing rougher, 55
Schneider, Elizabeth, 223n
Schoolmistress, The, 103n
SCHWARTZ, DELMORE
   In the Naked Bed, In Plato's Cave, 107n, 166
SCOTT, SIR WALTER
   *Proud Maisie, 130
Season of mists and mellow fruitfulness, 76
Seasons, The, 102
Selected Poems (Barker), 245
SHAKESPEARE, WILLIAM, 11, 15n, 19, 80, 98, 99, 114, 145, 158, 167, 172–73, 186–95, 198n, 199, 199n, 200, 250
   From A Midsummer Night's Dream, 18

From Antony and Cleopatra, 97
How like a winter hath my absence been, 111
From Macbeth, 145
My mistress' eyes are nothing like the sun, 168
Shall I compare thee to a summer's day, 79
*When to the sessions of sweet silent thought, 186, 193
Shall I compare thee to a summer's day, 79
SHAPIRO, KARL, 173, 173n
   The Fly, 174
*She dwelt among the untrodden ways, *32, 159n
She is not fair to outward view, 168
SHELLEY, PERCY BYSSHE, 16n, 20–21, 70, 103n, 105, 145, 160, 161, 223, 234
   From A Defence of Poetry, 4, 5, 16n
   From Hymn to Intellectual Beauty, 20, 223n
   From Ode to the West Wind, 40, 54, 114
   From Prometheus Unbound, 66
Shenstone, William, 103n
Sibelius, Jean, 12, 12n, 15n
Sidney, Sir Phillip, 4
Sinai, 107
Sir Gawain and the Green Knight, 138
*Sir Patrick Spens, *125, 160, 161
Sleep and Poetry, 4, 69
So here hath dawning, 46
*Soldier, A, 233, 240
Soldier, The, 233
Soliloquy of the Spanish Cloister, 151, 152
Somebody wished you luck . . ., following 183
Song for St. Cecilia's Day, A, 61–62, 81
Song of Myself, 112
Song of Saul Before His Last Battle, 45, 47
Song (When I am dead, my dearest), 41, 42n, 44
Song (Why so pale and wan, fond lover), 44
*Sonnet to My Mother, 107n, *244, 256
Sonnets from the Portuguese, 106, 169

Sonnets (Shakespeare), 79, 98, 111, 168, 186, 193
Sophocles
From **Antigone,** 118n
Southey, Robert, 74
SPENDER, STEPHEN, 107n
The Express, 106, 243
SPENSER, EDMUND, 75, 98, 99, 103n, 135, 138
One day I wrote her name upon the strand, 78
Stallman, Robert Wooster, 16n
Stanzas from the Grande Chartreuse, 177, 178
STARKWEATHER, PAULINE, 54n, 107n
Two Mountains Men Have Climbed
Sinai, 107
Palomar, 108
Sterling, George, 106
Stevick, Robert, 159n
Story of Rimini, The, 104
SUCKLING, JOHN
Song (Why so pale and wan, fond lover), 44
SURREY, HENRY HOWARD, EARL OF, 96, 98
From Aeneid, 49
SWINBURNE, ALGERNON CHARLES, 89, 90n, 232, 254n
Cor Cordium, 57
From Nephilidia, 59
Synge, John Millington, 144

Tamburlaine, 97
Tam o' Shanter, 144
Task, The, 102
TEASDALE, SARA
Night Song at Amalfi, 170
Tempest, The (Incidental Music), 12, 13
TENNYSON, ALFRED, LORD, 40, 49, 105, 138, 154
Break, Break, Break, 42, 116
From In Memoriam, 72, 177
Ring out, wild bells, 61
From The Lady of Shalott, 110
From Morte d'Arthur, 105
That's my last Duchess painted on the wall, 154
That which hath made them drunk hath made me bold, 145
The good flat earth . . . and not so very high, 107
The king sits in Dumferling toune, 125

The Lord is my shepherd; I shall not want, 175
Then Hrothgar went with his hero-train, 134
There is another, 95
There was a boy, ye knew him well, ye cliffs, 67
There was a faith healer of Deal, 93
The salt spray swings itself with shining flash, 89
The sea is calm tonight, 118
These equal syllables alone require, 53
The trumpet's loud clangor, 61
The Way My Ideas Think Me, 87n, 178, 179
The world of half reality, 88
This evening, 95
Thomas, Dylan, 216, 243
Thomson, James, 102, 103n
Thoughts of a Briton on the Subjugation of Switzerland, 107
Thou shalt have one God only; who, 178
Three years she grew in sun and shower, 114
Thrown backwards first, head over heels in the wind, following 183
Time, stop, 94n
To Autumn, 76, 77, 83n
To a Writer, 105
To Cyriack Skinner, 99
To-Day, 46
Today I met a stranger, 95
To My Friend Whose Parachute Did Not Open, 36n, 182, following 183
To Theocritus in Winter, 90
Tristram, 105
True ease in writing comes from art, not chance, 68
Tschaikowski, Petr Ilich, 15n
Twenty-Third Psalm, The, 87n, 175
Two Mountains Men Have Climbed, 107–8
Two voices are there, one is of the sea, 107

Ulysses, 154
Under the surface of the reaching lake, 55
Unhallowed wight, grim and greedy, 134
Upon Julia's Clothes, 10n, 170
Upon Prue His Maid, 180

Upon the Death of Sir Albert Morton's Wife, 180
VERGIL, 135
  From Aeneid, 14, 49, 97
VILLA, JOSÉ GARCIA, 87n
  The Way My Ideas Think Me, 179
Vitas Hinnuleo, 91

WAGONER, DAVID, 182
  To My Friend Whose Parachute Did Not Open, following 183
Waking of a City, 165
Waller, Edmund, 100
Wandering between two worlds, one dead, 178
Warriors and chiefs! should the shaft or the sword, 45
We fools who cannot sleep have heard it waken, 165
West, Ray B., Jr., 16n
Whan that Aprille with his shoures soote, 96
What dire offense from am'rous causes springs, 136
What Shall Endure, 73
Whenas in silks my Julia goes, 170
When I am dead, my dearest, 41
When I consider how my light is spent, 196, 203
When I heard the learn'd astronomer, 86
When I saw you last, Rose, 93
When Lilacs Last in the Dooryard Bloomed, 86
*When to the sessions of sweet silent thought, 186, 193
Where, like a pillow on a bed, 113
Where was you last night, Johnny Randall, my son, 128
While yet a boy I sought for ghosts, and sped, 20
WHITMAN, WALT
  From Song of Myself, 112
  When I heard the learn'd astronomer, 86

Why so pale and wan, fond lover, 44
*Windhover, The, 89n, *216, 231, 250, 251, 253
With a puling infant's force, 69
Woodhouse, Richard, 26
Wordsworth, John, 31
WORDSWORTH, WILLIAM, 21, 22n, 27, 31, 32–36, 74, 77n, 105, 109, 111, 159n
  A slumber did my spirit seal, 180
  Composed Upon Westminster Bridge, 165
  *London, 1802, 40, *51, 66
  From Lyrical Ballads (Preface), 4, 5, 19, 24, 26, 109
  From Ode: Intimations of Immortality, 81–82
  From The Prelude, 19, 102
  *She dwelt among the untrodden ways, 32
  There Was a Boy, 67
  Thoughts of a Briton on the Subjugation of Switzerland, 107
  From Three years she grew in sun and shower, 114
WOTTON, SIR HENRY
  Upon the Death of Sir Albert Morton's Wife, 180
Wyatt, Sir Thomas, 98

YANAGIWARA, AKIKO
  Four haikus, 95
Ye banks and braes o' bonnie Doon, 71
Ye blessed creatures, I have heard the call, 81
Ye flowery banks o' bonnie Doon, 71
YOSANO, AKIKO
  Four tankas, 95
You are a tulip seen to-day, 112
You bid me try, 92
Young, Edward, 102
You shun me, Chloe, wild and shy, 91